Narrative in Fiction and Film

Narrative in Fiction and Film

An Introduction

Jakob Lothe

OXFORD

UNIVERSITY PRESS

Oxford University Press, Great Clarendon Street, Oxford OX2 6DP

Oxford New York

Athens Auckland Bangkok Bogotá Bombay Buenos Aires
Calcutta Cape Town Dar es Salaam Delhi Florence Hong Kong Istanbul
Karachi Kuala Lumpur Madras Madrid Melbourne Mexico City
Nairobi Paris Singapore Taipei Tokyo Toronto Warsaw
and associated companies in
Berlin Ibadan

Oxford is a registered trade mark of Oxford University Press

Published in the United States
by Oxford University Press Inc., New York

British Library Cataloguing in Publication Data
Data available

Library of Congress Cataloging in Publication Data
Data available

ISBN: 0-19-875232-6

1 3 5 7 9 10 8 6 4 2

Typeset by Best-set Typesetter Ltd., Hong Kong
Printed in Great Britain
on acid-free paper by
T.J. International Ltd, Padstow, Cornwall

To my mother
and the memory
of my father

Preface

Narrative theory (or 'narratology') is an area of research that is experiencing rapid development. Narrative theory discusses central questions concerning human communication; it also investigates the conditions for, and form and content of, such communication. The stories studied by narrative theory take various forms. Our culture is based on different types of story: novels, films, television series, strip cartoons, myths, anecdotes, songs, advertisements, biographies, and so forth. All these tell stories—even though the stories may not necessarily be complete, and may be presented in many different ways.

Since the forms of story that surround us are so many and so varied, narrative theory is relevant not only to literary studies but also to subjects such as history, the history of religion, theology, social anthropology, sociology, linguistics, psychology, and media studies. Crossing the borders between subjects, narrative theory thus brings to light a problem in the traditional establishment of discipline boundaries. For although it is often necessary to isolate a field of research or a particular problem in order to study it systematically, borders between subjects may be more arbitrary than we realize. The basis for this book is literary studies. Beyond formalism we may be, but we owe to formalism our understanding that literary texts are meaningful not just because of their 'content' but because of the totality of their verbal presentation. Narrative theory builds upon and extends this fundamental insight, and this is the basis for its contribution to literary studies. Additionally, as the book's title indicates, I wish to relate narrative theory to film: a different medium, but one that is a form of narrative (particularly the narrative fiction film). Of particular interest to a literary critic are 'film adaptations'—films that are based (more or less directly) on literary texts.

This book has a two-part structure. Part I provides an introduction to narrative theory. Although the discussion is oriented towards narrative fiction and centred on literary texts, the film aspect is brought into each chapter. Part II then analyses five prose texts by means of the narrative concepts (and theories associated with these concepts) introduced in Part I. I also comment on film adaptations of four of these texts, which are all central works in world literature.

In the period following the publication of the Norwegian version of this book in 1994, narrative theory has developed further. One striking feature of this development is the diversification of narrative theory: insights and terms from narrative theory are being used within critical trends that are not primarily, or not only, concerned with the study of literary form and narrative structure. Examples of such trends are theories of reading, variants of new historicism, and post-colonial studies. While much is positive in these developments, there are also examples of the ignoring or marginalizing of insights from narrative theory as it has developed in our century from the Russian formalists onwards. In some contributions to post-colonial studies, for example, there is a tendency to reduce literary texts to relatively stable carriers of ideological positions. But this is to distort and simplify both narrative fiction and the narrative fiction film, which depend for their originality and significance as cultural documents on aesthetic form, and on the interplay of form and content. Although we live in an age of post-structuralism, it does not follow that insights accrued by formalist and structuralist critics, without whose contributions narrative theory would not exist, are irrelevant or useless. If, as critics now tend to stress, reading is a social activity that is influenced by the society beyond the author and reader, then it is important to study narrative texts as diverse manifestations of such social activity.

Another characteristic of recent developments is that, partly as a result of the decreased differentiation between fiction and history, narrative theory is being used to a greater extent in research which is not primarily (or not only) concerned with literature. The link between narrative theory and film studies has also been strengthened. Again, this kind of diversification suggests the continuing relevance of narrative theory—especially if, as the analyses in Part II aim to do, we understand narrative inclusively as a form of textual dynamics rather than as formalist schematization. Narrative is part of history, yet it also contributes to historical processes from within. Narrative is dynamic and changing, yet because the significance of its contribution to history and culture is inseparable from the way in which it is produced, narrative needs to be studied as form—as literary structure. It is to further investigation of this question that this book hopes to contribute.

I should like to thank Scandinavian University Press for co-operation on the Norwegian version of this book, and also for approving its publication by Oxford University Press in English. I am most grateful to Jon Haarberg, who read and commented on both the Norwegian and English versions, offering a number of constructive criticisms. Working with the English text, I had the pleasure of co-operating with Patrick Chaffey, who has translated most of the manuscript. I should like to express my thanks to Patrick Chaffey for his kind assistance and professional competence as a translator. The person to whom I owe the greatest debt of gratitude is Jeremy Hawthorn. In his constructive and academically inspiring way, Hawthorn read and commented on several versions of the manuscript: he is the best scholarly contact I could ever imagine. I am also grateful to Per Buvik and

Atle Kittang, who read and commented on the Norwegian version, and to Terence Cave, Andrew Lockett, and Sophie Goldsworthy for wise advice and professional publishing assistance. Last but not least I thank Elin Toft for her invaluable support.

J. L.
Oslo
December 1998

Contents

PART I

1
Introduction

Narrative text and narrative fiction

A narrative presents a chain of events which is situated in time and space. There are narratives not only in literature but also in other cultural utterances that surround us. Part of the explanation for the importance of, and our fascination with, narrative lies in the fact that it is fundamental not only to different forms of cultural expression but also to our own patterns of experience and to our insights into our own lives. For instance, our conversations with other people contain narrative sequences—we often report something we have experienced. Our thoughts often assume a narrative form, and even our dreams are like incomplete and confusing stories. Human beings have a deep-seated need to establish narrative patterns, something that is again connected with the tendency we have to see life as a story—a temporally limited line of development from beginning to end, from birth to death, in which we like to find each stage meaningful and to justify the choices we make.

Let us illustrate the definition above by a couple of examples. First an agency report printed in a newspaper:

WITH FATHER IN HIS SUITCASE

Security guards at Ben Gurion Airport in Israel recently stopped a 33-year-old Indian who had a skeleton in his suitcase. 'These are my father's remain,' said the Indian. 'I am keeping his bones with me until I can find a place to live. Then I shall bury them,' he said.

Is this a narrative? The answer to this question will depend on what we understand by the term (which I shall use synonymously with 'narrative text'). Gerald Prince gives this example of a 'minimal story': 'John was happy, then he saw Peter, then, as a result, he was unhappy' (Prince 1991: 53). Here we have only *one* event, which marks a *transition* from the happy state John was in to the unhappy state he is in now. Our example above also has a dominant event: the discovery of the skeleton in the Indian's suitcase. On the other hand, no transition in the man's state of mind is indicated, but must if necessary be read out of the explanation he gives. What most clearly 'pulls' this report in the direction of a narrative is that in condensed form it exhibits a three-link progression of events: first the Indian is stopped by airport security, then the skeleton in the suitcase is discovered, and finally the Indian gives an explanation. This explanation (i.e. the third link in the chain of events) is in itself virtually a narrative. It not only sketches a journey, but furthermore relates the bones in the suitcase to a desire to end this journey. Brief as it is, the Indian's explanation thus highlights the temporal aspect of narrative. Yet since the central point of this text is a situationally determined explanation, it is its *narrative potential* that is most striking.

Since this newspaper report refers to an event that did in fact take place, the report does not constitute literary 'fiction' as we normally understand the term. However, although this book deals primarily with texts usually called 'fictional' (i.e. literary fiction and screen fiction), many of the narrative terms, techniques, and variations we discuss will be relevant for other text types as well. Our inclusive definition of narrative refers by no means only to literary fiction. Still, even though narrative theory has a relatively high transfer value to other subject areas, our primary concern is 'narrative fiction'. Here is an example of such a text:

> 'Ach', sagte die Maus, 'die Welt wird enger mit jedem Tag. Zuerst war sie so breit, dass ich Angst hatte, ich lief weiter und war glücklich, dass ich endlich rechts und links in der Ferne Mauern sah, aber diese langen Mauern eilen so schnell aufeinander zu, dass ich schon im letzten Zimmer bin, und dort im Winkel steht die Falle, in die ich laufe.' 'Du musst nur die Laufrichtung ändern,' sagte die Katze und frass sie. (Franz Kafka, *Sämtliche Erzählungen*, 368)

> 'Alas', said the mouse, 'the world is growing smaller every day. At the beginning it was so big that I was afraid, I kept running and running, and I was glad when at last I saw walls far away to the right and left, but these long walls are narrowing so quickly that I am in the last chamber already, and there in the corner stands the trap I am running into.' 'You only need to change your direction,' said the cat, and ate it up. (My translation)

I shall be returning to this text in Part II, where I shall discuss it in connection with Kafka's novel *The Trial*. The reason for presenting it at this early stage is to illustrate the definition of narrative given above. In addition to being narrative this text is *fictional*: it presents in words fictitious events that follow one another.

'Fiction' comes from the Latin *fingere* (original meaning: 'to make by shaping')—to invent, to think up, to make up (cf. Italian *fingere*, French *feindre*, English *feign*, German *fingieren*). By verbal fiction we understand in this book a literary narrative in prose that has been made up or invented. Fiction does not accurately describe events that have in fact (historically) taken place. In his *Apology for Poetry* (1595), Sir Philip Sidney said of the poet that he 'nothing affirmes, therefore never lyeth'. A modern version of this point of view is that even if fictional utterances are meaningful, and conform to the rules of ordinary, non-fictional discourse, they nevertheless do not present themselves as 'facts' in the usual sense (and cannot therefore be falsified in the way that a historical account can). This does not at all imply that we cannot learn something important by reading and working with narrative fiction. The poet's task, as Aristotle believed, is to tell of such things as might happen; fiction can, as Theodor Adorno has observed, serve as a form of subconscious writing of history, and it can show us how man has experienced, and been formed by, what has happened down through the ages.

Having said this, it needs to be added that the borderlines between fiction and non-fiction can be blurred. Nor is 'fiction' understood in the same way in all cultures. When we say that fiction does not represent facts, this is partly on account of prevailing conventions in our cultural community, that is to say that author and reader understand fiction in the same way and mean roughly the same thing by the term. Salman Rushdie assumes the knowledge of such conventions when he writes in his essay 'Imaginary Homelands' that in *Midnight's Children* the narrator, Saleem, uses the cinema screen as a metaphor to discuss human perception (Rushdie 1992: 13). Both 'narrator' and 'metaphor' function, in the way Rushdie uses the terms here and in the way we normally understand them in connection with novels, in a fiction-constituting sense: we use these and other terms to show how fiction is created and how it operates. The fact that our understanding of such concepts is partly conventional (located in a social practice and influenced by European culture and history) helps to explain the extreme reaction to another of Rushdie's novels, *The Satanic Verses*, in Islamic societies. In spite of numerous aestheticizing and fiction-creating elements, *The Satanic Verses* was considered blasphemous in these cultural communities, as readers will know.

Having ventured these introductory comments on the concept of fiction, let us return to the Kafka text. The two verbs that in this case constitute the fictional events are 'run' and 'eat'. Note that the order of these two verbs is absolutely crucial to the meaning expressed by the text. A narrative *development* takes place between the two events, and this development is created by the verbal presentation. That the text is fictional is in this instance clearly indicated through the narrative device of making a mouse talk. In Chapter 5 we shall come back to the thematic effects of this device. What must be stressed already at this point is the narrative-constituting aspect, the *narrativity*, in the way in which the events are presented here.

Brief as it is, Kafka's text illustrates fundamental characteristics of narrative. The text presents not only events that follow one another but also indicates (albeit ever so briefly) that these events are situated in time and space and have dramatic effects. In extremely concentrated form this text shows a *combination* of events. The way such combinations are carried out involves different narrative devices and variations. Furthermore these point towards the interplay between three fundamental aspects of narrative fiction that we shall now look at a little more closely.

Narrative fiction: Discourse, story, and narration

This classification of narrative fiction was proposed by Gérard Genette in his seminal essay 'Discours du récit' (1972; published in English as *Narrative Discourse* in 1980). Genette's starting-point is the term *récit* (narrative), which in French has (at least) three meanings: a statement, the content of the statement, and the action one performs when producing the statement. In his argument Genette distinguishes between these three meanings of the word by giving each of them its special term: discourse (*récit*), story (*histoire*), and narration (*narration*). The explanation of the three concepts that now follows is provisional and will be refined as we go along.

1 *Discourse* is the spoken or written presentation of the events. Put in simple terms discourse is what we read, the text to which we have direct access. In discourse the order of events is not necessarily chronological, people are presented through characterization, and the transmitted content is filtered through narrative voices and perspectives.

2 *Story* refers to the narrated events and conflicts in narrative fiction, abstracted from their disposition in the discourse and arranged chronologically together with the fictional characters. Thus story approaches what we usually understand by a summary of the action. Part II gives several examples of such versions of stories; here is a suggested summary of the action in Miguel de Cervantes's *Don Quixote* (1605, 1615):

> A wise man goes out of his senses as a result of reading chivalric romances and travels out into the world as a knight errant to help those who need it and to punish those who deserve it. On account of his lack of any sense of reality he achieves the opposite of what he wants: he harms innocent people and himself, sets the guilty free, etc. Outwitted by a friend he finally returns home for good, curses chivalric romances, and dies.

This kind of summary of the action is a story, a *paraphrase*. Paraphrasing the action is something we all do (more or less subconsciously) as we work our way through a text—it is included in the structuring activity that reading consists of. But a story is something other than an interpretation, for which we must analyse the discourse in a completely different way. (Note, however, that story can also be used synonymously with 'narrative'.)

3 *Narration* refers to how a text is written and communicated. The process of writing, of which narration is a trace, carries with it a number of narrative devices and combinations, which all contribute to constituting discourse. As Shlomith Rimmon-Kenan puts it: 'In the empirical world, the author is the agent responsible for the production of the narrative and for its communication. The empirical process of communication, however, is less relevant to the poetics of narrative fiction than its counterpart within the

text' (Rimmon-Kenan 1983: 3), a process in which the *narrator* has a key function. Yet we shall see that there are important links between the author *of* a text and the narrator *in* it.

As Peter Larsen has pointed out, these three basic categories of Genette's are primarily connected with written discourse:

> In oral cultures the story is produced and received in one and the same situation— it is immediately available to the listener as the narrator's 'speech' (as 'discourse' in the original meaning of the word). But it is not this form of 'discourse' Genette has in mind. Although he . . . consciously defines his basic categories in such a manner that in principle they can cover all types of story . . . he deals in his own analytical practice exclusively with 'literature', with *written* stories, in other words with statements which by virtue of the written word's 'preserving' quality circulate 'freely', isolated from the original act of narrating. (Larsen 1989: 11; my translation)

Larsen links this commentary to Genette, but it may also be related to the points in Chapter 2 on 'the epic proto-situation' and the author as writer. While Genette's classification of narrative fiction has exerted a great influence on recent narrative theory, he in his turn owes a debt to the pioneers of this theory: the Russian formalists, who as early as around 1920 used the conceptual pair *fabula/syuzhet* in a way that pointed towards the distinction between story and discourse. *Fabula* is a paraphrasing summary of the action, which the formalists relate to what Viktor Shklovsky calls the 'material' for narrative construction (Erlich 1981: 240). *Syuzhet* on the other hand refers to the oral or written *design* of the story, to the different procedures and devices in the text that make it literary. Thus the formalists' concept of *syuzhet* is linked to the word 'discourse'. *Syuzhet* is an element of form which extends over into the text's content side. In this way *syuzhet* is related to *plot*. Aristotle in the *Poetics* explains plot as 'the construction of the events' (Aristotle 1995: 49, 1450a). Central to Aristotle's understanding of plot is the notion of transformation 'in a probable or necessary sequence of events' (1995: 57, 1451a); compare the relation of cause and effect in the 'minimal story' presented above. In narrative fiction causality can either be implied or gain an explicit status. Rimmon-Kenan rightly notes that 'the very notion of causality is by no means unproblematic' (Rimmon-Kenan 1983: 17), and it needs to be stressed that causality in narrative fiction is not directly comparable with causal relationships in the empirical world. For example, elements of causality can be supplied by the reader of a fictional text. Even so, aspects of causality are commonly associated with the concept of plot. In *Reading for the Plot* (1984), Peter Brooks links this concept directly to *syuzhet* (in the 1920s the formalists were unknown outside Russia). For Brooks, plot is 'the dynamic shaping force of the narrative discourse' (Brooks 1984: 13). The term thus refers not only to *how* a fictional narrative is presented—as linguistically formed discourse and through an act of narrating (narration)—but also draws attention to the relationship between textual form and content and the reader's vital role in the understanding of narrative.

Narrative fiction as film

With reference to narrative texts in general I have so far outlined the major characteristics of narrative fiction. In the case of literary fiction we usually think of short stories, novels, and so on. Yet although my central focus is on *verbal* fiction (i.e. written texts), each chapter will also devote some attention to film, which can have an important narrative dimension. Now clearly the narrative aspect is not equally clear in all films (nor, incidentally, in all prose texts), but often the narrative aspect is absolutely crucial both for the way the film functions and for its effect on the audience.

This said, it must be emphasized that literary and screen texts are in many ways very different. The cinema audience is, as the Russian formalist Boris Eikhenbaum stressed as early as 1926,

> placed in completely new conditions of perception, which are to an extent opposite to those of the reading process. Whereas the reader moves from the printed word to visualization of the subject, the viewer goes in the opposite direction: he moves from the subject, from comparison of the moving frames to their comprehension, to naming them; in short, to the construction of internal speech. (Eikhenbaum 1973: 123)

For Eikhenbaum and many later film theorists the transposing of literature to film (often referred to as 'adaptation') involves neither the staging nor illustration of literature but a *translation to film language*. Although film language is essentially different from language in literature, however, the most important components of the definition we have given of a narrative—time, space, and causality—are central concepts in film theory as well. Narrative terms such as plot, repetition, events, characters, and characterization are also important in film—even though the *form* of presentation and the way in which these concepts are actualized vary greatly in these two art forms.

The relationship between narrative prose literature and narrative film thus confirms the point that those narratives which are part of the world around us assume different forms and are expressed in many ways. By linking literature to film this book will examine more closely this central characteristic of narrative. The combination of the enormous appeal films have in themselves and the development of the modern media society is causing film to become a more and more important art form, which to an increasing extent influences the way in which we read and understand literature. In this evolutionary picture narrative theory helps us understand both what ties literature and film together and how they differ.

If the focus of this book is on narrative fiction, the film sections deal primarily with the narrative fiction film. And yet, as David Bordwell and Kristin

Thompson put it, 'not everything shown or implied by a fiction film need be imaginary ... [and fiction films] often comment on the real world' (Bordwell and Thompson 1997: 45). As in verbal narratives, the borderlines between fictional and documentary films can be blurred, and narrative is crucially important in many films which base themselves on actual events (for example, Steven Spielberg's *Schindler's List* (1994) or James Cameron's *Titanic* (1998)).

Narrative theory and analysis

The theory on which this book is based can, as has already been shown, be traced back to Russian formalism in the 1920s, and it has since become a truly international phenomenon, inspiring extensive research in many countries. That French theorists have been central to this development is reflected by the status of Genette's *Narrative Discourse* as a major theoretical reference. This standard work in narrative theory has been supplemented by theories and concepts developed by other scholars. Narrative theory has been combined with studies that also refer to film (such as Seymour Chatman's *Coming to Terms* (1990)) and with film theory (such as David Bordwell's *Narration in the Fiction Film* (1985) and Edward Branigan's *Narrative Comprehension and Film* (1992)). The present study is distinguished from these works by the manner in which it relates the filmic aspect to narrative literature, and by the weight it gives to narrative analysis.

This kind of critical emphasis implies that, although my approach is selective in that I refer to (and am indebted to) various theories of narrative, there are also significant contributions I do not use because they investigate forms of narrative not subjected to discussion here. An example of such a study is Monika Fludernik's *Towards a 'Natural' Narratology* (1996). In this important study, Fludernik presents a new paradigm which is explicitly historical and which does not restrict itself to canonical (and fictional) forms of narrative. This is an important area of study, yet the kind of narrative theory we need in order to explore narrative in this wider sense is not unproblematically applicable to the study of, for example, the modern novel. Thus, Fludernik's study is an illustrative example of the diversification of narrative theory on which I commented in the Preface.

Why include analyses in an introductory book on narrative theory? First, brief references to fictional texts are often too short to illustrate the critical possibilities (and problems) of narrative theory. As James Phelan and Peter J. Rabinowitz have observed, 'If the untheorized interpretation is not worth reading, the untested theoretical proclamation is not worth believing' (Phelan and Rabinowitz 1994: 9). Second, narrative theory is primarily understood as a tool for analysis and interpretation—a necessary aid to a better understanding of narrative texts through close reading. In order to exemplify the theoretical terms presented in Part I, I use prose texts that are central to literary studies (such as Cervantes's *Don Quixote*). To illustrate and test the theory, Part II analyses five texts that are all complex and critically challenging, both narratively and thematically: the biblical parable of the sower in Mark 4, Franz Kafka's *The Trial*, James Joyce's 'The Dead', Joseph Conrad's *Heart of Darkness*, and Virginia Woolf's *To the Lighthouse*. On the basis of these narrative analyses Part II also discusses adaptations of four of these texts: Orson Welles's *The Trial*, John Huston's *The Dead*, Francis Ford Coppola's *Apocalypse Now*, and Colin Gregg's *To the Lighthouse*.

A critical attempt of this kind requires respect for the literary text and a wish to bring the reader of the analysis back to the text. At the same time it is clear that although a narrative commentary will be helpful in different interpretations, it is itself interpretative—among other things through the selective use of critical terms and through the choice of textual extracts on which comments are made. There is no ultimate interpretation of, for example, Kafka's *The Trial*, and I invite the reader of the analyses in Part II to supplement, refine, and problematize the attempts at interpretation I make. In theoretical terms Paul Armstrong formulates this problem as follows:

> Every interpretive approach reveals something only by disguising something else, which a competing method with different assumptions might disclose. Every hermeneutic standpoint has its own dialectic of blindness and insight—a ratio of disguise and disclosure which stems from its presuppositions. To accept a method of interpretation is to enter into a wager—to gamble, namely, that the insights made possible by its assumptions will offset the risks of blindness they entail. (Armstrong 1990: 7)

A word on ways of using this book: the theoretical Part I is divided into four chapters. In order that the different narrative theories and concepts can be used to supplement and explain one another, it will be an advantage to read these chapters chronologically. Although Part II is an integral part of the book, one need not read this part sequentially to derive benefit from it in relation to Part I, because although the texts here have been chosen with narrative variation in mind, the analyses are so designed that they can also be read independently of one another.

2
Narrative Communication

That a text is narrative implies that it verbally relates a story. Another term for this story-telling is *narrative communication*, which indicates a process of transmission from the author as addresser to the reader as addressee. A useful point of departure to enable us to discuss and analyse such narrative communication is what we call the *narrative communication model*. After the model has been presented, I shall comment on the different links it illustrates, with examples taken from narrative texts. I shall also relate the model to different narrative variants, to the term 'film narrator', and to central narrative concepts such as distance, perspective, and voice. First, however, some comments on narrative communication in film.

Film communication

From the previous chapter we will recall that the central concepts in the definition we gave of a narrative—time, space, and causality—are also important in the narrative fiction film. It is implicit in the premisses of this book that film should be considered as a variant of narrative communication: the fiction film is narrative in the sense that it presents a story, but in contrast to literary fiction it communicates filmically.

What then is film communication? We first note its strikingly visual quality. A film holds us firmly in the optical illusion that images displayed in rapid succession (usually shot and projected at a rate of twenty-four frames per second) come to life. The intensely visualizing force of film is fundamental to the colossal breakthrough this art form has had in our century. If we then ask what film's visualizing force involves, we immediately touch upon a much-discussed topic in film theory. 'The visual is *essentially* pornographic,' claims Fredric Jameson. Films 'ask us to stare at the world as though it were a naked body' (Jameson 1992: 1, original emphasis). The visualizing aspect of film gives it an oddly superficial nature. Film is formally 'light' in a way Philip Kaufman exploits thematically in his adaptation of Milan Kundera's *The Unbearable Lightness of Being* (1984); the fiction film shows us an illusory real world that resembles to the point of confusion the world we know ourselves, a world into which we are free to peep for a couple of hours without participating.

Much of film's power to fascinate lies in the manner in which it combines the dimensions of space and time. The spatial dimension of film links it closely to photography, on which film is totally dependent—and which it constantly violates. 'I liked', writes Roland Barthes in *Camera Lucida*, 'Photography *in opposition* to the Cinema, from which I nonetheless failed to separate it' (Barthes 1982a: 3, original emphasis). In the terms of G. E. Lessing's classic aesthetic study *Laokoon* (1766), still photography—like the art of painting, which Lessing distinguishes from poetry—is a 'spatial' art form. In a photograph the elements exist simultaneously in space, whereas filmic elements reveal themselves to us sequentially. What characterizes film is this chaining of successive images, in which film's temporal dimension is superimposed on the spatial dimension in the photograph.

The special relationship between film and photograph has led such different film theorists as Rudolf Arnheim, George Bluestone, André Bazin, and Siegfried Kracauer to study film on the basis of its spatial and photographic elements. For a film theorist such as Sergei Eisenstein, on the other hand, time (succession) is primary in film. If one places emphasis on this temporal dimension, the linguistic and narrative aspects of film become absolutely central. As Gerald Mast puts it:

> Because cinema is a sequential process, it demands comparison with that other sequential human process which serves the purpose of either communication or art—namely, language. Just as verbal (or linguistic) structures can produce communication between a speaker and a listener, as well as works of art (novels, poems, and plays), the cinema can both communicate information and create works of art. The 'listener' (audience) can understand the statement of the 'speaker' (the film's director, producer, writer, narrator, or whoever). (Mast 1983: 11)

If we link film communication to linguistic communication in this way, with the French semiologist Christian Metz we can answer the question of what film communication is as follows: film is a complex system of successive, encoded signs (Metz 1974). 'Semiology' (or semiotics) means the study of signs, and the word is apt since film, while being a form of language, is a hybrid form in which the visual aspect dominates the verbal, and in which the signs become meaningful not only by virtue of themselves (whether they be spatial, temporal, or objects), but also through the film context into which they fit. Semiotics represents perhaps the most important theoretical point of contact between linguistic/literary studies and film. Yet interestingly, as Mast among others has pointed out, an influential semiotically oriented film theorist such as Metz is extremely cautious about drawing analogies between film and verbal language.

First, Metz reminds us, there is nothing in film that corresponds to the word (or morpheme, the smallest unit of meaning) in verbal language. The closest we get to the verbal-language notion of word in film is not the frame but the shot, i.e. 'one uninterrupted image with a single static or mobile framing' (Bordwell and Thompson 1997: 481). Metz finds that such a camera shot is at least as complex as a sentence, perhaps a paragraph. The minimal, indivisible unit in film is not 'horse' but 'Over there is a horse'—and then almost inevitably at the same time—'that is jumping', 'that is white', 'by the tree', and so forth. Second, Metz emphasizes that compared with verbal language film is a 'language' without a code. In verbal language we understand immediately what 'horse' means. The content of a camera shot is not fixed in the same way, but may on the contrary vary to the point of infinity. Thus, Metz argues, effective camera shots are complicated and original tropes, which work on the viewer through their kinetic energy (i.e. through the impression made on our senses) and through chaining with other filmic images.

Discussions (and conclusions) concerning film communication are easily marked by whichever aspect one chooses to emphasize within the enormous register of functions that film possesses. Many film theorists have seen a parallel between film and music and have found that film, like music, works through atmosphere, resonance, and rhythm. Since film is unique when it comes to reflecting the external, real world, one may maintain that the greatest (utilitarian) value of film lies here—something which perhaps makes one consider the documentary film as more important than the fiction film. But since film (through directors such as Luis Buñuel and Alain Resnais) may represent the unreal and logically impossible, one may equally claim that film is best suited to showing, for instance, dreams and fantasies. Finally, one may believe that the task of film is to *combine* as many as possible of the elements in the uniquely varied repertoire of functions that the medium possesses.

To sum up: on the basis of these brief comments we can state that although film communication clearly has points of contact with verbal communication, the film medium is very different from the verbal form of communication we meet in narrative texts. As I now proceed to present the narrative communication model, I must therefore stress that it refers to verbal language and not to film. On the other hand, although the *forms* of communication vary, film also communicates; and the differences between the ways in which these art forms operate can be just as critically interesting as their similarities.

The narrative communication model

The narrative communication model has been developed on the basis of different theories about language and narrative fiction. Theorists have designed the model in many versions (for a survey see Martin 1986: 153–6; cf. Onega and Landa 1996: 4–12). Yet most of them are concerned with central concepts such as author, narrator, narrative text, narratee, and reader. Constituent elements in the model can be traced right back to Plato and Aristotle. I shall be commenting on Plato's contribution later in this chapter, in the section on 'narrative distance'. As for Aristotle, he points out in the *Poetics* that 'as regards narrative mimesis in verse, it is clear that plots, as in tragedy, should be constructed dramatically, that is, around a single, whole, and complete action, with beginning, middle, and end, so that epic, like a single and whole animal, may produce the pleasure proper to it' (Aristotle 1995: 115, 1459a). Although the context of Aristotle's discussion is tragedy, he comments on narrative composition and progression. Moreover, Aristotle touches on the question of narrative communication when he praises the conveyance of language and thought in Homer's epics; and he places decisive weight on plot and artistic composition. Attaching great importance to form, Aristotle assumes that a work of art is not a random collection of elements. Such an assumption also informs the present work.

An important part of the foundation of the narrative communication model is brought to light in that section of *Das sprachliche Kunstwerk* in which Wolfgang Kayser discusses 'the structural elements of the epic world'. Here Kayser introduces the concept of 'die epische Ursituation': 'the epic proto-situation is this: a narrator tells some listeners something that has happened' (Kayser 1971: 349; my translation). This narrator, Kayser stresses, is at a distance from the story he is relating, and in Kayser's opinion this distance leads to a fundamental difference of genre between epic and lyric poetry. Such a generic distinction is not unproblematic, but the concept of distance is important in narrative theory and will be discussed in more detail. Kayser's notion of the epic proto-situation is helpful because it includes three of the links in the narrative communication model: the narrator, 'something that has happened' (i.e. the story the narrator relates), and the listener or 'narratee'. We note that all the links here refer to a narrative 'proto-situation', i.e. an 'original' narrative situation in which the story is told orally. The relationship between author and narrator is thus not captured by this definition, nor is that between the text and its reader. Himself aware of these limitations, Kayser in other contexts points out that the novelist is a writer who creates a fictional world, a world in which the narrator is included. By thus emphasizing that an author is something other than an oral narrator, Kayser distinguishes a constructive act of writing from an oral act of narrating. That this distinction also has important consequences for the text's reading is something Walter Benjamin brings out in his classic essay 'The Storyteller'. 'A man listening to a story is in the company of the storyteller,' observes Benjamin; 'the reader of a novel, however, is isolated' (Benjamin 1979a: 100). Benjamin implies that, although the distinction between storyteller, listener, author, and reader is general (typological), it is not unrelated to, or unaffected by, historical and cultural alterations. All the authors discussed in Part II of this book were acutely aware of the changing conditions of writing, narrative, and reading and listening.

Roman Jakobson's contributions to the narrative communication model usefully supplement those of Kayser. Jakobson was a central figure in Russian formalism and in the branch of structuralism represented by the Prague School. Much of Jakobson's research lies at the point of intersection between

CONTEXT

ADDRESSER   MESSAGE   ADDRESSEE
CONTACT
CODE

Figure 2.1

linguistics and poetics. Most relevant for my purposes is his model of verbal communication (Jakobson 1987: 66), a model he summarizes in the sentence 'The addresser sends a message to the addressee', and schematizes as shown in Fig. 2.1. This general model applies, Jakobson emphasizes, to all verbally communicative acts. For a message to be operative, he argues, it requires a *context* that is seizable by the addressee and that is either verbal or capable of being verbalized. Further, there is a need for a *code*, i.e. a system of norms and rules that is fully or at least partly common to the addresser and the addressee. Finally, the message requires a *contact*: 'a physical channel and psychological connection between the addresser and the addressee, enabling both of them to enter and stay in communication' (Jakobson 1987: 66).

The connection between this model and Kayser's epic proto-situation becomes clear if we replace addresser, message, and addressee by narrator, story, and listener. Obviously, these concepts do not necessarily correspond exactly. Jakobson's concept of addresser, for instance, is so general that it can include both author and narrator, and furthermore it refers most directly to spoken language. Jakobson links the model to six different ways of using language, six language functions, which may be summarized as follows:

1 *Referential function*: orientation towards the referent (cf. the context of the narrative text).
2 *Emotive function*: focus on the addresser (cf. author, writer, narrator).
3 *Conative function*: orientation towards the addressee (cf. listener, reader).
4 *Phatic function*: focus on the communication itself in order to establish, prolong or discontinue it (cf. narration).
5 *Metalingual function*: focus on the code (cf. the language, style, or genre of the narrative text).
6 *Poetic function*: 'the set (*Einstellung*) toward the message as such, focus on the message for its own sake' (Jakobson 1987: 69).

Of these functions one will be *dominant* according to Jakobson, thus playing a determining and shaping role with respect to the meaning of the message the addresser sends to the addressee. That one function is dominant, however, does not mean that the others are turned off: 'The poetic function is not the sole function of verbal art but only its dominant, determining function' (Jakobson 1987: 69).

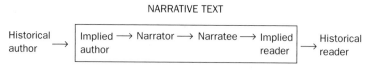

Figure 2.2

On the basis of these brief references to Aristotle, Kayser, and Jakobson I can now present the model of narrative communication shown in Fig. 2.2. Note the distinction in the model between the narrative text in the middle and the historical author (as a kind of addresser) on the one side and the historical reader (as a type of addressee) on the other. I shall now first situate 'narrative text' in a larger context and relate it to the two extreme points in the communication model. After that, by commenting on the other links in the model, I shall gradually approach the central concept of narrator.

Narrative communication through narrative text

As this model illustrates, the narrative text is fundamental to both narrative theory and analysis. Modern narrative theory would have been unthinkable without the focus on the literary text that has been characteristic of much literary criticism in this century, from Russian formalism onwards. Yet this kind of textual emphasis does not imply that the concepts of author and reader become unnecessary links in the communication model. As we shall see in Part II, we need them both in narrative analysis. Moreover, they relate narrative theory to other aspects of literary criticism and, more broadly, to different ways of reading literature.

Like language the narrative text creates meaning indirectly. In so far as narrative theory tends to isolate the text as its working area, it implies that literary meaning (and literary versatility of meaning) are established through verbal language, textual structure, and narrative strategies. For a theorist such as Roland Barthes the literary text has multiple meanings; thus the author's intention behind the text becomes difficult, and in one sense unnecessary, to determine (Barthes 1988). Here we are touching upon a controversial issue in literary theory that we cannot go into in greater depth. We note, though, that narrative theory tends to situate itself in an intermediate position in this debate. Narrative theory contends that narrative structures serve to constitute the text's meaning; it furthermore claims that these narrative structures can not only extend but also delimit the meanings which they themselves create. Thus narrative structures contribute to establishing what Umberto Eco in *The Limits of Interpretation* calls 'the rights of the text', and which he links both to a right to be interpreted and to a right not to be over-interpreted: 'The limits of interpretation coincide with the rights of the text (which does not mean with the rights of its author)' (Eco 1990: 7; cf. Eco 1992: 64). Part II of this book responds to the challenge to draw out by analysis some of the ways in which narrative texts can perform this double operation.

I use 'narrative text' synonymously with 'discourse'. The narrative text is the short story or novel we read, in which a series of narrative techniques and variations is included. Yet while narrative theory is still text-oriented, it now puts more emphasis on, and takes a greater interest in, the outer links in the narrative communication model: the addresser as the writing author and the addressee as the reader. As both are part of history and of one or more cultural communities, the recent (re)orientation of literary theory towards history and context does not reduce the relevance of narrative theory. There is a sense in which the opposition between 'history' and 'narrative structure' is factitious, possibly even theoretically untenable. As Tzvetan Todorov argues, 'it is only on the level of structures that we can describe literary development; not only does the knowledge of structures not impede that of variability, but indeed it is the sole means we possess of approaching the latter' (Todorov 1981: 61).

Historical author and historical reader

The historical author is the man or woman who writes a narrative text, for example Miguel de Cervantes, who wrote *Don Quixote* and published the novel in two parts, the first in 1605 and the second in 1615, the year before his death. Correspondingly—at the other extreme of the model—the historical reader is the man or woman who reads, for instance, *Don Quixote*, whether in, say, Britain today or in Spain in the time of Cervantes.

Thus far the concept of author may seem clear and unambiguous. However, what actually is an author? The word does not only refer to a specific historical person but also to a *writer of a text*. Both the notion and concept of author are linked to the text (and its reading), not only to a personal biography. That authors themselves may also experience such a combination as problematic is exemplified in the short text 'Borges and I'. Here the narrator, who identifies himself as the historical person Jorge Luis Borges, wanders about in Buenos Aires experiencing distance from—almost a feeling of being in competition with!—the author Borges, whom he sees on show in bookshops and reads about in periodicals and so forth.

More important than such a difference, however, is the main distinction in narrative theory that we touch upon once we connect the concept of author with the writing of a text: the difference between the author *of* a text and the narrator *in* the text. This is how J. Hillis Miller puts it in connection with Virginia Woolf's *To the Lighthouse*:

> A distinction must be made here, as always, between Virginia Woolf sitting at her desk with a blank sheet of paper before her, composing *To the Lighthouse*,

extending the line of words further and further out into the void of not-yet-written-on paper, and, on the other hand, the imagined and imaginary narrator of the novel. The latter is a different person, is located in a different place, and possesses quite different powers. (Miller 1990: 155)

This distinction between author and narrator, which is one of the most important in narrative theory, will become clearer when the concept of 'narrator' is explained below. As the quotation from Miller shows, the author stands in principle outside the literary universe he or she creates by means of language. A finished and published novel is much more sharply separated from the author than is the linguistic message from the addresser in Jakobson's communication model. I understand the author primarily as a writer, as the producer of the text of narrative fiction that forms the starting-point of the narrative analysis. This does not imply that there is not a crucial connection between the author and the text (the text does not arise by itself any more than it exists in a hermetically sealed room), but it means that this relationship is *indirect* and influenced by the sort of language and literary techniques the author uses.

The *historical reader* thus refers to the person who reads the text. As Wallace Martin comments, readers themselves are the most obvious source of variety in interpretation, since each and every one of them brings with him or her different experiences and expectations to the reading of narrative texts:

> Reader-response theorists emphasize an important point: narratives do not contain a definite meaning that sits in the words waiting for someone to find it. Meaning comes into existence only in the act of reading. But it is equally wrong to conclude that interpretation must therefore be 'in' the reader, regardless of the words on the page. In order to read them, we must know the language—the 'code' in Jakobson's communication model—though we need not be conscious of its complex rules. (Martin 1986: 160–1).

This is a sensibly nuanced view of the relationship between the text and its reading. 'Endless variety is possible in interpretation', notes Paul Armstrong, 'but tests for validity can still judge some readings to be more plausible than others' (Armstrong 1990: p. ix). The fact that interpretations may vary strongly from reader to reader does not mean that all are equally valid or important: here a narrative analysis can provide one basis for establishing interpretative validity.

Implied author and implied reader

So far I have made general comments on the narrative text, relating it to the author on the one hand and to the reader on the other. If we now enter the 'box' illustrating the narrative text in the communication model, we see that the two extreme links are called 'implied author' and 'implied reader'. Although the analyses in Part II do not make extensive use of these concepts, they are so important in narrative theory that it is necessary to be familiar with them.

The concept of *implied author* was first introduced by Wayne Booth in *The Rhetoric of Fiction*, a pioneer study in American narrative theory. Subsequently it has been used by, among others, Seymour Chatman, who points out that 'Unlike the narrator, the implied author can *tell* us nothing. He, or better, *it* has no voice, no direct means of communicating. It instructs us silently, through the design of the whole, with all the voices, by all the means it has chosen to let us learn' (Chatman 1978: 148, original emphasis). For Chatman, the implied author is in other words silent and without any voice. As Rimmon-Kenan rightly emphasizes in *Narrative Fiction*, this means that the implied author must be seen as a construct which the reader assembles on the basis of all the textual components. The implied author is best considered as 'a set of implicit norms rather than as a speaker or a voice (i.e. a subject). It follows, therefore, that the implied author cannot literally be a participant in the narrative communication situation' (Rimmon-Kenan 1983: 88). Although I share this view, I include the implied author in the narrative communication model. But I understand the concept in a particular way: as 'an image of the author in the text' (Genette 1988: 141) and as an expression of 'textual intention' (Chatman 1990: 104). The implied author then becomes practically a synonym for the ideological value system that the text, indirectly and by combining all its resources, presents and represents.

Like the implied author, the *implied reader* is also a construct, and just as the first is different both from the historical author and the narrator, so the second is distinguished both from the narratee and the historical reader. The concept of the implied reader takes us into the border area between narrative theory and theories of aesthetic response. A major representative of this area of study is Wolfgang Iser. For Iser, the literary work arises through the interplay, the *interaction*, between text and reader. The implied reader, who enters into this interaction, is a 'role' or a 'standpoint' which 'allows the (real) reader to assemble the meaning of the text' (Maclean 1992: 131). The implied reader is thus both active and passive: active by making the text meaningful, passive since the premises of the text's production of meaning are given in its discourse and narration. The author has, according to Iser, a certain control of the way in which we read, but this form of control is indirect and based on shared conventions which have matured over time—a repertoire of social, historical, and cultural norms regulating the manner in which fictional prose works and communicates. The meaning of a text arises in *productive tension* between the role or model reader the text presents and the historical reader's dispositions and interests. The implied reader's activity is very much a structuring process, in which we not least attempt to establish a connection between the text's 'blanks'. For Iser, fictional prose is characterized by such *Leerstellen*—points of 'suspended connectability in the text' (Iser 1980: 198) that need to be arranged by the reader to become comprehensible as textual aspects of an overall aesthetic structure.

Narrator and narratee

With these two concepts we have reached the 'centre' of the communication model—that part of the model that is most clearly related to 'the epic proto-situation'. We have already seen that narrator and narratee form two of the links in this 'original' communication model. (The third and final link, the story the narrator relates, has in the more complex model become 'narrative text'.)

As Rimmon-Kenan puts it, the narrator is 'the agent which at the very least narrates or engages in some activity serving the needs of narration . . . the narratee is the agent which is at the very least implicitly addressed by the narrator' (Rimmon-Kenan 1983: 88–9). If the narrator explicitly addresses one or more narratees, the narrative situation in one sense resembles that of the oral proto-situation. As we shall see in Part II, Joseph Conrad's *Heart of Darkness* provides a particularly interesting example of such a narrator and such narratees. Yet as *Heart of Darkness* also illustrates, this kind of resemblance is superficial because in fictional prose texts narrative communication is generally more complex, varied, and indirect than it is in oral narrative. When in Charlotte Brontë's *Jane Eyre* (1847) the narrator exclaims, 'Reader, I married him' (p. 473), the meaning of 'reader' approximates to that of narratee as explained here. In this case, then, the narratee is explicitly addressed, and this kind of address tells us something about Jane as narrator (and, by implication, about Charlotte Brontë as author). Correspondingly, that the narratee in Albert Camus's *The Outsider* (1942) is just implied serves, in conjunction with other textual signals, to indicate the narrator's fundamental loneliness. In some texts, if the narratee is only addressed implicitly, his or her function may approach the role of the implied reader.

As I have already emphasized, the narrator in a narrative text must be clearly distinguished from the author of the text. The narrator is an integral part of the fictional text written by the author. The narrator (or the combination of narrators) is a narrative instrument that the author uses to present and develop the text, which is thus constituted by the activities and functions that the narrator performs. Gerald Prince defines the narrator as follows: 'The one who narrates, as inscribed in the text. There is at least one narrator per narrative, located at the same diegetic level as the narratee he or she is addressing' (Prince 1991: 65). By 'diegetic level' Prince means 'the level at which an existent event, or act of recounting is situated with regard to a given *diegesis* . . . [i.e.] the (fictional) world in which the situations and events narrated occur' (Prince 1991: 20, original emphasis). Prince's use of the word 'inscribed' about the narrator is useful since it so clearly brings out that the narrator is a part of the diegesis: he is in the fictional text while also helping the author to constitute and communicate it. (Note that 'diegesis' can also be used synonymously with narration.)

If we say that the narrator is an important narrative instrument for the author, there can be no doubt that the concept of narrator is useful and productive of insights in narrative analysis. 'The narrator', argues Mieke Bal, 'is the most central concept in the analysis of narrative texts' (Bal 1997: 19). Much of the reason for the key position held by the concept of narrator in narrative theory lies in the text's narration aspect: the narrator is the narration instance within the narrative text. This function is crucial to the production of fictional prose, yet it brings to light a problem that Paul de Man (1979: 139) has put his finger on: if we give the narrator qualities such as personal identity and creative skills, we have in a way done nothing but introduce a new concept of author. It needs to be stressed, therefore, that the narrator is a part of the narrative text (as the communication model also makes clear), and that he does not exist outside the linguistic structure which constitutes him. Having said this, I hasten to add that the function of the narrator as a 'narrative instrument' is most clear in narrative texts in which he serves as a 'pure' narrator, i.e. without at the same time being an active character in the plot. This brings us to the distinction between two main types of narrator.

Third-person and first-person narrator

Since the concepts of third-person and first-person narrator are most readily definable in relation to each other, I shall start with a quotation from Franz Stanzel:

> The contrast between an embodied narrator and a narrator without such bodily determination, that is to say, between a first-person narrator and an authorial third-person narrator, accounts for the most important difference in the motivation of the narrator to narrate. For an embodied narrator, this motivation is existential; it is directly connected with his practical experiences, with the joys and sorrows he has experienced, with his moods and needs . . . For the third-person narrator, on the other hand, there is no existential compulsion to narrate. His motivation is literary-aesthetic rather than existential. (Stanzel 1986: 93)

In addition to being a narrator, the first-person narrator is in other words *active in the plot*, i.e. in the dynamic shaping of the text's action, events, and characters. The third-person narrator is on the other hand outside or 'above' the plot, even though he is also in the text. Since he does not participate in the action, the function of the third-person narrator is more purely communicative. It is on the contrary typical for the first-person narrator to combine the functions of narrator and character.

The transitions between these two main variants of narrator may be unclear. For instance, a third-person narrator may well link the presentation to characters in the plot (as when the third-person narrator in *The Trial* does so with K.). Yet the distinction between third-person and first-person narrator is an important one—not only theoretically but also in analysis. Tzvetan Todorov has emphasized that 'there is an impassable barrier between the narrative in which the narrator sees everything his character sees but does not appear on stage, and the narrative in which a character–narrator says "I". To confuse them would be to reduce language to zero. To see a house, and to say "I see a house," are two actions not only distinct but in opposition. Events can never "tell themselves": the act of verbalization is irreducible' (Todorov 1981: 39).

As the use of the personal pronoun 'I' shows, Todorov justifies the distinction between third-person and first-person narrator not only existentially (like Stanzel), but also linguistically/grammatically. As a basis for this distinction these two criteria supplement each other. For it is often the *combination* of first-person pronoun and active plot engagement that marks the narrator as first-person. In other words a third-person narrator can also use the 'I' reference without having to enter into the action as a participant. This was quite normal, not least in the nineteenth-century novel. Consider the first paragraph of Fyodor Dostoevsky's *The Karamazov Brothers* (1879–80): 'Aleksei Fyodorovich Karamazov was the third son of Fyodor Pavlovich Karamazov, a landowner of our district, extremely well known in his time (and to this day still remembered in these parts) on account of his violent and mysterious death exactly thirteen years ago, the circumstances of which I shall relate in due course' (p. 9). We note that the narrator here places one of the characters in 'our district' before going on just afterwards to refer to himself as 'I'. Such an opening may seem to indicate a first-person narrative. However, this 'I' is not individualized, it does not participate in the action, and overall the novel's narrative method is third-person. A slightly different variant that was common in the nineteenth century is to position the narrator temporarily among the characters, in order, so to speak, to provide a personal anchorage point for the third-person narration. Examples of this variant are observable in Charles Dickens, George Eliot, and Wilhelm Raabe, but the best known is in the opening of Gustave Flaubert's *Madame Bovary* (1857). Here the narrator is first introduced as a classmate of Charles. However, he soon withdraws completely from the action, something which is crucial for Flaubert's development of a variant of third-person narrative in which the events are peculiarly autonomized. Developing a narrative method which prefigures that of James Joyce (see Chapter 6), Flaubert makes his third-person narrator record the events and then communicate them to the reader without evaluating them in the manner of, for example, a narrator in a novel by Balzac.

The question of the personal pronoun not only applies in this case to the marking of a narrator as third-person or first-person, but also moves over to the question of how a third-person narrator can or should be identified. As we shall see below (in the analysis of the second part of Virginia Woolf's *To the Lighthouse*), one may refer to a third-person narrator as 'she', 'he', or 'it'. The problem is that even if the third-person narrator is also in principle distinct from the author, she/he/it can nevertheless express opinions, viewpoints, feelings, and so forth that are not neutral with respect to gender. In this book I choose to refer to the third-person narrator as 'he' (where 'he' refers to a narrative tool or instrument), while in discussions of literary texts I use 'she' of the narrator if the author is female, and 'he' if the author is male. A related problem is that although we may refer to the third-person narrator as he/she/it, there is a sense in which all narrative situations (within the narrative communication model) presuppose a first-person narrator. There is no simple solution to this problem, partly because the alternatives to 'third-person' narrator also have terminological drawbacks ('external' narrator is easily misunderstood as meaning that the narrator is outside the fiction: 'authorial' narrator may suggest too close a relationship between narrator and author). However, the analyses in Part II suggest that my use of the term third-person narrator has a heuristic justification. First, it enables us to distinguish between two main types of narrator. Second, although the identity of the third-person narrator is unclear, the term does indicate that the narrator is outside the action (but within the fiction), and that he/she/it is an indispensable narrative instrument in the service of the author as writer.

The choice between a third-person or first-person narrator is not necessarily a definitive choice the author must make before he or she sets about writing. We may well have both a third-person and a first-person narrator in the same text. One of the best examples of how thematically productive such a combination of narrators can be is William Faulkner's *The Sound and the Fury* (1929). In this modernist novel, the first three parts are told by three very different narrators who are also main characters, Benjy, Quentin, and Jason respectively. The final part has a third-person narrator who is outside the action he presents (but whose perspective is interestingly related to that of Dilsey, a Black servant in the Compson household).

It is also possible to combine these two main variants in a short narrative text. 'Tiger', a short story by the Norwegian author Sissel Lie, opens thus:

> She awakens while it is still night, sees unclear shadows in the room that she knows will disappear with the morning light, presses her eyelids together to make these shadows less dangerous. With the morning light the sun shines straight onto the red dress hanging on the cupboard door, and the fear releases its grip. An amulet against evil spirits. She imagines a woman quite unlike herself to whom she will give the role of author. She is to write about the dress.
>
> I had written the first lines of a short story, but something happened, I did not get any further . . . (p. 7, my translation)

The important thing here is not so much the metafictional (i.e. fiction-revealing) elements at the beginning of the second paragraph as the sudden transition from a third-person narrative situation to a first-person one. (That the element of metafiction is used to *motivate* the transition is another matter.) We cannot assume that 'I' is identical with the author. As author, Sissel Lie constructs both narrative situations, the third-person as well as the first-person one. The two narrative variants mutually influence each other in the short story, just as they do throughout the collection of stories of which it is the first.

The characteristics of both the third-person and first-person narrator will become clearer when I relate these terms to concepts such as narrative level, distance, perspective, and voice below, and when in Part II I analyse examples of texts with both main variants. However, let us first see how an author can alternate between first-person and third-person narrator from one novel to another. Knut Hamsun's *Hunger* (1890) opens thus: 'It was in those days when I wandered about hungry in Kristiania [the name of Oslo in 1890], that strange city which no one leaves before it has set its mark upon him . . .' (p. 3). The text immediately characterizes itself as first-person—communicated by an anonymous 'I'—a narrator who wants to relate something he has experienced and who therefore, we suspect, will become both narrator and main character. What this narrator is called, we do not yet know (and are in fact never told), but, even here at the beginning, his narrative appears to have what Stanzel calls 'existential' motivation. That the novel's focus will be on the main character during a difficult period is something we sense as we relate the key-word 'mark' in the first paragraph to the very first word that we read: the title-word 'hunger'.

See now how Hamsun opens his next novel, *Mysteries* (1892):

> In the middle of the summer of 1891 the most extraordinary things began happening in a small Norwegian coastal town. A stranger by the name of Nagel appeared, a singular character who shook the town by his eccentric behaviour and then vanished as suddenly as he had come. At one point he had a visitor: a mysterious young lady who came for God knows what reason and dared stay only a few hours. But let me begin at the beginning . . . (p. 3)

We first note a detail: as in *Hunger* Hamsun ends the first paragraph with an ellipsis—successive dots that as blanks (to use Wolfgang Iser's term) typographically mark the narrative situation for the further presentation of the events. However, while in *Hunger* we immediately link the narrator's voice to the 'I' we meet in the very first line, the first paragraph in *Mysteries* rather indicates a difference and distance between the narrator and the stranger who turns up in the town. As Atle Kittang puts it:

> The differences apply first and foremost to the narrative form. True enough, *Mysteries* is also a work in which the inner life of the main character is in focus. Nagel is the text's central consciousness, and central sequences take us into his mental processes in a way that prefigures the techniques of the modern psychological novel (inner monologue, 'stream of consciousness'). Yet by choosing the third-person

form, Hamsun opens the way for an interplay between first-person and third-person instances that one only finds pale glimpses of in *Hunger*. The independent narrator's voice makes it possible to establish a level of insight outside the main character and thereby to pass judgements, mark distance. (Kittang 1984: 73, my translation)

While it is necessary to emphasize this difference in narrative communicative form between the two novels, it must be pointed out that the third-person position of the narrator in *Mysteries* does not in itself make him 'objective' or his assessments 'right'. As we read our way through the text, the third-person narrator's perspective seems to approximate to the perspective of the social surroundings made mysterious by Nagel, and we cannot therefore be quite sure that his account is reliable. Still, this problem does not make the distinction between first-person and third-person narration unnecessary. Hamsun's innovative use of a third-person narrator is on the contrary decisive both for the structure and for the formation of thematic tensions in *Mysteries*.

Reliable and unreliable narrator

Unless the text happens to provide indications to the contrary, the narrator is characterized by *narrative authority*. By way of illustration let us take the same example that Wayne Booth uses at the beginning of *The Rhetoric of Fiction*: 'There was a man in the land of Uz, whose name was Job; and that man was perfect and upright, one that feared God, and eschewed evil' (Job 1: 1; all biblical quotations are taken from the Authorized Version). This is the first sentence of the book of Job, a text in the Old Testament. We do not know who the author of the book of Job was, nor do we know with any certainty when the book was written (probably *c*.600 BC). A striking feature of the text's beginning, however, is the storyteller's narrative authority. As Booth points out, here we get at one stroke the kind of information about Job that we never obtain about people we know ourselves, not even our most intimate friends. 'Yet it is information that we must accept without question if we are to grasp the story that is to follow' (Booth 1983: 3). All those who know Job will know that the development of the plot is wholly dependent on the moral quality of the life led by the main character: it is precisely the fact that Job loses everything he owns without having done anything wrong that makes his situation so desperate and conflict-provoking. The essential point, however, is not what sort of person Job is, but the fact that we as readers so directly and without reservation accept the narrator's valuation of him. The narrator, Booth stresses, has an 'artificial authority' (Booth 1983: 4). This demonstrates how strongly our attitude to narrative texts is influenced by conventions, i.e. customary notions and expectations that are so ingrained that we do not (or only to a partial extent) think about them. A fundamental convention in narrative fiction is that we believe the narrator, unless the text at some point gives us a signal *not* to do so.

If the text does give such signals, the narrator's authority may be under-mined and the narrator becomes *unreliable*. The borderline between reliable and unreliable narrator may be blurred. For instance, even an unreliable nar-rator can give us necessary information. Yet the fact that he is unreliable will reduce the trust we place in this information (and to an even greater degree the trust we place in the narrator's evaluation of the information). How does a narrator betray the fact that he is unreliable? Let us stick to the notion that as a starting-point he is reliable, that he has the 'artificial authority' the narrative function ascribes to him. Each narrative act has its own features and charac-teristics, and features that may indicate a narrator's unreliability include:

1   The narrator has limited knowledge of or insight into what he is narrating.
2   The narrator has a strong personal involvement (in a way that makes both his narrative presentation and evaluation strikingly subjective).
3   The narrator appears to represent something that comes into conflict with the system of values that the discourse as a whole presents.

Often these three factors will mutually affect each other. By 'system of values' I mean the text's ideological orientation, i.e. the combination of those view-points, priorities, evaluations, and criticisms we can read out of the text as a narrative language system. Such a value system is seldom 'simple' in the sense that it can be summarized in a few sentences. The concept is related to the term *thematics*: the most significant problems and ideas that the text (as fictional discourse) presents and explores. The thematics of the texts analysed in Part II are complex and multi-faceted, and this kind of thematic richness comes not least from the narrative technique through which the fictional content is gen-erated and presented.

The text's value system is linked to what I have called textual intention, a concept related to that of the implied author. When a narrator becomes un-reliable, a form of communication is established between the implied reader and the implied author, 'above' the narrator. We can illustrate this in Fig. 2.3. Seymour Chatman, who presents this diagram, comments that 'the broken line indicates the secret ironic message about the narrator's unreliability' (Chatman 1990: 151). Two examples will serve to substantiate these theoretical comments.

I have said that the first three parts of *The Sound and the Fury* are told by

Figure 2.3

three very different narrators, while the narrative position in the fourth and final part is third-person. What becomes apparent as we approach the end of the novel (and becomes even clearer when we read it again) is that the third of the first-person narrators, Jason, is unreliable. Why? The reasons are complicated and can be linked to all three characterizing features of the unreliable narrator. Yet the most important reason why Jason becomes unreliable lies in the contrast that arises between his judgements and views on the one hand, and those we can read out of the novel's fourth part on the other. For in *The Sound and the Fury* this concluding, third-person narrative instalment is instrumental in establishing the text's value system, which—even though it is far from simple—manifests itself as radically different from the system of values for which Jason stands.

If we go from Faulkner to an author whose narrative experiments Faulkner carried further, Joseph Conrad, we meet in the latter's *Under Western Eyes* (1911) a novel which even in its own title announces the limited perspective the narrator has on the events he is to report. The narration in *Under Western Eyes* is first-person, and the narrator's limited perspective signals that his account is potentially unreliable. Conrad presents the whole novel, apart from the title and an accompanying 'motto', as told by an English-language teacher. Working in Switzerland, the teacher comes into contact with a group of Russians, including the novel's main character. What makes us sceptical about this narrator, on whom we are wholly dependent as readers, is that although he proclaims how little he understands of Russia and eastern Europe (both culturally and historically), he narrates, and generalizes, in a manner that presupposes great knowledge and insight. Thus the narration undermines its own authority, while paradoxically presenting themes that are more complex than the narrator realizes. Since the novel's title in this connection appears as an ironic commentary on the novel's narrator, we can relate it to the implied author of *Under Western Eyes*. We can do the same thing with the motto, which is an inaccurate quotation from the novel's own text.

Film narrator

Is the concept of narrator critically productive for film? I believe it is, but I emphasize at once that the film narrator is very different from the literary narrator. From the section on film communication above, we recall that in the 1960s Metz and other film theorists attempted to apply linguistic principles to the study of film. However, as Chatman comments, Metz soon realized that 'film is not a "language" but another kind of semiotic system with "articulations" of its own' (Chatman 1990: 124). Film narration is an economic and effective system. As John Ellis puts it in *Visible Fictions*, film narration balances 'familiar elements of meaning against the unfamiliar, it moves forward by a succession of events linked in a causal chain' (Ellis 1989: 74). The concept of *film narrator*, as it is used here, refers primarily to David Bordwell's *Narration in the Fiction Film* (1985) and Seymour Chatman's *Coming to Terms* (1990).

Bordwell believes that film has narration but no narrator: 'in watching films, we are seldom aware of being told something by an entitiy resembling a human being . . . [Therefore film] narration is better understood as the organization of a set of cues for the construction of a story. This presupposes a perceiver, but not any sender, of a message' (Bordwell 1985: 62). In other words, at the same time as he sees narration as completely central in film communication, Bordwell bases his theory on what the *viewer* does when she or he sees a film. As Chatman has pointed out, Bordwell thus accords priorities and works in a manner reminiscent of reader-response theorists. Bordwell's theory of film narration is also interestingly related to Boris Eikhenbaum's assertion that understanding a film is 'a new kind of intellectual exercise' (Eikhenbaum 1973: 123). Bordwell's viewer is not passive but actively participating: on the basis of an indeterminate number of visual and auditory impressions the viewer first constructs connected and comprehensible images and then a story. There is no doubt that the emphasis Bordwell puts upon the viewer's active role is critically illuminating, and so are his comments on narration. Yet as Edward Branigan has observed in *Narrative Comprehension and Film* (1992: 109–10), since Bordwell, in his discussion of film narration, uses a number of metaphors which can also be attributed to the film narrator, the difference between the two terms is perhaps less obvious than it appears to be at first sight.

'Film', writes William Rothman in *The 'I' of the Camera*, is 'a medium limited to surfaces, to the outer, the visible . . . [And yet film is] a medium of mysterious depths, of the inner, the invisible' (Rothman 1988: p. xv). It is to Bordwell's credit that he has given theoretical grounds for this fundamental paradox in the way in which film functions. From a literary perspective it is interesting that his theory is based on the Russian formalists' distinction between *fabula, syuzhet,* and *style*. Even though Bordwell understands these terms in a particular way (partly because he uses them to construct his own theory, partly because he applies them to film), their relevance illustrates an important point of contact between film theory and narrative theory (a point of contact strengthened by Bordwell's use of Genette).

For Bordwell, 'the *fabula* (sometimes translated as "story") . . . embodies the action as a chronological, cause-and-effect chain of events occurring within a given duration and a spatial field . . . The *syuzhet* (usually translated as "plot") is the actual arrangement and presentation of the *fabula* in the film' (Bordwell 1985: 49, 50). Crucial to Bordwell's theory is that the *syuzhet* of film, as he sees it, only presents a small part of the total *fabula*, which is an implicit structure the viewer supports through assumptions and inferences. As the third component, style refers to the systematic use of cinematic devices. In contrast to *syuzhet*, which for Bordwell is a general characteristic of narrative, style is medium-specific (and, in film, thereby more technical).

By means of these three concepts Bordwell then presents his definition of film narration: '*the process whereby the film's syuzhet and style interact in the course of cueing and channeling the spectator's construction of the fabula*' (Bordwell 1985: 53, original emphasis). This definition activates and builds on all the three elements Bordwell collects from Russian formalism. Yet Chatman finds that

> It is a little unclear how this process occurs, whether it is internal to the viewer— in which case style and *syuzhet* 'interact' only within her perception and cognition—or whether there is some kind of interchange between the screen and the viewer. If the latter, then 'narration' at least partly inhabits the film—in which case, we can legitimately ask why it should not be granted some status as an agent. (Chatman 1990: 126)

Bordwell's theory is remarkably comprehensive and broadly persuasive, yet it is indeed difficult to imagine that a film is 'organized' without being 'sent'. Film as an effective communication system presupposes some form of 'sender' (the fact that this sender is composed of many links and may be impossible to identify is another matter). Therefore it makes more sense to say, as Chatman does, that the viewer reconstructs the film's narrative than to say that he or she 'constructs' it. This does not mean that all viewers reconstruct alike, but it indicates that film narration both lays a foundation for reconstruction and governs it—somewhat in the same way that the narration in verbal prose governs the reading process.

The concept of 'film narrator' becomes critically helpful set against this theoretical background. Understood as a complex form of communication, film, like verbal prose, has a sender. Again, in both media, no matter how different they are, it is useful to differentiate the concept of sender into (implied) author and narrator. For films as for novels,

> we would do well to distinguish between a *presenter* of a story, the narrator (who is a component of the discourse), and the *inventor* of both the story and the discourse (including the narrator): that is, the implied author—not as the original cause, the original biographical person, but rather as the principle within the text to which we assign the inventional tasks. (Chatman 1990: 133, original emphasis)

Chatman illustrates this distinction with Alain Resnais's *Providence* (1977). The first half of this film presents the fantasies of the main character, the ageing author Clive Langham. Gradually it dawns on the viewer that the film's voice-over is in this case in charge of the images passing across the screen. These fragmentary images show more or less hypothetical drafts of the novel Langham is trying to write. The point is that in these fantasies that the film visualizes for us, it is the voice of Langham that determines what we see, not some impersonal 'narration'. Thus Langham functions here as a kind of first-person narrator, what Chatman with Genette calls a 'homodiegetic' narrator. Later on in the film this narrator disappears, and an 'impersonal' (third-person) narrator takes over the narration. Yet, according to Chatman, both are 'introduced by the overriding intent of the film, the implied author' (Chatman 1990: 13).

Let us summarize the argument so far. Film communication involves a presentation which is primarily visual, but which in addition also exploits other channels of communication. The superordinate 'instance' that presents all the means of communication that film has at its disposal we can call the film narrator. Guiding the viewer's perception of the film, the film narrator is the film-maker's communicative instrument. We will recall that this kind of function is something the literary third-person narrator may have. The great difference is that while the qualities of the third-person narrator are also 'human' in the sense that he communicates verbally (gives information, comments, and generalizes), the film narrator differs in that he is a heterogeneous mechanical and technical instrument, constituted by a large number of different components.

Chatman (1990: 134–5) presents this diagram (Fig. 2.4), which shows 'the multiplexity of the cinematic narrator'. The film narrator is the sum of these and other variables. A number of them (like the camera) are absolutely fundamental to film communication, while others (like off-screen sound) may be more or less important depending upon which film the diagram is related to. (Some of these concepts are so technical that I shall define them: *mise-en-scène* is all the elements—lighting, furniture, costumes, etc.—that are placed in front of the camera to be filmed; 'straight cut' means to move directly over from one framing to another, while 'fade' (or 'dissolve') is to superimpose one filmic image on another, so that the first one gradually disappears while the second comes into focus. For a helpful glossary of film terminology see Bordwell and Thompson 1997: 477–82.)

As this diagram illustrates, it is the *viewer* (not the film) who constructs such a 'narrative synthesis'. Much of the challenge to the film author lies in presenting the various elements that together form the film narrator in such a way that the viewer experiences all of them as necessary and thematically productive. The elements of film communication must be consistent in the sense that they provide the viewer with a foundation on which to construct the film narrator, and thus the film story. 'Voice-over' is one of the many elements that constitute the film narrator: a voice outside the film image. Sarah Kozloff stresses in *Invisible Storytellers* that all three constituents in the term 'voice-over narration' are fully operative. *Voice* determines the medium: we must hear somebody speaking. *Over* applies to the relationship between the sound source and the images on the screen: the viewer cannot see the person speaking at the time of hearing his or her voice. *Narration* is linked to the content

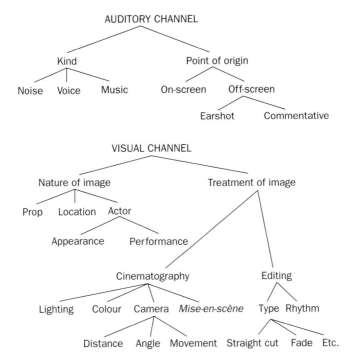

Figure 2.4

of what is said: somebody communicates a story—introduces, supplements, and comments on what is shown visually (Kozloff 1988: 2–3). The female voice-over in Gabriel Axel's *Babette's Feast* illustrates all these three characteristics of voice-over and furthermore exemplifies the narrative distance that may obtain between the voice-over and the action that is shown on screen (see Chapter 4).

Now if the film narrator is as complex and fragmented as Fig. 2.4 shows, who then is the film *author*? While writing a novel is normally something done by a single individual, a narrative fiction film is usually so expensive and so technically complicated that it can only be realized through a complex production process in which many of the links are 'co-creative'—the author of the script, the producer, actors and actresses, photographers, etc. The main reason why the *director* is usually regarded as the film's 'author' is that he or she not only has overall responsibility for according priorities and co-ordinating the activities that are part of the production process, but also functions creatively in relation to the screenplay and the thematics of the film. In keeping with this convention, in Part II I shall consider, for example, John Huston as the 'author' of *The Dead* because he is the film's director and clearly left his creative imprint on it.

Narrative levels

After this excursion into film, I shall now return to narrative communication in fictional prose. But initially we recall a point that the concept of 'film narrator' illustrates: in spite of the great difference in medium, elements in a narrative theory that has a literary basis may well be relevant to film. Before refining the concept of narrator further by means of the terms distance, perspective, and voice, I shall outline the different narrative levels we can have in a fictional prose text.

In the same way that an author can write a text by combining the use of third-person or first-person narrators the author may also design the discourse by combining different *narrative levels*. Thus, a character who performs actions that are narrated may himself serve as the narrator of an embedded story. Inside this story there may in turn be another character who tells another story, and so on. In this hierarchical structure the highest level is that which is placed right 'above' the action in the first story. We call this narrative level *extradiegetic*. Traditionally it is on this level that the third-person narrator is placed, with a full view of the action and usually also knowledge of the characters' thoughts and feelings. On the extradiegetic level the narrator in Chaucer's *The Canterbury Tales* (c.1390–1400) presents the pilgrims, and it is on a corresponding level that the narrator in *Don Quixote* introduces the main character:

> The age of our gentleman bordered upon fifty years. He was of a robust constitution, spare-bodied, of a meagre visage; a very early riser, and a keen sportsman. It is said his surname was Quixada, or Quesada (for in this there is some difference among the authors who have written upon this subject), though by probable conjectures it may be gathered that he was called Quixana. But this is of little import to our story; let it suffice that in relating it we do not swerve a jot from the truth. (p. 23)

'Our story' points to the dominant level of action in the novel, the *diegetic* level which the third-person narrator (on the extradiegetic level) presents but does not participate in. Since all narrators are by definition part of texts, the narrator is clearly entitled to refer to his own presentation as 'the truth'. Here we again touch on the question of narrative authority: because the brilliant idea from which Cervantes develops his novel turns on Don Quixote's madness, it becomes crucial to the fiction's sustainability that the reader believes in the account the narrator gives of the hero's daredevil actions. Thus it is far from a matter of chance that the narration at the beginning of the novel establishes a series of parallels between the narrator's evaluation of Don Quixote *as* mad and actions apparently confirming his madness. For similar reasons the diegetic level, with Don Quixote laboriously riding Rocinante in the Spanish landscape, is presented in graphic detail.

Yet although the diegetic level of Don Quixote and Rocinante (and on the second and third expeditions Sancho and the donkey as well) is dominant in *Don Quixote*, the novel provides in addition a good illustration of what we call a *hypodiegetic* level—the narrative level 'below' the diegetic. After a long day Don Quixote and Sancho arrive at some goatherds' huts where they are received in a friendly manner and decide to set up camp for the night. After a good meal and after 'one of the two wine-bags that hung in view' (p. 85) have been emptied, Don Quixote first makes his speech about the golden age, before the goatherd, Pedro, tells the story of Chrysostom who has died of love for Marcela. The narrative technique Cervantes uses here resembles structurally what Conrad does at the beginning of *Heart of Darkness* when he constructs an oral narrative situation on board a sailing vessel on the Thames. Although both authors establish an oral narrative situation inside the written fiction, however, there is a limit to how far these texts can be compared. While Marlow in *Heart of Darkness* tells his own story (which forms the diegetic level), Pedro tells a relatively brief story which is inserted into the main action and which is marked as hypodiegetic when Don Quixote (as a 'diegetic character') comments on it. This happens in two stages. First, Don Quixote cannot refrain from correcting Pedro's language and choice of words—he goes on doing this until Pedro becomes so irritated that he threatens to stop telling the story. Then Don Quixote changes his attitude, and his subsequent comments are encouraging rather than critical.

There are also other features of the inserted stories in *Don Quixote* that relate the hypodiegetic level to the diegetic. Such a feature is linked to the portrayal of characters, as when Dorothea turns up again on the diegetic level after she has previously been introduced on the hypodiegetic. As Viktor Shklovsky has shown, these inserted, short-story-like hypodiegetic texts enrich and complicate the novel's plot (Shklovsky 1973: 104–5). This applies not least to the longest embedded text, 'The Novel of the Curious Impertinent' (pp. 310–57), in which the main character Anselmo appears partly as a contrast to, and partly as analogous to, Don Quixote. When the hypodiegetic level operates in this way, Genette speaks of a thematic function. Broadly, a hypodiegetic narrative can have this function, an explanatory function, or a function which takes the form of a more independent contribution to the plot. In *Don Quixote* these functions blend, partly because the thread of action in the plot revolving round Don Quixote and Sancho is not particularly strong and the hypodiegetic narratives serve to supplement it. The classic example of hypodiegetic narrative in world literature is *The Arabian Nights' Entertainments*. Just before daybreak, Scheherazade, who has just been asked by her sister to tell 'one of those pleasant stories you have read', 'addressed herself to the sultan, thus: Sir, will your majesty be pleased to allow me to give my sister this satisfaction? With all my heart, answers the sultan. Then Scheherazade bid her sister listen, and afterwards addressing herself to Schahriar, began thus . . . ' (p. 17). Scheherazade's life is directly dependent upon her ability to narrate, and the only condition her stories (which constitute the text's hypodiegetic level) must satisfy is to retain the king's attention. In *The Arabian Nights' Entertainments*, the hypodiegetic level dominates in terms of quantity. Yet since Scheherazade has to continue narrating in order to survive, this kind of imbalance is redressed by the obvious need for many stories that the diegetic level provides.

Narrative distance

The distinction between third-person and first-person narrator actualizes the terms 'distance' and 'perspective', which both require a more detailed explanation. The concept of distance has a long history which can be traced right back to the third book of Plato's *Republic*. Here Plato sees narrative as 'execute[d] . . . either by simple narrative or by narrative conveyed by imitation (*mimesis*) or by both' (Russell and Winterbottom 1998: 29). Although Plato has difficulty in identifying the specifically epic (or narrative) by means of these categories, they are relevant to the concept of distance since the first variant—'simple narrative'—is more distanced and mediated than the second—'imitation (*mimesis*)'. For Aristotle, this distinction is partly neutralized since his understanding of *mimesis* is different from that of Plato. Aristotle uses *mimesis* to refer to literature in general, and he appears to assume that the concept is familiar and unproblematic. In spite of his use of other concepts, however, Aristotle distinguishes between epic and dramatic literature in a manner reminiscent of Plato: 'There is . . . a third distinction—in the *mode* of mimesis for these various objects. For in the same media one can represent the same objects by combining narrative with direct personation, as Homer does: *or* in an invariable narrative voice; *or* by direct enactment of all roles' (Aristotle 1995: 35, 1448a).

The classical tradition was not very much concerned with the question of narrative discourse, but in our century Plato's distinction has been reactualized through the conceptual pair *telling* versus *showing*. This pair of concepts is associated with the American novelist Henry James and the critic Percy Lubbock. In *The Craft of Fiction* (1921), Lubbock argues that it is practically a precondition for the art of the novel that the action be *shown*, and not told. This assertion (which not only systematizes but also simplifies the more sophisticated views of Henry James) is repudiated by Wayne Booth in *The Rhetoric of Fiction*. Since, for Booth, the art of narration is primarily *telling*, the concept of distance again becomes important.

Commenting on the *telling–showing* debate, Genette emphasizes that 'no narrative can "show" or "imitate" the story it tells. All it can do is . . . give more or less the *illusion of mimesis*—which is the only narrative mimesis . . . [because] narration, oral or written, is a fact of language' (Genette 1980: 164). As a contribution in support of narrative fiction as *telling*, this criticism is aimed not only at Lubbock but partly also at Aristotle's understanding of *mimesis* as representation of 'people in action' (Aristotle 1995: 33, 1448a). Genette emphasizes that 'mimesis in words can only be mimesis of words. Other than that, all we have and can have is degrees of diegesis' (Genette 1980: 164). 'Degrees of diegesis' means for Genette (and Booth) degrees of narrative distance—both between the author of a narrative text and the text itself (as a linguistic structure), and between the text's narrator(s) and the events/characters in it.

The concept of distance reveals a fundamental characteristic of narrative fiction (and in particular the novel): if narrative fiction is unusually flexible and can present events and conflicts with great intensity, it constitutes itself through a series of distancing means. In his classic essay 'Psychical Distance', Edward Bullough in 1912 defined distance as the quality through which expression becomes aesthetically valid: 'Distancing means the separation of personal affections, whether idea or complex experience, from the concrete personality of the experience' (Bullough, quoted in Hayman 1987: 19). By 'distancing' Bullough means a generalizing or objectivizing process: the writing activity which (through literary devices and strategies) can create an aesthetic product of more general interest. Combined with Genette's understanding of 'narrative mimesis', Bullough's concept of distance, as David Hayman presents it in *Re-forming the Narrative* (1987), provides a basis for a tripartite division of the concept. The term 'distance' now refers particularly to the relationship between the narrator and the events/characters in the narrative text.

1   *Temporal distance.* As we shall see in Chapter 3, narration in fictional prose is normally retrospective. This involves a temporal distance between the act of narration and the events that are narrated. Such a temporal distance is often a motivating factor for the narration, but it may be less clear when the narrative act begins. Let us go back to the beginning of Hamsun's *Hunger.* In the first paragraph, which ends with an ellipsis, the act of narration is clearly retrospective: 'It was in those days when I wandered about hungry in Kristiania . . .' (p. 3). This is how the second paragraph opens: 'Lying awake in my attic room, I hear a clock strike six downstairs. It was fairly light already and people were beginning to walk up and down the stairs'. Here we not only have a transition from past to present; the tenses are important to *show* the transition. It is as if the first-person narrator is carried into, or back to, what he is to relate. For the reader this has an intensifying effect, while also reducing the temporal distance that the first paragraph indicates.

2   *Spatial distance.* Temporal distance is often combined with distance in space, i.e. a distance between the narrative situation and the place where the (main) events unfold. In Part II we shall see that Conrad's *Heart of Darkness* marks both temporal distance (an unspecified time-span between Marlow's act of narration and the experiences he relates) and spatial distance (the distance between 'civilized' London and 'primitive' Africa). However, as the inverted commas in the parentheses suggest, even a great distance may be reduced and problematized. Although *Hunger* and *Heart of Darkness* are very different novels, in both narratives the ways in which suspense is generated involve variations of both temporal and spatial distance.

3   *Attitudinal distance.* This variant is the most complex—not only because it is connected with the different levels of insight of the narrator and the characters in the text, but also because the concept of distance here functions more metaphorically and is more closely related to interpretation. By 'attitude' I understand the narrator's level of insight, judgements, and values. Attitudinal distance is a useful concept in order to discuss, and perhaps clarify, the relationship between the narrator and the characters. It may also be a helpful term in discussions of the narrator's position and function in relation to the intention and value system of the text.

Attitude may in other words refer to characteristic features of a character as well as of the narrator, whether the narrator be third-person or first-person. For even if a third-person narrator is outside the action, he may nevertheless express opinions about the characters, judge them, and so forth. In addition, particularly if the narrator is unreliable, an attitudinal distance may arise between the narrator and the implied author (as an abstract entity representing the text's overall intention). Faulkner's *The Sound and the Fury* is a ready example. Jason's attitudes, which involve contempt for his brothers Benjy and Quentin and a generally egoistic and cynical view of life, contrast both with the subsequent third-person narration (in which the narrator's attitude is associated with, and curiously influenced by, that of Dilsey) and with the two preceding first-person parts. In addition to characterizing Jason, this form of double contrast contributes to establishing him as an unreliable narrator.

A narrative text that marks distance in attitude may in the next instance complicate this distance through *narrative sympathy.* This may be achieved in several ways. An example of a character who is presented sympathetically in a novel in which the third-person narration is consistently distanced and ironic is that of Stevie in Joseph Conrad's *The Secret Agent* (1907). Like Faulkner's Benjy Compson, Stevie is mentally retarded. Sympathy for Stevie is established partly through the plot (he becomes the victim in an unsuccessful act of terrorism, an innocent person blown to pieces by a bomb), partly contrastively through the ironic characterization of the other characters.

Irony As *The Secret Agent* illustrates, attitudinal distance is often related to irony. This is a complex concept which I shall only comment on briefly here, though I shall return to it in the discussions of 'The Dead' and *To the Lighthouse*. Part of what makes the concept of irony so complex is that it is not only defined as a rhetorical term or a figure of speech. It can also be understood more philosophically: as an existential experience of distance between the outer world of reality and man's ability to comprehend it— including experiencing the fact that language (on which we are dependent to be able to think and comprehend) cannot reach beyond itself. In what follows I shall use the concept of irony in a rhetorical sense (even though the philosophical implications necessarily come into play to a certain extent). We can distinguish between verbal irony, stable and unstable irony, and dramatic irony.

Verbal irony was traditionally classified as a *trope*, i.e. a figurative expression on a par with metaphor (see p. 131) or metonymy (see p. 187). It is an utterance in which the speaker (the person who is speaking or writing) actually means something quite different from what she or he in fact says directly. A literary example of verbal irony is the first sentence of Jane Austen's *Pride and Prejudice* (1813): 'It is a truth universally acknowledged, that a single man in possession of a good fortune, must be in want of a wife' (p. 1). An ironic implication here is that unmarried women strive to catch rich men. Another implication is that men with good fortunes do not necessarily share the surface sentiments of the narrator's utterance.

Stable and unstable irony is a distinction developed by Wayne Booth in *A Rhetoric of Irony* (1974). *Stable* irony is what we have if the author (through the narrator and the shaping of the discourse) presents the reader with an assertion or a position that gives a firm basis for subverting the surface meaning. In *The Secret Agent* we have stable irony in the narrator's presentation of the anarchists in London: their rhetoric is unveiled as pompous since nothing comes out of it, their politically 'progressive' ideals are compromised by naïve brutality (such as the killing of Stevie). Here we can bring in D. C. Muecke's explanation of irony as a 'two-storey phenomenon' (Muecke 1969: 19), in which there is always opposition or distance between the ironist (Conrad's third-person narrator) on the top floor and the irony's victims (the anarchists) on the ground floor.

Unstable is used of irony if the basis for subverting the surface meaning or the alternative to this meaning becomes uncertain. In this case, what we usually call *ironic regression* occurs: layer upon layer of irony that complicates the reading by making all judgement, choice, and ranking of priorities difficult, not to say impossible. Samuel Beckett's novel trilogy—*Molloy* (1951), *Malone Dies* (1958), and *The Unnamable* (1960)— illustrates unstable irony: each time the reader thinks he or she has found a point of orientation in this fiction (and in the next instance perhaps an explanatory model for it), it is undermined by new narrative variations and thematic complications. In *Malone Dies* (Beckett's own English version of *Malone meurt* (1951)), for example, Beckett frustrates the reader by making Malone the first-person narrator, the main character, and the author of inserted, constructed stories. Malone claims that for him the characters in the stories are fictitious, and that he tells about them—writes about them with an ever shorter pencil—in order to entertain himself while he is waiting to die:

> I think I shall be able to tell myself four stories, each one on a different theme. One about a man, another about a woman, a third about a thing, and finally one about an animal, a bird probably. I think that is everything . . . Perhaps I shall not have time to finish. On the other hand perhaps I shall finish too soon. (p. 7)

Just the same the transitions become unclear between these stories, which form a kind of hypodiegetic level of action, and the sober (but perhaps also desperate) account of Malone's own death process. *Malone Dies* does not have a plot in the usual sense. The most certain event in the novel is that the main character dies—which the title of the book has already announced, but which the main character as first-person narrator ironically enough cannot report himself. The novel's narration gradually approaches a zero point it never reaches.

Dramatic irony. The unstable irony in *Malone Dies* is ascribable to a series of narrative, structural, and thematic elements in which dramatic irony is also included. Such irony involves a situation (in a play or a narrative) in which the spectator or reader gains knowledge that a character in the drama or narrative text does *not* possess. The lack of such knowledge usually causes the character to act 'mistakenly' (i.e. against his or her own interests) without knowing this; she or he will then also without realizing it say things that prefigure the ending (the disaster). The Greek tragedies provide classic examples of dramatic irony, as in Sophocles' *Oedipus the King* (*c*.425 BC). Oedipus can see, but he does not see what he has done until he is told by the blind Tiresias. This is typical dramatic irony, which here can also be called *tragic*. The dramatic irony is never this clear in Beckett's *Malone Dies*, in which (in my reading of the novel) it can be detected in the paradoxical parallels between Malone's 'constructed' characters and himself.

Narrative perspective

When we relate the narrator's attitudinal distance to his level of insight and judgements, we imply that he 'sees' the events he relates in a special way, and

that the way in which he sees and judges the events and characters has consequences for how he presents them. This feature of narrative communication is
associated with the linguistic term *deixis*, which refers to all those elements of
language that have a specifically demonstrative function. Examples of such
words are *the, this, that, here, there, now, I, you, tomorrow, yesterday*. None of
these words can be understood properly unless we bring in 'the point of orientation' (both in space and time) of the person (addresser) uttering them. If
we go from the linguistic level of word to narrative discourse, here too the narrator's (or addresser's) point of orientation is often crucial to how we understand the text. We call this point of orientation the narrative *perspective*. Even
in the first sentence of *Hunger*—'It was in those days when I wandered about
hungry in Kristiania'—several words and tenses have a demonstrative function: 'in those days', 'I', and 'in Kristiania'. They signal that the narrative perspective is linked to a character, that the narration is probably first-person,
that the perspective is distanced and retrospective, and that the story-events
have perhaps been decisive for the main character.

Even if the concept of perspective can be anchored linguistically, these comments show that narrative perspective has functions that go beyond the linguistic ones. One reason for this is that perspective is linked to the utterances
of the narrator or character. Such individual utterances contribute to constituting narrative discourse as 'translinguistic' and pragmatic (Bakhtin 1982; cf.
Todorov 1984: 24). Utterances are further related to the viewpoints, judgements, or experiences of the narrator or character. This enables us to determine more precisely the concept of perspective according to what aspect of it
is important in a given narrative text. Perspective is a question of what makes
a narrative presentation probable (or improbable) and distinct from other
(alternative) presentations. The narrative perspective will also, in different
ways and to a varying degree, appeal to the perspective of the narratee or
reader.

'The phenomena that compose the fictive universe are never presented to
us "in themselves" but from a certain perspective' (Todorov 1981: 32). Narrative perspective is not only a matter of the narrator's visual perception
of events and characters, but also of how he or she experiences, judges, and
interprets them. Mieke Bal puts it this way: 'Perception depends on so
many factors that striving for objectivity is pointless. To mention only a
few factors: one's position with respect to the perceived object, the fall of the
light, the distance, previous knowledge, psychological attitude towards the
object; all this and more affects the picture one forms and passes on to others'
(Bal 1997: 142).

Perspective, then, indicates the vision through which the narrative elements
are presented. As Bal shows, it 'covers both the physical and the psychological
points of perception . . . [but not] the agent that is performing the action
of narration' (Bal 1997: 143). Because it is possible for both a narrator and a

character 'to express the vision of another', perspective needs to be distinguished from 'the identity of the voice that is verbalizing that vision' (Bal 1997: 143). (Bal uses the term 'focalization', which I reserve for film, in a way that broadly corresponds to 'perspective'.)

Let us illustrate what we have said so far with two examples from *The Stories of Eva Luna*, a collection of short stories by Isabel Allende. This is how 'Walimai' begins:

> The name given me by my father is Walimai, which in the tongue of our brothers in the north means 'wind'. I can tell it to you, since now you are like my own daughter and you have my permission to call my name, although only when we are among family. The names of persons and living creatures demand respect, because when we speak to them we touch their heart and become a part of their life force. (p. 86)

Walimai is the short story's main character. He is also a first-person narrator: he consistently uses I-reference and is the most important player in the plot. If we bring in the concept of narrative perspective, we can better see how Walimai's two main functions (as the main character and a first-person narrator) are combined, and how they function thematically. Even in the first sentence several of the words indicate narrative perspective, 'Walimai', 'tongue', 'our brothers', 'in the north'. The text rapidly and demonstratively establishes a time dimension, a temporal difference between before and now (and between three generations: father, Walimai, daughter). Furthermore, by repeating the main character's name that the title has already announced, it signals that this name not only identifies a character but also marks respect both for this character and for the group of people (the Indian tribe) to which he belongs. Such an indication of respect (for other people and other cultures) may suggest that in other contexts respect is lacking. We have a feeling that this short story will give us examples of precisely such a shortcoming, and thus perhaps dramatize problems of power and freedom. Several of the effects of this opening depend on Walimai's status as a first-person narrator. The perspective of the short story is influenced by the first-person narrator's perceptions, yet textual perspective (which here approximates to a variant of textual intention) also informs the narrator's judgements and experiences. For they are not only his—they are also related to his father, anchored in his culture, and influenced by 'the tongue of our brothers in the north'.

Now consider the first sentence of another short story from *The Stories of Eva Luna*, 'Phantom Palace': 'When five centuries earlier the bold renegades from Spain with their bone-weary horses and armour candescent beneath an American sun stepped upon the shores of Quinaroa, Indians had been living and dying in that same place for several thousand years' (p. 201). While the first-person narration in 'Walimai' links up with that of Allende's novel *Eva*

Luna (1987), the narrative method of 'Phantom Place', as in most of the short stories in this collection, is third-person. Yet the fact that the narrator in this case is outside the action, which she observes without participating in it, does not mean that the narrative perspective is neutral. The first sentence not only establishes a distinction between 'before' and 'now'; it also links *before* to the natives and *now* to the European immigrants. Put another way, temporal distance is linked with spatial distance; and while the past is related to the Indians, the present is linked to the Spaniards. This linking of temporal and spatial distance marks an attitudinal distance: the narrator distances herself from the invading Europeans, while she sympathizes with the Indians and 'the shores of Quinaroa'. It is difficult, and hardly desirable either, to read the short stories in *The Stories of Eva Luna* in total isolation from one another. A point of contact, both narrative and thematic, between the two stories considered here is that the third-person narration which serves to establish the perspective in 'Phantom Palace' gives greater weight to the perspective of 'Walimai' as a first-person narrative.

As Genette was the first to point out, it is necessary in the analysis of prose fiction to distinguish between the two questions *who sees?* and *who tells?* The first question comes under the heading of discourse, and can be linked to the concept of perspective as explained above. The second comes under that of narration, and is related to narrative voice and speech presentation. Discussions of 'point of view' have often overlooked this important distinction. The term 'point of view' is confusingly imprecise as it may alternately refer to both perspective and voice. Although in much narrative theory perspective has come to indicate both narrator and vision, the two narrative agencies actually supplement rather than duplicate each other. Thus it can be fruitful to study the relationship, whether it be stable or variable, between perspective and narration in the text. Take James Joyce's *A Portrait of the Artist as a Young Man* (1915). After the novel has opened by presenting the beginning of a fairy-tale-like story, the second paragraph starts as follows: 'His father told him that story: his father looked at him through a glass: he had a hairy face' (p. 3). The narrative voice is that of the narrator, who is third-person and outside the action. Yet the perspective is *Stephen's*—it is ascribed to the main character as a child, to Stephen's retrospective experience of the oral narrative situation when his father told him stories.

Generally speaking, the narrative perspective may be either 'external' or 'internal' in relation to the story the discourse presents. An *external* perspective can be associated with a third-person narrator who 'sees' the events without participating in them (cf. the last Allende example). This does not imply that an external narrative perspective is necessarily stable throughout the text. It may well vary, and such changes are often linked with variations in distance. An illustrative example of such perspectival variation is a short story by

Nadine Gordimer, 'Is There Nowhere Else Where We Can Meet?' In common with Isabel Allende, Gordimer contrasts two cultures with each other, one white and one black. A white woman meets a black man, but what in another place might have been a meaningful encounter in this short story becomes a confrontation marked by fear—fear of the other, but at the same time fear of oneself. The narrative perspective, which is external and related to the third-person narrator, associates itself with the perspective of the white woman as she perceives the situation. Yet this orientation towards the woman, which to begin with has elements of sympathy, is modified towards the end through a clear marking of distance:

> She was trembling so that she could not stand. She had to keep on walking, quickly, down the road. It was quiet and grey, like the morning. And cool . . . Why did I fight, she thought suddenly. What did I fight for? . . . The cold of the morning flowed into her.
>
> She turned away from the gate and went down the road slowly, like an invalid, beginning to pick the blackjacks from her stockings. (p. 20)

The narrative voice in this text remains stable; as in the example from Joyce's *Portrait* it is the narrative perspective that varies. This perspective is first informative and soberly observant, then seems to approximate to the vision of the female main character, only to distance itself finally from her.

The varying, external perspective is associated with the third-person narrative of this short story. In first-person narration too the perspective may at times give the impression of being external. An example from Albert Camus's *The Outsider* (1942):

> Mother died today. Or maybe yesterday, I don't know. I had a telegram from the home: 'Mother passed away. Funeral tomorrow. Yours sincerely.' That doesn't mean anything. It may have been yesterday.
>
> The old people's home is at Marengo, fifty miles from Algiers. I'll catch the two o'clock bus and get there in the afternoon. Then I can keep the vigil and I'll come back tomorrow night. (p. 9)

The voice speaking here belongs to the novel's main character. In so far as the narration is first-person, the narrative perspective is basically linked to the main character. Yet at the same time Camus tries various ways of separating or distancing this perspective from that of the main character, Meursault. For example, the title-word 'outsider' (*étranger*) not only applies to Meursault as a stranger in the world and to his immediate family (for instance, he shows no sign of sorrow over his mother's death), but also invites us to understand Meursault as a stranger to himself. Is this perhaps why he later kills the Arab, apparently for no other 'reason' than the bright sunlight on the beach?

If the narrative perspective is *internal*, the point of orientation will as a rule be linked to a character. The reader has no choice but to see the fictional events with the eyes of this character, and will therefore in principle more easily accept the vision she or he presents. A characteristic example of internal perspective is Charlotte Brontë's *Jane Eyre* (1847), a novel with first-person narration. In this novel the perspective is closely, and lastingly, linked to Jane as narrator and main character. Her internal perspective influences, and in part governs, how the reader judges Jane, Mr Rochester, and the other characters.

Such internal perspective is common in first-person narratives such as *Jane Eyre*. Yet although in such texts perspective is associated with the narrator, it is not identical with, or limited to, the narrator's voice. For example, in the first chapter of Ian McEwan's *Enduring Love* (1997) the first-person narrator draws attention to perspective by attempting to see himself from above: 'I see us from three hundred feet up, through the eyes of the buzzard we had watched earlier, soaring, circling and dipping in the tumult of currents: five men running silently towards the centre of a hundred-acre field' (p. 1). The visualizing force of this sentence owes something to the perspectival modulation it incorporates; more indirectly, it also suggests that the narrator may regard his own narration as unsatisfactory or too partial. We can also have internal or person-oriented perspective in novels with third-person narrators, such as Woolf's *To the Lighthouse* and, as we have seen above, Joyce's *Portrait*.

In narrative fiction perspective is related to distance, voice, and different variants of third-person and first-person narrator. Inspired by Boris Uspensky (1973) Rimmon-Kenan systematizes the concept of perspective by dividing it into a perceptual, a psychological, and an ideological facet. If, as the analyses in Part II suggest, such a systematization is difficult to carry out in critical practice it is because the different aspects of perspective continually blend and modify one another in narrative discourse. What Rimmon-Kenan's systematization clearly shows is that perspective is something more than 'perceptual viewpoint'. It is partly for this reason that the concept of perspective is preferable to that of 'focalization' in discussions of fictional prose,

In film, however, focalization is an indispensable term, even though the concept of perspective can be usefully applied to the film medium too. Once we connect focalization with film we think of the film camera. From the diagram illustrating the film narrator (Fig. 2.4) we will recall that the camera is only one of the many elements that constitute the cinematic narrator. Yet the camera has a special place among the narrative devices of film because of its diverse methods of focalization. The camera decides not only what the viewer sees, but also how and for how long we see what we see. Among the factors that govern the orientation of the camera in relation to the filmed object are distance and level—whether the camera is far away from or close to the object being filmed, and whether it films 'from below' (low angle) or 'from above' ('bird's-eye perspective'). However, such focalization components are not only combined with one another, they also become more complicated as the camera only exceptionally focuses stably on objects that are at rest. Moreover, the camera itself is often in movement (partly because it will be moved during filming, but mostly through advanced zoom techniques and technically sophisticated panning and tilting camera movements).

In *Narrated Films* Avrom Fleishman points out that discussions about films often have a tendency to 'personify' the camera, as I also do when I say that the camera 'decides' what we see. Fleishman reminds us that although this is partly correct, it is also misleading since the camera is steered by the cinematographer and (more indirectly yet just as importantly) by the film's director (Fleishman 1992: 3). A film in which camera focalization is clearly related to the perspective of the main character is Henning Carlsen's *Hunger* (1966), an adaptation of the Hamsun novel to which I have already referred. As Lars Thomas Braaten shows in *Filmfortelling og subjektivitet* (Film Narrative and Subjectivity), we can see the film's mobile framing, including variations of camera focalization, as a filmic equivalent to the subjectively personal perspective that permeates Hamsun's novel. Several of the points made in Braaten's analysis of Carlsen's *Hunger* are associated with the concept of subjective camera movement (Braaten 1984: 87–9; cf. Bordwell and Thompson 1997: 245). For instance, the camera focalizes over the shoulder of the main character (Per Oscarson) on a sheet of paper on which he is writing. The viewer understands this as a key image:

> It is here that we most closely approach what he is actually up to and why he is lingering by the railings on the bridge. He is writing, making notes on his little sheet of paper. There is fine thematic logic in the fact that this subjective camera setting is held for as long as eight seconds, while the others, as has been mentioned, are only kept for a couple of seconds, as short and involuntary penetrations of his field of attention. Yet we can see from his hand movements that there is also something nervous and unconcentrated about this writing activity . . . (Braaten 1984: 89, my translation)

In Carlsen's *Hunger* such close-ups have a characterizing function not only by virtue of themselves but just as much through the relationship between the near and that which is at a distance. Together with montage, this kind of spatial interplay (typically combining long shots and close-ups, as in the helicopter sequence in Coppola's *Apocalypse Now*) is fundamental to the structure of the narrative fiction film. For example, in the classic film made by the Lumière brothers, *Leaving the Lumière Factory* (1895), we see the workers in front of the factory gate at a distance; here, as in Orson Welles's *The Trial*, the use of long shots makes the viewer see the people on the screen as moving figures without any real identity. In the introductory scene in

Carlsen's *Hunger* too, the narrative distance associated with long shots is striking. Yet as Braaten points out, an important difference from the Lumière film is that, in Carlsen's film, this kind of narrative distance is contrasted with the subsequent close-ups. Using camera focalization combined with a variety of other filmic means, film brilliantly visualizes both what is distant and what is near, and it can present not only external but also internal perspective.

Voice and speech presentation

Even Plato, as we recall, in his day attempted to answer the question of *who tells* in a narrative text. Narrative communication in fictional prose involves distance, a form of distance which (greatly simplified) arises through the combination of two factors. First, the use of a narrator is in itself a means of distancing, partly since he or she is the narrator *in* the text while the author *writes it*, partly since the words the narrator uses can only imitate other words (and cannot, like drama, show action). Second, the signifying linguistic structures in fictional prose have a tendency to 'break free' from the external world of reality to which fiction stands in an indirect relationship.

Since all literary prose exists linguistically (as writing), it is not possible to imitate or show directly the events or the physical phenomena that the text says something about. If the narrator has a distancing function, he thereby also acquires a communicative function. Even when the narrative text presents direct speech, a narrator 'quotes' what a character says so that what is 'shown' is further communicated to the reader (sometimes also filtered through a narrative frame). We can distinguish between *narration* and *speech*. The narrative function is linked to the narrator. Speech is what the characters utter, and this speech is then presented by the narrator. In some texts of narrative fiction (for example Conrad's *Heart of Darkness*) a first-person narrator both participates in (part of) the plot and then communicates it. Generally speaking, the first-person narrator often has a key function in the presentation of speech.

Having established that in narrative fiction all speech is communicated, and that the crucial distinction is between various degrees and kinds of narration (rather than between 'telling' and 'showing'), I present a progressive scale from 'purely' narrative speech presentation to 'purely' mimetic. The following presentation is indebted to the progressive scale suggested by Brian McHale (1978: 258–9), and to Rimmon-Kenan's helpful survey in *Narrative Fiction* (1983: 109–10). I use McHale's examples, which are all taken from Dos Passos's novel trilogy *U.S.A.* (1938). (The following scale is somewhat simplified compared to those presented by McHale and Rimmon-Kenan.)

1 *Diegetic summary*: a short report of a speech act, without any specification of what was said or how it was said, for example:

When Charley got a little gin inside him he started telling war yarns for the first time in his life. (*The Big Money*, 295)

2 *Indirect content paraphrase (or indirect discourse)*: a summary of the content of a speech event, without any account being taken of the style or form of the 'original' utterance:

The waiter told him that Carranza's troops had lost Torreón and that Villa and Zapata were closing in on the Federal District. (*The 42nd Parallel*, 320)

3 *Free indirect discourse*: grammatically and mimetically in an intermediate position between indirect and direct discourse (more about this variant below):

Why the hell shouldn't they know, weren't they off'n her and out to see the goddam town and he'd better come along. (*1919*, 43–4)

4 *Direct discourse*: a 'quotation' of a monologue or dialogue in the text. This creates the illusion of 'pure mimesis', although the 'quotation' is communicated and stylized:

Fred Summers said, 'Fellers, this war's the most gigantic cockeyed graft of the century and me for it and the cross red nurses.' (*1919*, 191)

5 *Free direct discourse*: direct discourse without conventional orthographic cues. This is the typical form of first-person interior monologue:

Fainy's head suddenly got very light, Bright boy, that's me, ambition and literary taste . . . Gee, I must finish *Looking Backward* . . . and jez, I like reading fine (*The 42nd Parallel*, 22, Dos Passos's ellipses)

If orthography and syntax are in complete disarray, free direct discourse may take the form of a stream of consciousness. The classic example of such a speech presentation is the last sixty pages of James Joyce's *Ulysses* (1922), a textual segment practically without punctuation, in which Joyce lets the female main character, Molly, present her thoughts through first-person narration. A short excerpt:

yes he said I was a flower of the mountain yes so we are flowers all a womans body yes that was one true thing he said in his life and the sun shines for you today yes . . . (pp. 931–2)

Free indirect discourse

Of these variants of speech presentation narrative theory has taken a particular interest in what we call free indirect discourse (corresponding to the German *erlebte Rede* and the French *style indirect libre*). The reason for this interest can in part be inferred from the survey given above: since free indirect discourse is placed in the middle of the scale of speech presentation, it reflects in a unique way *both* the narrator's voice and the voice of the person speaking. However, although free indirect discourse is usually explained as a linguistic combination of two voices, this phenomenon is not 'purely linguistic' because it can also have important literary effects, both narratively and thematically.

How can we identify free indirect discourse in the fictional text we are reading? Let us look at three discourse variants of the same sentence:

1   *Direct discourse*: 'She said: "I like him!" ' (present).
2   *Indirect discourse*: 'She said that she liked him' (past).
3   *Free indirect discourse*: 'She liked him!' (past).

As we can see, free indirect discourse (like indirect) has third-person reference and the past form of the verb 'like'. Yet by leaving out the reporting verb and the conjunction 'that', the utterance approximates to or 'slides' towards the quotation which direct discourse cites. Thus, free indirect discourse falls linguistically and narratively midway between direct and indirect discourse: 'rendering the content of a figural mind more obliquely than the former, more directly than the latter' (Cohn 1983: 105).

Since free indirect discourse can communicate both the speech and thoughts of a character, we can differentiate this concept by means of the terms *free indirect speech* and *free indirect thought*. These two concepts cover the two main variants of free indirect discourse. I have already given a non-literary example of free indirect *speech*; a literary example of free indirect *thought* which I shall discuss in more detail in Part II is the narrative presentation of how K. is stopped by the priest when he wishes to leave the cathedral in the penultimate chapter of *The Trial*: 'He had almost got clear of the pews, and was nearing the empty space between them and the door, when for the first time he heard the priest's voice. A powerful, well-trained voice. How it rang through the expectant cathedral!' (p. 234). The last two sentences are both free indirect thought. If we are unsure whether we have free indirect discourse here, we can 'test' the first of the two sentences. As indirect discourse it would run: 'He thought that the priest's voice was powerful and well trained', and as direct discourse: 'He thought: "The priest's voice is powerful and well trained"'. We notice that the fact that K. *hears* the priest's voice contributes to identifying this sentence as free indirect thought. If free indirect thought is even more clearly marked in the following sentence (the final one in the quotation), it is because the effect of free indirect discourse is reinforced here by the exclamation mark.

This example from *The Trial* illustrates the fundamental ambiguity that is characteristic of free indirect discourse. It confirms Dorrit Cohn's point that 'narrated monologue [Cohn's term for free indirect discourse] is at once a more complex and a more flexible technique for rendering consciousness than the rival techniques' (Cohn 1983: 107). Who is speaking here, the narrator or the character? This question, which is essentially linguistic and may appear simple and delimited, rapidly flows together with other questions in a narrative text such as *The Trial*: who has control, authority, power? What does it involve to have these things, what are the consequences of *not* having them? The path is short from narrative observation to thematic discussion.

3
Narrative Time and Repetition

Time is a fundamentally important category for human beings, but the concept of 'time' is so diffuse that it is practically impossible to define. Part of what makes the concept of time so complex is that it is linked both to the physical world and to our perception of the world (and thereby of ourselves). Furthermore, our perception of time *varies*. An indication of how difficult the problem of time is to tackle from a philosophical angle is that one of the factors that creates this variation is precisely the age in which we live. The perception of time in agricultural communities of the European Middle Ages, for example, was different from ours if only because of the way in which work was conditioned by the changing seasons. Our own experience of time is influenced and changed by the rapid developments within such fields as information technology and the mass media. Literature provides a continual response to these changes, which means that questions of time are often included as part of the thematics in literary texts.

This chapter covers four main subject areas. Since narrative time cannot be separated from narrative space, I shall start with some comments on the concept of space. After that I shall outline the most important variants of time as presented in narrative fiction, before giving a brief discussion of the concept of time in relation to film. The last part of this chapter deals with repetition in narrative fiction and film.

Narrative time and narrative space

Since the concept of time is linked to both the physical world and our perception of the world, it is also related to *narrative space*, i.e. the fictional universe which the text presents through its narrative discourse. If this chapter puts more emphasis on narrative time and repetition rather than on narrative space, this is not because the latter concept is unimportant but because narrative theory has developed more terms and distinctions when it comes to narrative time than it has for narrative space. Typically, however, in order to be adequately understood these terms need to be seen in the context of narrative space.

In narrative texts the spatial dimension stands out most clearly in connection with the theme of travel. Of the texts I analyse in Part II, this is best illustrated in *Heart of Darkness*. The dominant space here is the vast African continent, but since the narrative structure takes the form of a journey that the narrator, Marlow, makes from Europe to Africa, the 'European space' also comes into play—narratively, structurally, and thematically. The fact that the journey takes place at sea and on the river we can identify as the Congo indicates that we can see sea/water/river as a third, more neutral and mediating space, inserted between Europe (powerful, dominant, 'civilized') and Africa (oppressed, exploited, 'primitive'). In theoretical terms Morten Nøjgaard formulates this point as follows: 'A journey, which can of course take place in inner space, is the expression of a strong spatialization of the experience of time and is therefore well suited to expressing the complex of problems associated with our realization of ourselves, which is fundamental to narrative texts' (Nøjgaard 1976: 194, my translation). Now of course narrative space is not dependent on the fact that the characters in the story actually travel, either physically or metaphorically. My reason for mentioning the travel motif in particular is that it illustrates the close relationship between narrative space and narrative time. Broadly, it can be stated that even if the spatial dimension is not equally important in all narrative texts, it often plays a crucial part. This applies especially if specific parts or characteristics of the narrative space influence and shape the characters, who normally appear in space and are thus also spatial elements of a kind.

In order to discuss how narrative space is presented in verbal fiction, it is important to know of the distinction between 'story space' and 'discourse space'. *Story space* is the space containing events, characters, and the place or places of the action as it is presented and developed in the discourse (i.e. as plot). It is elements from story space that we build on when we construct the story on the basis of the text we are reading. (Edward Branigan uses the term 'story world' (Branigan 1992: 33–6) synonymously about film.) *Discourse space* is the narrator's space. This can assume different forms and need not be indicated in the text at all, but it is in principle distinguished from story space. Again *Heart of Darkness* is a ready example, for in this short novel (or 'novella') the discourse space is in practice physically defined through the narrative situation with Marlow as a first-person narrator on board a sailing vessel on the Thames. Yet although the discursive space of *Heart of Darkness* seems to be sharply divided from the novella's story space, one of the effects of Marlow's narration is to destabilize this apparently safe distinction and to bring the two spaces closer to each other.

The relationship between narrative time and narrative space suggests that an author of fiction must use different forms of presentation according to whether she or he wishes to depict what the universe and the objects in it look like, or tell what happens to objects in the universe. On this basis Nøjgaard distinguishes between three forms of presentation:

1 *Narration*: as purely temporal presentation (i.e. only presentation of movements—'action' in the traditional sense).

Writers occasionally attempt to illustrate the narrative spaces of the fiction they produce. This map, drawn by William Faulkner and included in *The Portable Faulkner* (edited by Malcolm Cowley in 1946), is a well-known example. As the map shows, Faulkner situates a number of his most famous novels and short stories around the town Jefferson in Yoknapatawpha County, his fictional name for Lafayette County, Mississippi, USA.

2 *Description*: as purely spatial presentation (i.e. presentation of objects in space disconnected from the aspect of time).

3 *Comment*: which is neither spatial nor temporal presentation.

Although this tripartite division is illuminating in theoretical terms, it may be difficult to use it as a structuring aid in narrative analysis. For we rarely meet these forms of presentation as pure variants in prose literature: they are usually connected and they mutually influence one another. Thus even a 'descriptive pause' is *narrated*, and as a result is influenced by the temporal presentation inherent in the narrative. This applies to the extended descriptive pause at the beginning of Conrad's *Nostromo* (1904), to which I refer below. It is also the case that most comments, at any rate indirectly, will be related to both narration and description. For although a narrator's comment is in discourse space, it is still included in the narrative universe that the author constructs. Nøjgaard says of this characteristic feature of narrative fiction:

> Only comment can occur in a pure form, but we have seen that in such a case it really falls outside the narrative universe . . . One may therefore argue that none of the three basic forms can occur in a pure form within the confines of the narrative universe. Pure temporal presentation is an impossibility, because any movement is necessarily a movement of something and takes place somewhere (a place which must be described). Conversely, even the most detailed description (e.g. in Balzac's novels) sees objects as existing in time, i.e. in movement. (Nøjgaard 1976: 151)

If we link the concept of space to film, the first thing that strikes us is that film *displays* space superbly. Since film projection is also a form of conveying space-constituting elements (place, events, milieu, characters, etc.) the film-maker traditionally puts a lot of work into finding the best location. This of course also applies to film adaptation. If space and time complement each other in fictional prose, the same is certainly true in film. Film, says Gerald Mast, 'is a truly space-and-time art; it is certainly the only one in which space and time play a fully equal role' (Mast 1983: 10). 'Different film forms', suggests Thomas Elsaesser, 'would seem to be determined by a film-maker's ability to construct space and time—the two dimensions simultaneously present in filmic representation—in a comprehensible manner' (Elsaesser 1994: 12). We shall return to the spatial dimension of film in the section on filmic presentation of time below.

Temporal relations between narration and story   In order for story events to be presented narratively it seems logical that they first must have 'happened', i.e. they must have been realized within the fiction. Still, the temporal relationship between narration and events in a story can vary, and we distinguish between four main variants.

The first and most important is *retrospective narration*. In this variant, which is clearly the most common, events in a story are related after they have happened. The distance between the act of narration and the events that are related varies from text to text. In Dickens's *Great Expectations* (1861) the distance is approximately fifteen years, in Kafka's *The Trial* (1914–15) it is unspecified, in Hamsun's *Mysteries* (1892) it is one year (measured from the beginning of the novel). Yet even though retrospective narration dominates—and, as mentioned, is in one sense the only possibility—we can also have *pre-emptive* narration. Even if this variant is seldom found in modern literature, it is not unusual in texts such as the Old Testament books of the prophets (e.g. Isaiah 11: 1–2).

A third variant is approximately *contemporary* with the story events. A ready non-literary example is the broadcasting of a football match on the radio. It is hardly possible for narrative fiction to be *so* contemporary, since the written text necessarily indicates a difference, and thus a distance, from the act of narration (unless the writer is writing about his or her writing). Finally, as in novels written in the form of letters or a diary, we may have *embedded* narration. Here the narrative acts change with the actions that are being talked about. Chapter 9 in Part I of Cervantes's *Don Quixote* can be said to form such an embedded act of narration. Here the narrator claims that he has lost the source material he needs to be able to continue the story: 'This grieved me extremely: and the pleasure of having read so little was turned into disgust to think what small probability there was of finding much that, in my opinion, was yet wanting of so savoury a story' (p. 74).

Retrospective narration, then, is found in most fictional prose. This narrative form exists, as Genette puts it, through a fundamental paradox: on the one hand, retrospective narration is temporally related to the story it is telling; on the other hand, it has an 'atemporal essence' since it does not give any impression of the passage of time. For Käte Hamburger, this paradox contributes to making narrative texts fictional: only in narrative fiction, she argues, do we accept without reservation a sentence such as 'Morgen war Weihnachten' ('Tomorrow was Christmas Eve'), which in everyday speech would be an illogical construction (Hamburger 1968: 53–72).

Time in fictional prose

In the analysis of Virginia Woolf's *To the Lighthouse* in Part II I shall be discussing time as an important motif in fictional prose. Yet as this analysis shows, time is not only something authors write about: it is also a factor that constitutes both the story and the discourse. If on this basis I say that time in narrative fiction can be understood as the chronological relation between story and text, I have delimited the topic for this presentation, which takes Genette's *Narrative Discourse* as its basis by linking narrative time to three main terms:

1   Order (*ordre*): answers the question 'when?'
2   Duration (*durée*): answers the question 'how long?'
3   Frequency (*fréquence*): answers the question 'how often?'

Order   By 'order' we mean the temporal order of events in the story in relation to the presentation of these events in the narrative discourse. If a text is so narrated that it departs from the chronologically ordered story (as an abstraction that can first be assembled when we have read the whole text), there arises a type of difference which Genette calls 'anachrony', and which has two main variants: *analepsis* and *prolepsis*. To a certain extent these two terms correspond to 'flashback' and 'foreshadowing'. However, Genette's concepts are clearly preferable since they are more precise and more directly related to two complementary narrative variations.

Analepsis is an evocation of a story-event at a point in the text where later events have already been related, i.e. the narration jumps back to an earlier point in the story. This narrative variation, which is much more common than prolepsis, is divided by Genette into three types:

1   *External analepsis*: the time of the story in the analepsis lies outside and prior to the time of the main narrative (which Genette calls 'first narrative'). This means that the narration jumps back to a point in the story before the main narrative starts. For example, the Norwegian author Erik Fosnes Hansen's *Psalm at Journey's End* (1990) opens with a portrayal of Jason, the conductor of the orchestra on the *Titanic* and one of the novel's main characters, walking through the streets of London on 'April 10, 1912 . . . just before sunrise' (p. 7). At sunrise Jason stops:

    The sun rose. He put down his suitcase and violin and watched everything slowly changing, contours sharpening and deepening, the river acquiring colours.
    He looked at the redness for a while.
    *
    'It should be a little to the right below the sun.'
    His father's voice.
    'Will it be long?' That is his own voice, light, curious, a very long time ago, when he was ten. It all seems far, far away, and yet now it is coming closer. (p. 8)

    While this analepsis is linked to, and in a certain sense motivated by, the red colour of the rising sun, it is clearly marked in the text—and at the same time it sets the pattern for similar analeptic variations later on in the narrative. (Actually, in this novel these analepses are so long that they aspire to be 'main narratives' in their own right.)

2   *Internal analepsis*: the narration goes to an earlier point in the story, but this point is inside the main story. A well-known example of this variant is provided by Gustave Flaubert's *Madame Bovary* (1857). After we have been told about later events in Emma's life, the third-person narrator presents an internal analepsis which gives a concise account of the time she spent in

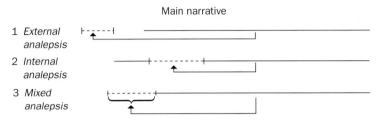

Figure 3.1

a convent (pp. 32–7). This period lies *after* the day when Charles starts at a new school, which is the event Flaubert uses to begin his novel.

3 *Mixed analepsis* means that the time period covered by the analepsis starts before but leads up to or jumps into the main narrative. The sophisticated narrative technique in Emily Brontë's *Wuthering Heights* (1847) combines this variant with external analepsis. The novel presents a strange love story through a series of analeptic manoeuvres. Emily Brontë carries out these manoeuvres via two main narrators, Lockwood and Nelly Dean. The effect is partly to present the plot, and the love affair between Catherine and Heathcliff, as mysterious and romantic. Yet the novel's distanced plot (and thereby also its potentially threatening and unmasking elements) is brought closer to the reader through a curiously tentacular effect. The narration infiltrates the reader into the action, among other things through the ways in which the novel's apparently closed and limited space is destabilized in the narrative discourse. Emily Brontë achieves this effect not least through the way in which she combines external and mixed analepsis.

We can illustrate the three variants of analepsis as shown in Fig. 3.1. Internal analepsis is the most important of these variants. The third variant is relatively uncommon, while the first (external) variant often takes the form of a supplement to the main narrative. An internal analepsis may, according to how extensive it is and how it is designed, intervene in the main narrative and in extreme cases may also 'threaten' it. This applies in particular to the variant of internal analepsis that Genette calls 'heterodiegetic'. Whereas an internal 'homodiegetic' analepsis deals with the same line of action as the main narrative, a heterodiegetic analepsis deals with an action different from the content of the main narrative. The stories that Malone constructs in Samuel Beckett's *Malone Dies* (1958) remind us of both these variants of internal analepsis.

Prolepsis is any narrative manoeuvre that consists in evoking in advance an event that will take place later. Prolepsis occurs much more seldom than analepsis, and most often in first-person narration. This anachronic variation also involves a narrative manoeuvre that represents a departure from the first, dominant narrative. Prolepsis is, in other words, the evocation of a story-event at a point before earlier events have been narrated. This form of narrative information can be extremely compressed; it may be so dense that we can hardly say that the prolepsis is 'narrated'. In such instances, as in the example from Fyodor Dostoevsky's *Crime and Punishment* (1866) below, one or just a few words that later become particularly significant may acquire a proleptic quality.

A question actualized by this point concerns the connection between the number of prolepses we believe we can identify in a text and how well we know the text. This question exemplifies one aspect of the relationship between narrative presentation and reading. If we re-read texts such as Conrad's *Heart of Darkness* or Dostoevsky's *Crime and Punishment*, we probably find more prolepses than when we read the novel for the first time. One of the reasons for this is that in the reading process the transition between 'calling up' a later event (which we perhaps know already) and 'referring to' it in a pre-empting way is easily blurred.

Thornton Wilder's *The Bridge of San Luis Rey* (1927) provides an illustrative example of how prolepsis and analepsis can be combined. The special thing about this example is that, in the novel's first sentence, it immediately plays on both these variants of anachrony: 'On Friday noon, July the twentieth, 1714, the finest bridge in all Peru broke and precipitated five travellers into the gulf below' (p. 3). Few novels have a more fascinating beginning. At the same time that we as readers can see the five travellers in our mind's eye, plunging to their certain deaths, we sense that the novel's action will be concerned with precisely these five. Indeed, this turns out to be correct, for Brother Juniper, who witnesses the accident, feels himself compelled by what he has seen to attempt to answer the question: ' "Why did this happen to those five?" If there were any pattern in a human life, surely it could be discovered mysteriously latent in those lives so suddenly cut off' (p. 6). In so far as the subsequent discourse develops from this question, we might say that most of the novel is analeptic in relation to the beginning. Yet in this long analepsis, which covers practically the whole book, the first sentence functions *proleptically*: as we know the whole time what is going to happen to the five characters, we interpret what we learn about them in the light of this knowledge.

A more debatable example of prolepsis ('debatable' because the prolepsis calls up a later event without identifying it) is to be found in Dostoevsky's *Crime and Punishment*. At the beginning of this novel the third-person narrator focuses on Raskolnikov, the impoverished student in St Petersburg, who becomes the novel's dominant main character. In a way that marks great narrative economy the characterization of Raskolnikov starts immediately. The omniscient narrator comments that Raskolnikov has an embarrassing feeling of fear, and in a summary of his thoughts we read: ' "To think that I can contemplate such a terrible act and yet be afraid of such trifles," he thought, and he smiled strangely' (p. 1). This combination of thought summary and narrative comment is indicative of the direction of the whole novel. 'Terrible act' we can read as a prolepsis for the dominant act Raskolnikov performs a little later (but nevertheless relatively early): the double murder of the landlady and Lizaveta. To those who object that 'terrible act' at first reading is simply suspense-creating in a general sense and that the word only functions proleptically when we re-read the book, it must be conceded that this prolepsis, like several others in *Crime and Punishment*, is more obvious on a second reading. Still, it is supported here by other textual elements. For example, a little later it is qualified and repeated through words such as 'evidence' and 'real project' (p. 3), and '*the thing itself*' (p. 4) which is even italicized so that the prolepsis is typographically reinforced.

Duration   To answer the question how long a narrative text 'lasts' is really impossible. For the only relevant yardstick is 'reading time'—something which varies from reader to reader. If we nevertheless say that story time and discourse time 'coincide' in what we call 'scene', this is based on conventional grounds; it is not because this necessarily *is* so. One reason why this convention has developed is that a dialogue in a scene communicates language in language; we reckon that words in the text stand for words that were uttered in the story. Linguistic communication of non-verbal events may on the other hand be carried out narratively in many different ways, also with respect to time.

Since the passage of time cannot be measured, both Genette and Rimmon-Kenan sensibly take their starting-point in another relation that combines the text's temporal dimension with the text's spatial dimension. The story *lasts* so long, and its duration (which may be anything from a few minutes to many years) stands in a relationship to the *length* of the text that presents the story. Consider the short story 'The Father' by the Norwegian author Bjørnstjerne Bjørnson. It is only a couple of pages long, yet in a manner reminiscent of Kafka's 'Before the Law' (which I shall be discussing in Chapter 5) this text presents, through the variant of third-person narrative Bjørnson employs, a whole life. At the opposite extreme to 'The Father' is a novel such as Joyce's *Ulysses*, in which the narrative discourse (that fills over 900 pages) presents a story which—true enough with innumerable digressions and complications—is limited to only one day.

Textual length, which is an integral part of an author's narrative technique, thus has an important temporal aspect. Genette proposes to use what he calls 'constant speed' as an imagined norm against which to measure different degrees of the passage of time. 'Constant speed' means that the ratio between how long the story lasts and how long the text is remains stable and unchanged, for example in the case of a novel which consistently uses one page to present each year in a character's life. On the basis of this norm the 'speed' may increase or decrease. The maximum speed is *ellipsis*, the minimum speed is *descriptive pause*. Between these two extremes we have *summary* and *scene*. We can define these four concepts as follows:

1 *Descriptive pause*: narrative time = n, story time = 0; i.e. for a text segment ('n') there is zero story duration in the story. Such pauses are common in narrative fictional prose, and they can have many different functions. An example to which reference is often made is the extended descriptive pause at the beginning of Joseph Conrad's *Nostromo* (1904). Here Conrad lets the third-person narrator depict the topography and analeptically sketch historical lines of development in the area where the action is to unfold, an unidentified country in Latin America. When we read the novel again, it is striking what great relevance this descriptive pause has to the subsequent events in the story and to the novel's thematics. Yet since we inevitably expect a *certain* progression in the story as we read, our patience and interest are really put to the test the first time we read the novel! Similarly, the reader of a very different kind of novel, Robbe-Grillet's *La Jalousie* (1957), may be struck, or even irritated, by the way in which the narration centres on an apparently static constellation of characters and constantly refers to the same hour of the clock.

2 *Scene*: narrative time = story time. There are two things to remember when it comes to scenic presentation in prose fiction. First (as I have already mentioned), it is only *conventionally* that we can say that narrative time corresponds to story time. Second, a scene too is *narrated*. This applies also to texts in which the author mostly uses only dialogue (which is commonly regarded as the 'purest' form of scene). A ready example is Ernest Hemingway's short story 'The Killers' (1928):

'I'll have a roast pork tenderloin with apple sauce and mashed potatoes', the first man said.
'It isn't ready yet.'
'What the hell do you put it on the card for?'
'That's the dinner', George explained. 'You can get that at six o'clock.'
George looked at the clock on the wall behind the counter.
'It's five o'clock.'
'The clock says twenty minutes past five', the second man said.
'It's twenty minutes fast.' (p. 57)

As Rimmon-Kenan (1983: 54) notes, 'consisting exclusively of dialogue and a few "stage directions", the passage looks more like a scene from a play than like a segment of a narrative'. The third-person narrator's contribution is sparse, yet we note his presence in reported statements such as 'George looked at the clock . . .'. Novels written in dialogue include Denis Diderot's *Jacques le fataliste* (1795) and (even more clearly) *Le Neveu de Rameau* (1805), and several books by the Spanish author Pío Baroja.

Extensive use of scenes may, but need not, result in a longer text. A text such as Bjørnson's 'The Father' illustrates that scenic elements are important in short prose too. The crucial turning-points in Thord's life are presented through the short dialogues which he has with the priest, and with his son just before he drowns:

Fourteen days after that day father and son were rowing across the lake to Storliden in calm weather in order to talk about the wedding. 'This thwart is not safely in place under me', said the son, getting up to put it in the right position. At the same moment the loose floorboard on which he is standing slips; he throws out his arms, utters a cry and falls into the water.—'Grab the oar!' yelled his father, getting up and sticking it out. But when his son had made a couple of grabs, he stiffens. 'Wait a minute!' yells the father, and he rowed up to him. At that moment his son falls backwards, fixes his gaze on his father—and sinks. (My translation)

Short though it is, the dialogue in this excerpt illustrates the dramatic and intensive function a scene can have. Much of the effect here lies precisely in the textual concentration and in the way in which the three pieces of dialogue are linked together with the narrative comments. That the third-person narrator is soberly informative rather than omnisciently explanatory also promotes the textual concentration of this narrative.

3   *Summary*: narrative time is less than story time. Together with scene this is an extremely common variant in narrative fiction, and the two are often combined. When we read right after the scene I have quoted that 'For three days and three nights people could see the father rowing around this spot without taking any food or getting any sleep; he was dragging the lake for his son', we have a simple example of summary: this sentence is shorter than the scene above, but the story time to which it refers is much longer.

4   *Ellipsis*: narrative time = 0, story time = n; i.e. for some story duration ('n') there is zero textual space. We have two main variants of ellipses: (*a*) *explicit ellipsis*: the text indicates how much of the story time it jumps over, as for example when the narrator in 'The Father' introduces the final paragraph with the sentence 'Perhaps a year might have passed since that day'; (*b*) *implicit ellipsis*: Here no direct indication is given of change or transition in story time. Sometimes the transition may be made clear in other ways (for example by the context), but an implicit ellipsis can also be disorienting, since we do not know what has been left out or how long a period of time the narration has jumped over. In some cases a subsequent analepsis may provide the answer to these questions (or parts of them). Faulkner's *The Sound and the Fury* has many such implicit ellipses, not least in the novel's first part. In this case the ellipses are unusually well justified (both narratively and thematically): the mentally retarded Benjy has no conception of 'normal' or 'connected' time; for him an event that made an impression ten years ago may be just as close as the present day, and he also in fact moves rapidly and frequently between different dimensions of time.

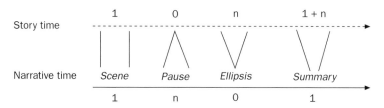

Figure 3.2

In the context of analysis, an implicit ellipsis is often more interesting than an explicit one. The ellipsis opens a chronological gap in the text, and for the reader it is a challenge to understand and explain what thematic effect the ellipsis has. Does it perhaps give an interpretative signal? This does not mean that all implicit ellipses *do* have a productive function—we may have to analyse the whole text to find out whether that is the case. Schematically, we can illustrate the four main variants in relation to 'constant speed' in a narrative prose text as shown in Fig. 3.2.

Frequency Frequency is an important temporal component in narrative fiction. For Genette, frequency refers to the relationship between how many times an event occurs in the story and how many times it is narrated (or mentioned) in the text. Thus frequency involves *repetition*, which in itself is such an important narrative concept that I shall discuss it in more detail below.

The relationships between story events and their narration in the text have three main variants:

1 *Singulative narration*: what 'happened' once is told once. This is the simplest and most common form of frequency. To this category also belongs a less common narrative phenomenon, namely telling several times what happened several times. Cervantes parodies this narrative method when in *Don Quixote* he lets Sancho tell the story of the fisherman who had to carry 300 goats in a boat and only had room for one at a time. When Sancho starts telling the story, it becomes clear that he is thinking of relating this event 300 times, corresponding to the number of trips the fisherman had to make.

2 *Repetitive narration*: what 'happened' once is told several times. This is an important narrative method in modern literature, though we also have examples that are much older. If we see the four gospels in the New Testament as 'one' story, we can say that they form a repetitive and self-consolidating narrative presentation of the life of Jesus. A modern master of repetitive narration is William Faulkner, especially in novels such as *The Sound and the Fury* (1929) and *Absalom, Absalom!* (1936). In the latter novel the narration returns again and again to a specific story-event: that Henry Sutpen kills Charles Bon. Faulkner then links these repetitions to other

narrative variations—of narrator, perspective, and passage of time. These variations create thematic complexity, among other things exploring how far-reaching (and different) the consequences of one single action may be.

In *The Sound and the Fury* the relationship that three brothers have to their sister, Cathy, is in one sense comparable to Sutpen's killing of Bon. These brothers are all first-person narrators, each in his own chapter, yet they are very different both as narrators and as characters. The presentation of the 'same' story-events thus becomes different too. Altogether the variations of presentation, language, emphasis, and consequence are so great that we must ask ourselves whether it really *is* the same story-events which the repetitive narrations refer to.

3 *Iterative narration*: what 'happened' several times is told once. This variant can have different forms. For Genette, Marcel Proust's *In Search of Lost Time* (1913–27) is a major example of iterative narration. This applies particularly to the first three main parts of this novel. The narrative text of *Combray* narrates 'not what *happened* but what *used to happen* at Combray, regularly, ritually, every day, or every Sunday, or every Saturday, etc.' (Genette 1980: 117–18, original emphasis). In Proust's fictional universe, this iterative narrative device has different forms and various thematic effects. Even in simple scenes Proust puts in iterative passages, which thus can have a generalizing effect. As well as being a significant part of the novel's overall structure, this narrative device also serves to engender and shape the content of *In Search of Lost Time*.

Both in the case of Proust and of other authors, an iterative narrative presentation can refer to story-events which together constitute a process or a complex of problems. Similarly, the iterative narration in Conrad's *Nostromo* signals that although the novel depicts one revolution, has one silver mine and one North American capitalist and so forth, it points to representative features of the historical development of the South American continent.

Graphically we can illustrate the three frequency variants as in Fig. 3.3. A narrative text need not limit itself to only one of these frequency variants. Many combinations are possible, and a number of theorists claim that in modern literature the presentation of time is so varied and sophisticated that

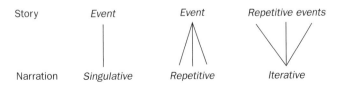

Figure 3.3

it undermines any systematized account. However, this in itself does not render these categories invalid, and the different combinations of narrative time are most interesting precisely *as combinations* of the systematized variants presented here. This means that the concepts which are relevant for use in narrative analysis will vary from text to text. The narrative characteristics and problems in the literary text under consideration will determine what concepts it is fruitful to apply.

Narrative time in film

It follows from what I have said about film communication and the film narrator in the preceding chapter that in a film narrative time is presented rather than narrated. Yet as we will also remember from Chapter 2, I see such film presentation as a variant of narration, and the expression 'film narrator' indicates the complex communication instance for this narration. When Gerald Mast claims that space and time have equal roles in film, it is not least film's unique presentation of time that he has in mind. On the one hand, film presupposes space (a film displays in rapid succession a series of images, and each image is a spatial print); on the other hand, film imposes a temporal vector upon the spatial dimension of the image. Film complicates and changes the image's stable space by setting it in motion and adding sound, and by introducing sequences of images and combinations of events. The result is an extremely complex and captivatingly effective art form, but film does not become less space-'based' or less space-dependent even though it continually destabilizes and complicates the spatial dimension of the image.

These comments touch upon one of the most interesting discussions in film theory: what is often called the 'Eisenstein–Bazin debate'. For Sergei Eisenstein (the Russian director of several classic films, including *The Battleship Potemkin*, which I shall be discussing below) film does not communicate so much by displaying images as through the way in which these images are combined: 'two film pieces of any kind, placed together, inevitably combine into a new concept, a new quality, arising out of that juxtaposition' (Eisenstein 1986: 14). This assertion, which is closely related to Eisenstein's montage technique, is countered by André Bazin, who argues that Eisenstein dubiously breaks up nature (the objective world of reality in which man is placed) into small pieces, both spatially and temporally. For Bazin, the value and human appeal of film lie primarily in presenting (and thus in a sense recreating) nature as 'whole' and 'complete'. Implicit in the arguments Bazin levels at Eisenstein there lies a conception of film as an art form in which space dominates. For Eisenstein it is on the contrary time that is more important, since film images can only be combined sequentially in the projection process.

If we link these views to my introductory comments on the presentation of time in film, both Eisenstein and Bazin seem to have good points. Yet Mast is right in saying that much of film's special appeal lies in the *cumulative* kinetic hypnosis of the *uninterrupted* flow of film and time. Because the art of cinema most closely parallels the operation of time, it imprisons the attention within a hypnotic grip that becomes steadily tighter and stronger (if the work is properly built) as the film progresses and it refuses to let go until it has had its way. (Mast 1983: 113, original emphasis)

Let us briefly look at the presentation of time in a film adaptation, the Russian director Lev Kulidzhanov's *Crime and Punishment* (1970). I shall limit myself to commenting on the way the film ends in relation to the ending of Dostoevsky's novel. In literary fiction as in film, beginnings and endings are extremely important: the beginning to arouse the interest of the reader/ viewer, the ending to maximize the total effect of the aesthetic product on the person reading (the book) or seeing/listening to (the film). As readers of Dostoevsky's *Crime and Punishment* will remember, the ending of this novel is designed as an epilogue. That the place for this epilogue is Siberia establishes a sharp spatial contrast with the plot, which takes place in St Petersburg. Siberia is the place for Raskolnikov's new life; there begins 'a new story' (p. 527) which lies outside the novel's universe but which presupposes Raskolnikov's confession of the double murder of the landlady and Lizaveta.

Why does Kulidzhanov omit the epilogue? Since the film version he gives us of the main action is relatively accurate in relation to the novel's plot, and since Georgi Taratorkin (as Raskolnikov) and Innokenti Smoktunovsky (as Porfiry) both bring out essential conflicts and thematic tensions in the novel, it may come as a surprise that he has not attempted to transfer the epilogue to film at all. The most plausible reason is probably that Kulidzhanov, a member of the Communist Party and a loyal 'Soviet artist', found it difficult to reconcile the novel's Christian ideology (which is perhaps most explicitly expressed in the epilogue) with the official Communist one. The relevant point in our context is that, by leaving out the epilogue, Kulidzhanov not only distorts the novel's ideas but radically changes its presentation of time. Put slightly differently: the fact that the adaptation omits the epilogue narrows down the novel's story time in a manner which eliminates an essential spatial contrast (St Petersburg ↔ Siberia) and which furthermore, by toning down the irrational aspect of the discourse, reduces the dialectic in the pressure to confess that both Porfiry and Sonya exert on Raskolnikov.

Narrative repetition

What is told again in a narrative prose text does not for that reason become true, but it probably becomes more important. Narrative repetition, which is closely related to narrative time (but also to other textual elements such as events and characters), is an important constituent aspect of prose fiction. Think again of Bjørnson's 'The Father'. Four times Thord comes to the priest: first to baptize his son, then to have him confirmed, then to get him married, and finally after his son has drowned. These visits constitute important stages in Thord's life, and they all contribute to presenting the drowning accident as a peripeteia-like climax. The effect of the repetitions is reinforced by the long story time which the concentrated narration spans, and the last repetition marks the end as final.

Of the many different forms narrative repetition takes, three are particularly clear. First, we may have repetitions of individual words (most often verbs, nouns, or adjectives), gestures, reactions, and so forth. The snow in 'The Dead' acquires a symbolic quality by being repeatedly referred to at important points in the text, and the same may be said of the lighthouse in *To the Lighthouse*. This form of repetition is often linked to characterization, as when Don Quixote is again and again described as 'mad'—both by the narrator and by those with whom he comes in contact. Such repetition can have a comic effect, but this effect may then be qualified through other narrative devices. For example, Don Quixote both confirms and complicates the picture drawn of him as being mad. Most clearly he seems to confirm his madness through his actions as a knight errant. Verbally he makes this most explicit in connection with the penance that he imposes on himself in Sierra Morena. Yet since in his ingenious narrative design Cervantes places the hero's proclamation of madness (pp. 213–30) *after* the speech Don Quixote makes on the golden age (pp. 86–7), the effect is different from what it would have been had the two passages changed places. For in his speech about the golden age Don Quixote appears far from mad; rather, he comes over as wise: he says things that are so surprisingly thought-provoking that the reader is startled when the narrator (who quotes the speech) expresses the view that 'this tedious discourse . . . might very well have been spared' (p. 87).

Second, a narrative text can repeat events or scenes in such a way that they appear alike, perhaps almost identical. Thord's visits to the priest in 'The Father' accord with this form—the fact that the pattern of action in the first three visits is very similar makes the variation in the fourth more dramatic. In *The Sound and the Fury* the narration in the first three parts circles around the same events. These events are ostensibly identical, but since they are variously presented and interpreted (through three very different narrators), Faulkner raises the question of whether they really are so.

Finally, if we extend our perspective from the single text to an author's works as a whole, we can see that many authors use again in later books characters, motifs, and events taken from what they have written before. Cedric Watts has introduced the term 'transtextuality' for this narrative variant (Watts 1984: 133). Such transtextuality does not mean the same as the concept of 'intertextuality' (which I shall be discussing in Chapters 4 and 7). Transtextuality is a more restricted concept for repetitions within a specific author's works, but it does not follow that these repetitions are simple or unambiguous. For example, Conrad's character Marlow is a narrator in four narrative texts, but the way in which he functions varies: Marlow as a narrator is thematically more productive in *Heart of Darkness* (1899) and *Lord Jim* (1900) than in the later novel *Chance* (1913).

One reason for mentioning Conrad's Marlow as an example is to emphasize that the narrator has an absolutely central function in the design of all these three forms of repetition, whether he or she functions as a narrative instrument or as a personal conveyor of his or her own experiences. This does not mean, however, that the repetition itself need be directly linked to the text's narration; it can also be formed through other aspects of the discourse. Since these three forms of repetition are relatively clear, in the context of analysis it is often more important to show how they operate, and what their effects are, than to identify them. Even if a narrative repetition (on a par with other narrative devices and phenomena) must first be detected in the text, this is usually only the first step in an analysis. Although it is necessary to say that *The Sound and the Fury* has three first-person narrators, this observation does not become important unless it provides the basis for questions we can *then* pose: why four narrators instead of one? Why is one of them mentally retarded? Why a concluding third-person part after the three first-person ones? If Faulkner 'needs' all three narrators, then this has thematic implications. Do the repetitions of narrators—who, in part, relate the same thing, but in different ways and with changing emphasis—mean that repetition is a means of exploring how different characters experience time? Such questions are critically interesting to pursue in reading and interpreting *The Sound and the Fury*. That the novel does not provide simple or unambiguous answers to them is connected with the thematic complexity these questions lead us into. The novel's narrative method, of which repetition is an integral part, is crucial to the presentation of its thematics.

Repetition is one of the narrative concepts that most clearly has a content dimension. Whether the interpreter places greater weight on the narrative or the thematic aspect will among other things be dependent on the way problems are posed and what critical approach he or she uses. In any case, the narrative and thematic aspects of repetition are linked together in analysis. Rather than making repetition less relevant as a narrative concept, this illustrates the interplay of narrative and thematic dimensions in narrative fiction.

'Platonic' and 'Nietzschean' repetition   In his *Fiction and Repetition* (1982), J. Hillis Miller investigates this 'double' dimension of repetition. Miller begins by referring to the three forms of repetition I have already presented. However, his own main distinction is between two *other* forms, which he calls the 'first' and 'second' forms of repetition. These two forms of repetition do not replace those mentioned above. Rather, they supplement the three first forms and contain elements from each of them. Furthermore, since they have an important content dimension they illustrate the close connection between narrative form and literary content.

The history of Western ideas of repetition begins, according to Miller's short summary, with the Bible on the one hand and with Homer, the pre-Socratics, and Plato on the other. The modern history of ideas about repetition goes by way of Vico to Hegel and the German Romantics, to Kierkegaard's *Repetition* (1843), to Marx, to Nietzsche's concept of the eternal return, to Freud's notion of the compulsion to repeat, to the aesthetics of modernism, 'on down to such diverse present-day theorists of repetition as Jacques Lacan or Gilles Deleuze, Mircea Eliade or Jacques Derrida' (Miller 1982: 5). The theorist Miller makes most explicit use of is the French philosopher Gilles Deleuze. In Deleuze's *Logique du sens* (1969), two alternative theories of repetition are set against each other by way of opposing Nietzsche's concept of repetition to that of Plato:

> Let us consider two formulations: 'only that which resembles itself differs', 'only differences resemble one another'. It is a question of two readings of the world in the sense that one asks us to think of difference on the basis of preestablished similitude or identity, while the other invites us on the contrary to think of similitude and even identity as the product of a fundamental disparity. The first exactly defines the world of copies or of representations; it establishes the world as icon. The second, against the first, defines the world of simulacra. It presents the world itself as phantasm. (Deleuze 1969: 302, Hillis Miller's translation)

What Deleuze calls 'Platonic' repetition is grounded in an archetypal model which is untouched by the effect of repetition and of which all the other examples are copies. 'The assumption of such a world gives rise to the notion of a metaphoric expression based on genuine participative similarity or even on identity . . . A similar presupposition, as Deleuze recognizes, underlies concepts of imitation in literature' (Miller 1982: 6). Positing a world based on difference, the other, Nietzschean, mode of repetition assumes that each thing is unique, intrinsically different from every other thing. 'Similarity arises against the background of this "disparité du fond". It is a world not of copies but of what Deleuze calls "simulacra" or "phantasms"' (Miller 1982: 6). These phantasms are not grounded in some paradigm or archetype, but are ungrounded doublings which arise from differential interrelations among elements which are all on the same plane.

These two variants of repetition are not mutually exclusive. Quite the reverse: the second form is related to the first and can to a certain degree be considered as a reaction to it—indeed, in many narrative texts *both* forms can be traced. If so, one can then go on to discuss what the relationship between the two forms is like, and whether there are special reasons for alternation, if it occurs, to arise between them. Such questions can lead to interpretative results which are not only interesting in relation to repetition but which can also be linked to other features of the text under consideration.

Even if the narrative aspect is more immediately visible in the first three forms of repetition, it is also present in the two basic variants Miller discusses. As has been mentioned, the snow in Joyce's 'The Dead' becomes more important through the repetition of the word 'snow' at various points throughout the text. To begin with this appears as a simple variant of the first form of repetition presented above. Yet as we shall see in the analysis of 'The Dead', these repetitions gradually become integrated in complex narrative and thematic patterns. In particular it is the central dinner scene in this short story which actualizes both the first and second forms of repetition.

Repetition in film Is the concept of repetition relevant for film? It obviously is, and yet the form and the functions repetition has in films are in part radically different from those we find in prose fiction. Let us first note three general points before briefly relating them to Orson Welles's *Citizen Kane* (1941) and Sergei Eisenstein's *The Battleship Potemkin* (1925).

1 Through its own production process film constitutes itself as a series of repetitions. That the projector 'stops' each frame in front of a light source at a rate of twenty-four frames per second represents a mechanically repetitive process which is uninterruptedly maintained through an apparently unending series of images—right up to the point when the film is over. The tendency of human vision to see movement creates the optical illusion that constitutes film. Forms of repetition are closely connected with film's uncompromising progression from beginning to end.

2 Repetition in film is closely related to filmic presentation of time, and especially to *sequence*. Succeeding frames can be practically identical, but they can also be very different, without the action becoming jerky and fragmented on that account. The reason is, as the Frenchman Méliès discovered just before the turn of the century, that the repetitive presentation of frames that the film projector provides makes the action in the film contemporaneous and coherent, even if it in fact is not. From this discovery, which represented an enormous step forward from the first film experiments of Edison and Lumière, it was only a short distance to *animation* or the animated cartoon film.

3 Repetition is an aspect of film that contributes to giving the medium a narrative dimension, since narrative progression, which we can relate to the development of time and action, combines known elements (i.e. elements that have already been introduced and are thus repeated) with the introduction of new ones. On this level, filmic repetition can operate in ways that may be compared with repetition in verbal fiction (even though the filmic means here too will be different from the linguistic ones). We shall be seeing examples of this in Part II, most clearly perhaps in the analysis of John Huston's adaptation of Joyce's 'The Dead'. This analysis places weight on the symbolic qualities associated with the snow in the short story. The film creates something of the same effect by linking images of the falling snow with key dialogue excerpts spoken by the characters (actors) in the film.

Repetition is a constituent element in all narrative film. Both *Citizen Kane* and *The Battleship Potemkin* have so many effective variants and combinations of filmic repetition that I must limit myself to a few selected points for comment. In Orson Welles's film, the most interesting repetitions are related to the main character, Kane. Their overall effect is reinforced by the structural device of presenting a life story as retrospectively 'ordered', but with chronological progression of action centred on crucial turning-points in Kane's life. Thus, relatively early in the film, an image shows Thatcher with his parents discussing Kane's future; in the centre background of the *same image* we can see Kane as a boy playing outside the house. Welles's combined use of framing, deep-focus photography, and low-key lighting to achieve this effect is repeated at a later point in the film. Here the viewer sees and hears Leland and Bernstein discussing Kane's integrity, and how reliable he is in relation to the projects they are themselves involved in. In the background between the two we can see—less clearly than the first time, but nevertheless clearly enough—the outline of Kane as an adult reflected on the window.

An obvious effect of this device is to supplement diegetic sound: the outline of Kane visualizes and illustrates what the dialogue is about. The background outlines of Kane as a boy and as an adult serve to integrate sound and image, thus reinforcing Kane's position as the film's main character. This effect is not only structural but also thematic: is Kane perhaps more vulnerable and less

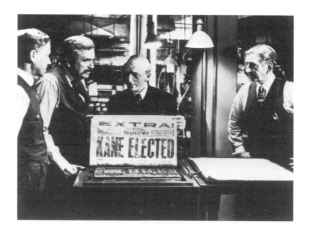

In Orson Welles's *Citizen Kane*, filmic techniques such as deep focus and low-key lighting are combined with elaborate forms of repetition and flashback (analepsis). The film starts with the dying Kane uttering the word 'Rosebud'. This name focuses the viewer's attention on Thompson's sustained attempt to reconstruct Kane's life in order to study his character traits.

From the Odessa Steps sequence in Sergei Eisenstein's *The Battleship Potemkin*, a classic example of Eisenstein's montage technique.

If the mutiny on the battleship *Potemkin* represents the Russian revolution, the ship itself symbolizes collective strength.

dangerous than he appears to be? This question can in the next instance be related to other aspects of the film, but the relevant point to make here is that Welles uses technical variants of repetition to achieve this kind of thematic effect. Not only are the framing and positioning of characters strikingly similar, with spaces between the characters to make room for the outline of Kane, but so is the use of camera angle and depth of field. Structurally as well as thematically, Welles's innovative use of the wide-angle, deep-focus lens is strikingly effective.

In Eisenstein's films as well, repetition is closely connected with other filmic means (and is therefore difficult to discuss in isolation). I shall briefly comment on the use of repetition in what Eisenstein himself called 'Act 4' of *The Battleship Potemkin*, the Odessa steps sequence. This deservedly famous sequence is the classic example of Eisenstein's montage technique. Generally speaking, montage describes how a film is assembled through editing. If montage refers to an approach to editing developed by Eisenstein and other Soviet film-makers of the 1920s, 'it emphasizes dynamic, often discontinuous, relationships beween shots and the juxtaposition of images to create ideas not present in either shot by itself' (Bordwell and Thompson 1997: 480). One constituent element of this particular montage sequence is that Eisenstein systematically integrates repetitive shots in other structural elements such as rhythm, contrast (mainly established through cross-cutting), and plot progression. For example, shot 1010 is an extreme close-up of a tsarist officer swinging a sabre across his shoulder. This shot is directly followed by shot 1011, which shows a woman with blood spurting from her right eye. As David Mayer points out, this image is logical: 'the woman has been slashed across the face with the sabre. The violent act, though unshown, is as real as if it were seen' (Mayer 1972: 11).

A different variant of montage is observable a few shots further on. In retaliation for the massacre on the Odessa steps, the battleship *Potemkin* bombards the tsar's military headquarters. Into the shots of this bombardment Eisenstein inserts three separate shots (on screen for just over two and a half seconds) of three marble statues: a sleeping lion, an awakening lion, and a standing lion. As Mayer notes, the image is striking but illogical. Together the shots of the lions 'form a stirring visual metaphor, the awakening anger of the Russian people' (Mayer 1972: 11). Yet although Eisenstein composes the shots of statues of lions so that they seem to come remarkably alive, this does not in itself reduce the effective contrast between this image and the repetitive shots of the people on the Odessa steps. Indeed one thematic effect of the image of the statues of lions is to invite the viewer to connect lions (as a classic image of human strength) with the strength of the revolutionaries in revolt. Following the low-angle shot (shot 1024) of the standing lion towering against the city there is a cut to the entrance gate, and as the panning camera dwells on all the dead bodies lying strewn over the steps the viewer is invited to compare them with the lion as a symbol of human strength. This kind of linking is logical and yet illogical— lifeless like the statues of lions, the bodies are those of human beings: victims of authoritarian violence. It is precisely this combination of different forms of montage which makes this sequence so exceptionally effective as film.

If finally we look at the relationship between the five 'acts' in *Potemkin*, we note that here too Eisenstein combines repetition with plot progression in a manner that creates suspense. In an essay written in 1939 as an introduction to the film's original screenplay, Eisenstein considers repetition as a central filmic device: 'The action in each part [of the film] is different, but the whole action is permeated and cemented, as it were, by the method of double repetition' (Eisenstein 1988: 9). What Eisenstein understands by 'double repetition' is made clear by his own example:

> In 'Drama on the Quarter-Deck' a handful of mutinous sailors—part of the battleship's crew—cry '*Brothers!*' to the firing squad. The rifles are lowered. The whole of the crew joins the rebels.
> In 'Meeting the Squadron' the mutinous ship—part of the navy—throws the cry '*Brothers!*' to the crews of the admiralty squadron. And the guns trained on the *Potemkin* are lowered. The whole of the fleet is at one with the *Potemkin*. (Eisenstein 1988: 9)

An image of revolutionary strength, the *Potemkin* supplements and reinforces the function that the statues of lions have in the Odessa steps sequence. And yet the *Potemkin* is something much greater than the lions. The ship has a significant structural and thematic function throughout, and may perhaps be considered the film's main character. The ship does not only symbolize strength but strength created by man—a collective strength which in the film's ideology is related to both progressive and reactionary forces, with the 'good' forces as the stronger. (Here Eisenstein deliberately breaks with the historical origin of the film: the mutiny on the *Potemkin* during the failed revolution of 1905 was unsuccessful.)

If structures of repetition in *The Battleship Potemkin* are thematically formative at the level of detail, this point can also be made about the film as a whole. In film as in fictional prose, an aesthetic element becomes as a rule more important if it is repeated. While repetition may indicate stability and raise fundamental questions of identity, repetition in narrative discourse is closely related to those factors that make this discourse dynamic, i.e. those creating suspense and advancing the plot. A key word here is the *characters* in verbal fiction and film, for it is usually the characters who initiate or destabilize a fictional event. Events, characters, and characterization are the topics of the next chapter.

4
Events, Characters, and Characterization

In fictional literature as in film, characters are characterized in many different and complementary ways. The characters are involved in the plot, and the actions they perform constitute a series of *events*. The first part of this chapter comments on such fictive events, which are then linked to the terms *character* and *characterization*. My main example is Cervantes's *Don Quixote*. Relating these concepts to that of film adaptation, the last part of the chapter briefly discusses Gabriel Axel's adaptation of a short story by Karen Blixen (Isak Dinesen), 'Babette's Feast'.

Events

In theory fictional events take place at the story level in a narrative text. The story is an abstraction—a chronologically ordered summary constructed from the discourse. An event is also abstracted from the text, and the same applies to the fictional characters. The difference between story and discourse usually becomes greater the longer and the more complicated the text is. Conversely, the difference is relatively small in short and simple stories. In the 'minimal story' which Prince presents, the narrative text is so short that story and discourse practically coincide: 'John was happy, then he saw Peter, then, as a result, he was unhappy.'

Although narrative theory has spent a great deal of time discussing how useful the concepts of story and event are, they are now as a rule considered to be absolutely necessary. One important aspect of the story is that it marks the text *as narrative*. For the story refers to the development of action, and it furthermore gives this development or change a temporal dimension. Time is a key word here; events are generally closely linked to narrative time. An event is an integral part of the action: it involves a change or a transition from one situation to another (cf. Prince's example), and this transition is usually caused or experienced by one or more characters. An event need not necessarily take the form of an external, dramatic action. To insist on any absolute distinction between state (as something static) and action (as part of a process) is difficult, for a process is usually composed of many complementary states and moments. As Mieke Bal has noted, two aspects of time are relevant here: 'The events themselves happen during a certain period of time and they occur in a certain order' (Bal 1997: 208). To stress the temporal dimenson of fictional events is not, however, to suggest that they are unrelated to space. On the contrary, fictional events can only happen in space—in the universe (be it Thomas Hardy's Wessex or William Faulkner's Yoknapataw-pha) constructed by the author through his or her use of language. Perhaps it is the energy associated with events which, combined with other factors, acti-vates the dimensions of both time and space. Henri Lefebvre finds that 'the relationships between force (energy), time and space are problematical. For example, one can neither conceive of a beginning (an origin) nor yet do without such an idea' (Lefebvre 1991: 22). Events, then, are related to both time and space; they are also, as Lefebvre implies, associated with various forms of repetition.

Let us briefly illustrate these theoretical comments with two extreme exam-ples. First we can look at an excerpt from a non-fictional narrative text, the *Annals of Saint Gall*, a list of events in Gaul during the eighth, ninth, and tenth centuries of our era:

709.   Hard winter. Duke Gottfried died.
710.   Hard year and deficient in crops.
711.
712.   Flood everywhere. . . .
1054.
1055.
1056.   The Emperor Henry died; and his son Henry succeeded to the rule.
1057.
1058.

(quoted in White 1990: 6–8)

Even though this text is very different from the short text 'With father in his suitcase', which I commented on in the introductory chapter, they are both on the verge of becoming narratives. The text above is unusually terse, it is a 'year-book' in which many years stand entirely without comment. As Hayden White has pointed out, this list has 'no central subject, no well-marked beginning, middle, and end, no peripeteia, and no identifiable narrative voice' (White 1990: 6). What perhaps most strongly 'pulls' this text in the direction of a story is the seed of temporal representation that we can read out of the succeeding years and out of the comments alongside the year 1056. What is striking about this example in relation to the concept of event is how visible and strongly pre-sent certain types of event are, even in a text in which most other narrative characteristics are lacking.

Hayden White none the less concludes that this text presents a story because 'there is surely a plot—if by plot we mean a structure of relationships by which the events contained in the account are endowed with a meaning by being identified as parts of an integrated whole' (White 1990: 9). What makes this text approach the form of an intelligible whole is the succession of dates. Note that, understood as a 'structure of relationships', plot is not identical with discourse. While discourse, put simply, is the text as it presents itself (with all its literary means, devices, and variations), plot refers to the way in which the events are combined, structured, and developed. As will be recalled from Chapter 1, plot has an important dynamic aspect. Paul Ricoeur finds that plot 'governs a succession of events in any story . . . [which] is *made out of* events to the extent that plot *makes* events *into* a story. The plot, therefore, places us at the crossing point of temporality and narrativity . . .' (Ricoeur 1981: 167; original emphasis). Such an understanding of plot implies a critical interest in, and focus on, the dynamics of narrative; this kind of critical interest informs, I hope, the analyses presented in Part II of this book. Moreover, defining plot in this way also indicates an interest in reading and in the relationship of reading and plotting—'that which makes a plot "move forward", and makes us read forward, seeking in the unfolding of the narrative a line of intention and a portent of design that hold the promise of progress toward meaning' (Brooks 1984: p. xiii). As Frank Kermode has observed in *The Sense of an Ending*, all plots thus have something in common with prophecy, 'for they must appear to educe from the prime matter of the situation the forms of a future' (Kermode 1981: 83). The texts subjected to analysis in Part II provide rich illustrations of these characteristics of plot.

After having commented on the dramatic, external events in the *Annals of Saint Gall*, I shall make a long leap forward to a fictional text characterized by a striking *absence* of such events. This is how Alain Robbe-Grillet's 'The Beach' opens: 'Three children are walking along a beach. They move forward, side by side, holding hands. They are roughly the same height, and probably the same age too: about twelve. The one in the middle, though, is a little smaller than the other two' (p. 13). As the beginning of a short story (or a novel) there is nothing special about this example; what is exceptional is that *the whole text* is descriptively observant in this particular way—through a third-person narrator's recording, camera-like perspective. Suspense in this short story comes partly from expectations on the part of the reader (from reading other short stories) that something (dramatic) is soon going to happen. The fact that very little happens beyond the opening paragraph does not mean that this short story is devoid of events, but rather that the text limits itself to giving supplementary observations of the one event that the first sentence presents.

Functions of events According to how it is presented in the discourse, an event can have different functions. These functions often become more complex when several events are combined with one another. By function I mean those properties of an event that give it one or more specific purposes, particularly in relation to the text's content aspect. Seen thus, functions of events are closely related to the characters in the text, for they usually set the action in motion (are action-initiating) on the basis of specific aims, wishes, desires, or experiences.

In a pioneer work on narrative theory originally published in Russian in 1928, Vladimir Propp links the concept of function to 'constant elements' that he abstracts from almost 200 Russian folk-tales. For Propp, the meaning of a function is 'an act of a character, defined from the point of view of its significance for the course of the action' (Propp 1968: 21). Functions can thus remain constant even if the performer's identity changes. Consider these examples that Propp provides:

1 A tsar gives an eagle to a hero. The eagle carries the hero to another kingdom.
2 An old man gives Súcenko a horse. The horse carries Súcenko to another kingdom.
3 A sorcerer gives Iván a little boat. The boat takes Iván to another kingdom.

The only constant element in these three events is that a person, with the aid of something he or she has received, is led to another kingdom. The identity of the participants in this event may change, and both their names and characteristics may vary from tale to tale. Therefore Propp insists that it is more important to study the events (i.e. *what* has been done) than who performs them and how they have been performed.

Such strong emphasis on events is not to be found in modern narrative theory, although the concepts of both event and character are now considered to be more important than was the case some years ago. That Propp finds himself able to limit the number of functions to thirty-one (1968: 26–63), is connected with the fact that it is folk-tales he is studying, since here the patterns of events are relatively similar. In longer and more complex texts the number of functions will be much greater, and it will also be more difficult to determine how many functions a given event has. Event functions may also change throughout the same text. A dominant function of the events in the first part of *Don Quixote* is to reveal the hero's madness. Gradually this function is combined with others, and in the novel's second part many of the events qualify and comment on the pattern-establishing events in the first part. That the function we can call 'illustration of the hero's madness' is closely connected to the parody of the chivalric romances establishes a point of contact between this epic sub-genre and the folk-tale.

Kernels and catalysts One factor determining what makes an event important is what consequences it has for the characters and for the development of the plot. Often the presentation of an event will signal to the reader how important the event is—through the narrator's comments, by means of repetition, or in other ways. In an influential structuralist essay first published in 1966, Roland Barthes distinguishes between two main types of event. A *kernel* is a 'cardinal function' which promotes the action by giving the character one or more alternatives to choose between; it can also reveal the results of such a choice. Barthes gives an illustrative, non-literary example: if the telephone rings, one can either answer it or let it ring. A *catalyst* accompanies and complements the kernel, but the action to which it refers does not 'open (or continue, or close) an alternative that is of direct consequence for the subsequent development of the story' (Barthes 1982b: 265). Before I answer the phone, I perhaps turn on the light, unlock the door, or wonder who is ringing.

Both kernels and catalysts may be more or less complex. In the first part of *Don Quixote* the attack on the windmills is a kernel event. Although we have our suspicions about the likely outcome, at this early stage we cannot be sure how Don Quixote will *react* to the outcome, and what new events his reaction will lead to. As a kernel the attack on the windmills is accompanied by various catalysts, such as Don Quixote's urging Rocinante into the fray and asking Dulcinea for help in the battle. Note that the way in which we understand a kernel event here means that it becomes more uncertain whether Don Quixote's subsequent attacks are kernels. For gradually we believe ourselves able to recognize in advance both the hero's pattern of action and pattern of reaction, something which is intimately connected with the parody of chivalric romances. Yet note too that in the novel's second part the concept of kernel is re-actualized, since to a higher degree the world around Don Quixote meets him on his own terms: the world around him acts as if it were mad, while the hero himself gradually becomes less mad.

The concept of character

The performing characters that narrative texts present are *fictional*. In literature they are part of a linguistically constructed fiction; in film they are indeed visualized for us, but they are nevertheless part of a complex film form with aesthetic devices and characteristics of its own. Both in literature and film the drawing of characters is based more on conventions than on unambiguous 'historical' references to 'real' people. This does not mean that fictional characters cannot be related to historical persons or to experiences from the reader's own life. Such contact is often crucial to what response and interest are aroused in the reader. Yet we do not expect the same of the fictional characters the author constructs as we do of historical people we know. There are a number of reasons for this, including literature's need to dramatize, concentrate, and intensify plot presentation. Much of the same applies to our expectations of characters in film, though it needs to be added that the viewer's expectations are influenced by film genre (as are the reader's by literary genre). Realistic Hollywood cinema, for example, asks us suspend our disbelief and to think of the film's plot as if it were real. This kind of request is made even though, as Richard Maltby points out in his reading of Michael Curtiz's *Casablanca* (1943), a cinematic narrative is temporally composed of a set of ellipses; it is a distillation of a series of events . . . The coherent narrative, however, attempts to disguise the elliptical nature of its temporal construction by subordinating both the actual time of a depicted event and the real time experienced by the spectator in the cinema to the artificial, perceived time presented by the narrative. (Maltby 1998: 285).

Narrative theory has been relatively little concerned with the concept of character. This kind of relative toning down is nothing radically new. In the *Poetics* Aristotle places action above character: 'because tragedy is mimesis not of persons but of action and life; and happiness and unhappiness consist in action, and the goal is a certain kind of action, not a qualitative state: it is in virtue of character that people have certain qualities, but through their actions that they are happy or the reverse' (Aristotle 1995: 51, 1450a). For Aristotle, characters are primarily important as performers of actions and are subordinate to the action itself. His concept of *éthos* is more closely related to drama than to prose fiction. Moreover, *éthos* does not correspond directly to our 'character' as it refers to the (conventionally determined) qualities of a person that express an idea or a direction of intent. In modern narrative theory too, there has been a tendency to grant a lower priority to the concept of character. Inspired by Propp, A. J. Greimas, a major representative of French structuralism, thus links his central concept of *actant* (i.e. a fundamental role or a fundamental function) not only to characters but also to things (e.g. a magic ring) or to abstract quantities (e.g. fate) (see Greimas 1966).

Yet is it right to make characters subordinate to those fictional events which precisely *they* have initiated and constituted? This is a crucial point in discussions of characters in relation to other textual elements. The problem is already apparent in Aristotle, for although he ranks the action above the characters, several of the key terms in his *Poetics* (such as 'reversal and recognition', Aristotle 1995: 67, 1452b) are closely related to the concept of character. The problem is also observable in the work of such an influential theorist as Roland Barthes. While in his 1966 essay Barthes sees action as more important than the characters, in *S/Z* (1970) he gives the category of character its own category or 'code'—the 'semic' code he presents in a detailed analysis of Honoré de Balzac's short story 'Sarrasine' (1830).

Barthes's *S/Z* also makes clear the *narrative* dimension of the concept of character. This dimension manifests itself in several ways. An obvious example is the first-person narrator. Here the narrative presentation is given by a person who is also an actor in the plot (as the main character or as a minor character). Yet even if to a certain extent they coincide, the concepts of 'character' and 'narrator' refer to two different levels in the narrative text: the concept of character to the level of story, that of narrator to the level of discourse and narration. This difference helps to explain why 'character' has been a controversial concept in narrative theory: as is the case with 'history' and 'event', the concept of character is an *abstraction* based on various character indicators in the discourse. In one sense this kind of abstraction is integral to the process of reading narrative fiction, especially fiction belonging to, or associated with, the strong tradition of realistic fiction in literature. As Hillis Miller notes in *Ariadne's Thread*, 'one of the powerful attractions of reading novels is the way the reading of a novel produces the powerful illusion of an even more intimate access to the mind and heart of another person than the reader can ever have in real life' (Miller 1992: 31). 'A character', continues Miller, 'is a carved design or sign . . . The word *character*, like the word *lineaments* and the word *person* (from the Latin word for mask) involves the presumption that external signs correspond to and reveal an otherwise hidden inner nature.' Yet as Miller also observes, the effect of encountering and knowing a character in a work of narrative fiction is an illusion, and while the plots of narrative fiction irresistibly invite us to construct mental images of its characters, narrative discourse can also (as we shall see in Part II) problematize 'belief in unitary selfhood' (Miller 1992: 31).

Miller's *Ariadne's Thread* is a forceful demonstration of the intricate ways in which our conception of character shapes, and is shaped by, our understanding of narrative. Another significant contribution to our understanding of fictional characters is James Phelan's *Reading People, Reading Plots*. Phelan's approach to the concept of character is different from Miller's. He begins by problematizing David Lodge's assertion, put forward in *Language of Fiction* (1966), that a character is an abstraction of verbal symbols. Lodge is not alone in holding such a view of the fictional character; on the contrary, his position is representative of a good deal of narrative theory. Now Phelan does not believe that Lodge's assertion is wrong, but that it is incomplete. As it is presented through verbal language, the concept of character has an artificial component that Phelan calls the *synthetic*—'part of knowing a character is knowing that he/she/(it?) is a construct' (Phelan 1989: 2). In addition he introduces two more components, the 'mimetic' and the 'thematic'. The *mimetic* component is linked by Phelan to the identifying activity we perform as readers when we switch from registering ('synthetic') characters to perceiving them as acting and thinking. The mimetic component, then, describes the activity we perform (as an integral part of the reading process) as we 'identify the concept implied in the phrase "this person"' (Phelan 1989: 2). The *thematic* component, a content component that builds further on this kind of identifying activity, is related to the reader's literary competence. Such competence is based on the ability we have to discuss questions such as: what is important and interesting about this character? To what extent is she or he representative, and what is the nature of the relationship between representativeness and individuality? Is the character credible and how does she or he develop/change throughout the text? Phelan finds that whereas the mimetic and thematic components may be more or less developed, 'the synthetic component . . . may be more or less foregrounded' (Phelan 1989: 3).

Consider this extract from William Faulkner's short story 'That Evening Sun':

> So the jailer heard the noise and ran up there and found Nancy hanging from the window, stark naked, her belly already swelling out a little, like a little balloon.
> When Dilsey was sick in her cabin and Nancy was cooking for us, we could see her apron swelling out . . . (pp. 291–2)

Relating the narration to Quentin's perspective as a somewhat detached first-person narrator, Nancy's swelling belly also occasions Quentin's transition back into the story's main plot. Pinpointing the child's characteristic fascination with visual details, this narrative variation accords nicely with Quentin's associative thought. Moreover, although the variation is essentially a narrative one, it serves to shape Quentin as a character, thus preparing the reader for greater specification and individualization of his role as a first-person narrator than ever afforded, for example, the anonymous narrator of Faulkner's short story 'A Rose for Emily': 'So father didn't look at me. I was the oldest. I was nine and Caddy was seven and Jason was five' (p. 294).

Enhancing Quentin's importance as a character in 'That Evening Sun', this kind of narrative identification strengthens what Phelan calls the mimetic component: it enables us to construct, from the narrative presentation in verbal fiction, a mental image of Quentin as a fictional character. As the borderline between Quentin's narrative functions and his significance as a character is blurred, his existential motivation to narrate becomes more noticeable. There is an odd affinity in this story between Quentin's urge to narrate and Nancy's insistence on telling the Compson children a story: 'She talked like her eyes looked, like her eyes watching us and her voice talking to us did not belong to her. Like she was living somewhere else, waiting somewhere else' (p. 302). Here as in *Absalom, Absalom!* (1936), an oral narrative situation is evoked (though not sustained)—thus signalling 'the significance of oral modes of narrative communication for sophisticated, written fictions' (Lothe 1997: 79).

Questions associated with Phelan's mimetic and thematic character components may be integrated in a narrative analysis (without the analysis thereby becoming any less a *narrative* analysis). If the analysis of character tends to become thematic only, it will have difficulty in mapping and discussing the various specifying and differentiating features (as they are shaped by the text) that characterize and distinguish the characters from one another. Character and plot are mutually dependent on each other. This becomes particularly clear if (as in the analyses in Part II) we relate the concept of character to *progression*. Progression refers to 'narrative as a dynamic event, one that must move, in both its telling and its reception, through time' (Phelan 1989: 15). A concept associated with plot, progression is related to the question of character development. What constitutes character are principles such as repetition, likeness, contrast, and (logical) implication. Between them these and other devices of verbal discourse form the character's essential qualities and identity—'the character and the discourse are each other's accomplices' (Barthes 1974: 178). The question of character development can be related to E. M. Forster's concept of a 'round' character: a character who develops and changes, who may surprise us, and whose actions we cannot predict. Forster contrasts such a round character with a 'flat' one, i.e. a character who does not develop, and who therefore appears more as a type (Forster 1971: 75). Even if Forster's dichotomy oversimplifies things, it may still be useful as a starting-point for character analysis.

A particularly interesting example of a character who starts 'flat' and later becomes 'round' is Don Quixote. For in Cervantes's novel the main character gradually becomes more complex in spite of the repetitive pattern of action in the first part. Critics have related this development of the hero to the novel's *Entstehung*, i.e. how it was conceived and written down over many years. It seems clear that Cervantes at first wanted to write a much shorter text, an 'exemplary short story' about the travels of a fool who had lost his wits through reading too much chivalric literature, and who returns home after some dramatic experiences and burns the books. Gradually fundamental changes were to come about: the introduction of the Sancho figure and his incipient proverbial wisdom after the fifth chapter, the linking of the experiences in the first part with the dialogues between master and servant, the pushing of the central point over towards social and ideological problems, the knight's growing insight, his release from error, and finally his illness and death.

These changes so to speak 'pull' Don Quixote from being a 'flat' character to being a 'round' one. Don Quixote's function as a flat character is essentially linked to the parody of chivalric romances. For as the narrator strongly emphasizes, the hero's madness has a specific cause:

> You must know then, that this gentleman aforesaid, at times when he was idle, which was most part of the year, gave himself up to the reading of books of chivalry, with so much attachment and relish, that he almost forgot all the sports of the field, and even the management of his domestic affairs; and his curiosity and extravagant fondness herein arrived to that pitch, that he sold many acres of arable land to purchase books of knight-errantry . . . With this kind of language the poor gentleman lost his wits . . . (pp. 23–4)

As a 'madman' (p. 25) Don Quixote is a 'flat character' in the sense that he acts on the basis of an ideal world inspired by notions of chivalry, thus repeatedly colliding with the real world as it is constituted in Cervantes's fictional universe. The hero's madness serves to initiate action, and Cervantes stresses the difference between Don Quixote's imaginary world and the world as it really is (in the fiction). An example of such a marked difference is observable in the second chapter. After the narrator has stressed that Don Quixote's 'frenzy [was] prevailing above any reason whatever' (p. 29), he reports how Don

Quixote, mounted on Rocinante and quoting from chivalric romances, 'began to travel through the ancient and noted field of Montiel' (p. 29). The narrator then comments: '(and true it is, that was the very field)'. 'True it is' refers to the diegetic level of action, which forms a supporting centre in the novel's plot. Don Quixote's madness is so vividly realized and convincing because of the correspondence between the narrator's *assertion* that the hero is mad and the fact that the hero's actions so clearly seem to *show* that he is (thus also indicating that the narrator is reliable). This madness is fundamental to establishing Don Quixote as a simple, 'flat' type: his madness introduces an element of mechanical repetition which enables us to imagine what his actions will or could be like (particularly after the pattern-setting confrontation with the windmills), and which contributes to making the figure comic. Yet although Don Quixote's madness is emphasized throughout the first part (by the narrator, by minor characters, and by the hero's own actions), the picture is at the same time gradually complicated. Don Quixote's speech about the golden age is such a modifying element—its surprisingly wise insights qualify and extend our picture of the hero, thus making him a 'rounder' character.

Characterization

In the extensive literature on Cervantes's masterpiece, discussions about the character of Don Quixote occupy a great deal of space. A. J. Close, for example, devotes roughly half of an introductory book (Close 1990: 53–108) on this novel to discuss the characters of Don Quixote and Sancho. His discussion illustrates an important point: although we can isolate the concept of character and discuss Don Quixote and Sancho in relative isolation from other textual elements, they are established as characters *through characterization*, i.e. through character indicators in the discourse. This means that the distinction between character (at the level of story) and characterization (at the textual level) is not absolute, something which the references to Don Quixote above also illustrate. Discussions of fictional characters become more convincing if they refer to, and are based on, characterization, for it is through such characterization that the characters are introduced, shaped, and developed.

We can distinguish between two kinds of character indicator in the text:

1 *Direct definition* means that a character is characterized in a direct, summarizing way—for instance by means of adjectives or abstract nouns. The persuasive power of such character definitions will vary, and it is as a rule greatest when the narrator who provides the definition appears as authoritative or omniscient. The perspective of literary history is interesting here: direct character definitions were more common in earlier (premodernist) fiction. This is how the narrator in the *Laxdœla Saga* (*c.*1250) introduces Gudrun Osvivsdottir:

Gudrun was their daughter's name, and she was the foremost of all women who grew up in Iceland, both in beauty and intelligence. She was so elegant and courteous that at that time the adornment that other women wore seemed merely childish in comparison with hers. She was more knowledgeable than other women and better at expressing herself in words; she was generous too. (p. 81; my translation)

We note the adjectives in this presentation and not least the use of the superlative ('the foremost'). Adjectives also have a characterizing function in *Don Quixote*: when the narrator presents the hero as mad, (p. 29), this is an example of direct definition. That Don Quixote himself (on the level of character in the same novel) defines himself as a knight is crucial to setting the plot in motion.

A special variant of direct definition is the *assigning of names* to characters. Of course, the names of characters *need not* have a characterizing function, but they *can* have (particularly in combination with item 2 below). Two well-known examples to be discussed in more detail in Part II are K. in Kafka's *The Trial* and Gabriel in Joyce's 'The Dead'. An interesting feature of both these examples is that the naming here complicates the characters' identities rather than determining them. This applies particularly to Kafka: both K. and Klamm (in *The Castle*) appear to be different both to different characters and at various stages of the plot. In pre-modernist literature the assigning of names often indicates more stable characteristic features. When a character in Dickens's *Hard Times* (1854) is named M'Choakumchild this tells the reader something about his attitude to education. That the hero in John Bunyan's *Pilgrim's Progress* (1678–84) is called Christian is connected with the text's allegorical meaning, indicating 'that life as a Christian brings problems comparable to those experienced by Bunyan's pilgrim' (Hawthorn 1997: 139).

The persuasive power of direct definitions of this kind becomes as a rule greater if the definition is coupled with the other main type of characterization:

2 *Indirect presentation.* This form of characterization is the more important of the two main variants. It demonstrates, dramatizes, or exemplifies a given character feature rather than naming it explicitly. This other main type has several variants:

   (a) *Action*: presentation either of a *single* action or of *repetitive* actions. An example of a single action is the double murder committed by Raskolnikov in *Crime and Punishment*. Now the reader will perhaps object that a double murder actually is *two* actions. Arguably, however, these two actions are so closely connected that we can see them as a dominant kernel event (framed by several catalysts).

   Characterization through repetitive action is something of which *Don Quixote* provides many examples, most clearly through the hero's repeated attacks on what he believes to be enemies. Such repetitions of action will be more or less important according to textual position, thematic emphasis, what consequences they have, and so forth. In *Don Quixote* it is crucial, particularly in the first part, that the hero's pattern of action is mechanically repetitive, thus making the character comic by constantly confirming his madness. Not only does this have the cumulative effect of making the novel's first part into 'the book of madness', the comically repetitive events here also lay the foundation for the second part as 'the book of the cure' (Togeby 1957: 40). The comic aspect of Don Quixote's repetitive actions does not mean, though, that they are without any variation—there is a significant difference between attacking windmills (chapter 8) and trying to release galley slaves (chapter 22). This variation on a fundamentally mechanical action pattern also has a characterizing function: our understanding of the main character becomes qualified and refined, and the characterization of him is related to the transitions between different narrative levels (such as the hypodiegetic level with the speech about the golden age in chapter 20).

(b) *Speech.* What a character says or thinks—whether it be in dialogue, direct speech, or free indirect discourse—often has a characterizing function through both content and form. This becomes particularly clear when the character's speech is individualized and distinguished from the narrator's discourse. Again we can use *Don Quixote* as an illustration. While 'knight' is Don Quixote's own definition, his speech characterizes him throughout the novel. This applies both to what he says and to the way in which he says it (for example, all the phrases he adopts from chivalric romances and which thus enter into the parody of this genre). The characterizing function of Don Quixote's speech is further reinforced as it is contrasted with the narrator's discourse on the one hand and with Sancho's speech on the other. An example from chapter 23 (just after Don Quixote and Sancho have been bombarded with stones by the galley slaves they have set free):

> Don Quixote, finding himself so ill treated, said to his squire:
> 'Sancho, I have always heard it said, that to do good to low fellows is to throw water into the sea. Had I believed what you said to me, I might have prevented this trouble; but it is done, I must have patience, and take warning from henceforward.'
> 'Your worship will as much take warning', answered Sancho, 'as I am a Turk'. (p. 192)

(c) *External appearance and behaviour* are usually presented, and interpreted as the case may be, by the narrator or another character. The narrator's introductory presentation of Don Quixote provides an illustrative example: 'The age of our gentleman bordered upon fifty years. He was of a robust constitution, spare-bodied, of a meagre visage; a very early riser, and a keen sportsman' (p. 23).

(d) *Milieu.* External (physical/topographic) surroundings may variously contribute to the indirect presentation of a character. Take Raskolnikov's garret in *Crime and Punishment.* The fact that it is small and confined reinforces the main character's depressed and brooding mood. Raskolnikov's bed is not for sleeping and resting but rather functions as a rack of torture: 'He was lying on his back . . . seized with such a violent fit of shivering that his teeth chattered uncontrollably, and every limb shook' (p. 84).

A larger and more complex milieu can also influence characterization, whether it be Dostoevsky's St Petersburg, the Yorkshire moors of the Brontë sisters, or Dickens's London. In *Crime and Punishment* the city reinforces the confined and claustrophobic quality of the room Raskolnikov rents in the tenement. The city on the Neva—with Kamenny Bridge, Sadovaya Street, and the Haymarket—is strangely isolated from the surrounding Russia, while the milieu of the city is contrasted with Siberia in the epilogue.

Various elements of characterization are as a rule combined with one another in the discourse. The total picture we form of a character can be ascribed to many different signals in the text. Not working each on its own, these textual signals influence one another through the ways in which they are combined, and their characterizing effect is enhanced through narrative variation and repetition. Thus, elements of characterization such as those mentioned above are related to other constituent aspects of narrative literature. One such aspect is genre: that *Don Quixote* parodies the chivalric romance is important for the depiction of the main character. In a novel such as *Don Quixote,* characterization is subtly nuanced through a series of textual modulations in which numerous narrative means and devices are combined with one another, with aspects of plot, and with imagery and metaphorical patterns to produce a novel of extraordinary richness.

A crucial point in discussions of Don Quixote concerns the hero's madness—both what 'madness' means here, how 'mad' he is, and the relationship between his madness in the novel's first and second parts. Some critics have found that Don Quixote's pattern of behaviour is characterized by playacting. His imaginative power is certainly very strong, and may possibly indicate a form of role awareness or role distance. A fundamental problem explored in *Don Quixote* concerns the incongruity between the fictional world of the chivalric romances (into which Don Quixote dreams himself) and Don Quixote's own world (as it is constructed in Cervantes's fiction). That this lack of compatibility results in actions that suggest Don Quixote is mad seems clear. Reasonably clear it is too that the novel's plot (and thus the form of madness that initiates and complicates it) changes character in the course of the narrative, partly because the surrounding world to a greater degree meets the main character on his own terms and responds to him with various forms of counterplay. On the other hand, *Don Quixote* characteristically calls into question a contrastive pair such as mad/normal. The elements of play-acting in the main character's pattern of speech and action support such a qualifying process, which is shaped through a complicated narrative pattern. In *Don Quixote*, the narrative and thematic complexity of the novel as a genre is reflected in the main character's ever-increasing complexity. This kind of complexity is illuminated by M. M. Bakhtin's concept of *heteroglossia*:

> Heteroglossia, once incorporated into the novel . . . is *another's speech in another's language*, serving to express authorial intentions but in a refracted way. Such speech constitutes a special type of *double-voiced discourse*. It serves two speakers at the same time and expresses simultaneously two different intentions: the direct intention of the character who is speaking, and the refracted intention of the author. (Bakhtin 1982: 324; original emphasis)

The concept of heteroglossia is closely connected to Bakhtin's understanding of the novel as a *dialogic* form: a narrative in which different voices, forms of consciousness, and opinions are played out against each other without being united or ranked. For Bakhtin, both these concepts are *relational* since they define consciousness and identity in relation to other characters, values, and priorities (cf. Holquist 1990: 18–19). To read *Don Quixote* dialogically is to respond to its narrative complexity and thematic heterogeneity. This means, for example, becoming more critical of the narrator's categorical statements on the main character. For one dialogic feature of *Don Quixote* is that while the narrator to begin with shows great authority in his evaluation of Don Quixote, this authority is problematized (without the narrator's thereby becoming unreliable) through the hero's incongruous and gradually more complex patterns of speech and action. In all his madness Don Quixote becomes a sort of artist—perhaps even a symbol of the poet.

Events, characters, and characterization in film adaptation

Although all three key words for this chapter are relevant to film, the presentation of events and characters in film is radically different from that in literary fiction. In literary fiction events are shaped through a combination of narrative devices, plot and character components, and metaphorical patterns to which the reader is invited to respond as he or she works through the text. Film's surface character and unusual kinetic force cause filmic events to 'hit' the viewer in a completely different way; film events manifest themselves as definitive even as they are being visually presented to us—and then disappear. Similarly, in film as in fictional prose the concept of character is related to characterization, but the ways in which the characters are presented are strikingly different in the two media. When it comes to external features, for example, film can *show* them with sovereign conviction. Moreover, film can easily combine external features with characterizing patterns of speech and action—just think of characters such as Chaplin, a typical Western hero, or James Bond. On the other hand, a film cannot convey a character's thoughts, feelings, plans, and so forth in the way fictional literature can—partly because the film narrator's functions are so unlike those of the literary narrator. A systematic discussion of events, characters, and characterization in film is a large venture which cannot be attempted here. Instead I have chosen to link these concepts to a particular adaptation, while also relating them to other relevant concepts introduced above. First, however, I will make some more general comments on film adaptation; these comments will be supplemented in the discussions of four different adaptations in Part II.

To 'transfer' a work of art from one medium to another is in one sense impossible. We speak of 'filming a book' almost as if the characters in a novel could step out of the story and become actors in front of the camera, but this expression simplifies the complicated transformation involved. As Stuart McDougal puts it in *Made into Movies*: 'Every art form has distinctive properties resulting from its medium; a filmmaker must recognize the unique characteristics of each medium before transforming a story into a film' (McDougal 1985: 3). An adaptation makes great demands, even from the very starting-point, on those who perform in it. In addition to media-specific characteristics, other factors further complicate the transformation from one medium to another. One such factor is that since making a film is a technically complicated process, problems confronted during production can distract the film's creators from an aesthetic evaluation of the literary starting-point. This said, many directors (such as Welles, Huston, and Coppola) have created adaptations that demonstrate intimate knowledge of the literary text to which they respond as creative artists.

A young art form, in our century film has developed techniques, structural patterns, and a thematic range that have taken other media—literature, music, dance, the pictorial arts—hundreds of years to work out. For many people, film is the most vital and exciting of artistic media. It is interesting therefore that literature, both through drama and narrative fiction, has made and is still making significant contributions to the development of film. For example, Akira Kurosawa's *Rashomon* (1951) and *Ran* (1985) are both important films. Yet for many viewers *Ran* is the more engrossing because of the way in which it filmically responds to the plot and thematics of Shakespeare's *King Lear* (1605), transforming Lear's three daughters into sons and transferring the plot's action from England to Japan in the seventeenth century.

Although *Ran* is only one of many examples of films inspired by drama, it is striking how many films (approximately one in three narrative fiction films) take as their starting-point a literary prose text, whether it be a short story or (more commonly) a novel. In 1926 Boris Eikhenbaum noted that 'the competition of cinema with literature is an undeniable fact of our present culture' (Eikhenbaum 1973: 126). This observation is even more valid today. But Eikhenbaum adds a point which is also still valid. Although, he acknowledges, film has its own methods, 'it needs material. It takes literature and translates it into filmic language.' It needs to be added, though, that since the interest and appeal of the 'material' of literature is in large measure ascribable to literary presentation, the narrative means and devices of a literary text may also influence the adaptation of it. As Eisenstein points out in a classic essay, narrative equivalents to the techniques of film composition are to be found in verbal fiction: 'Perhaps the secret lies in Dickens's (as well as cinema's) creation of an extraordinary plasticity. The observation in the novels is extraordinary—as is their optical quality' (Eisenstein 1992: 396). Adapting a literary text, even a director who believes that filmic techniques are *not* equivalent to literary ones will tend to search for forms of presentation which do justice to, and highlight the artistic quality of, the literary starting-point. We note that this characteristic of adaptation applies whether it be relatively direct (like John Huston's adaptation of Joyce's short story 'The Dead') or more indirect (like Coppola's *Apocalypse Now* in relation to Conrad's *Heart of Darkness*). One obvious yet important difference between adapting a short story and adapting a novel, however, is that with a short text as starting-point the adaptation can present the plot of the literary text in greater detail.

   In an influential essay on adaptation, Dudley Andrew identifies three basic modes of relation between film and literary text. *Borrowing* means that 'the artist employs, more or less extensively, the material, idea, or form of an earlier, generally successful text' (Andrew 1992: 422). Examples of this mode include numerous adaptations from Shakespeare and, in other art forms, adaptations from literature to music, opera, and painting. A key question here concerns artistic fertility, not the adaptation's 'fidelity' to the original text. *Intersecting* indicates a different attitude to adaptation: 'Here the uniqueness of the original text is preserved to such an extent that it is intentionally left unassimilated in adaptation' (Andrew 1992: 422). In one sense the concept of adaptation does not apply to intersecting, because what the viewer is presented with is rather 'a refraction of the original'. As examples of films in the intersecting mode, Andrew mentions Pier Paolo Pasolini's *The Gospel According to St Matthew* (1964) and *Canterbury Tales* (1972). 'All such works fear or refuse to adapt. Instead they present the otherness and distinctiveness of the original text, initiating a dialectical interplay between the aesthetic forms of one period with the cinematic forms of our own period' (Andrew 1992: 423). The third mode concerns *fidelity and transformation*: 'Here it is assumed that the task of adaptation is the reproduction in cinema of something essential about an original text' (Andrew 1992: 423).

Like André Bazin, who in *What is Cinema?* champions the intersecting mode, Andrew is sceptical about faithful transformations as they tend to 'become a scenario written in typical scenario form' (Andrew 1992: 423). One problem with this kind of tripartite distinction is that the points of transition between the three modes can be blurred, and one and the same adaptation can incorporate elements of more than one mode. Coppola's *Apocalypse Now*, for example, could be seen as an example of borrowing as well as intersecting—it is an adaptation and yet in one sense it is not. Still, Andrew's survey of the range of adaptations is critically helpful, and his classification provides a possible starting-point for further discussion of the phenomenon as well as for analysis of individual films. Andrew rightly notes that we cannot dismiss adaptation since it is a fact of human practice. He follows Christian Metz and Keith Cohen in regarding narrative as the most solid link between verbal and visual languages. As Cohen puts it *Film and Fiction: The Dynamics of Exchange*, 'In both novel and cinema, groups of signs, be they literary or visual signs, are apprehended consecutively through time; and this consecutiveness gives rise to an unfolding structure, the diegetic whole that is never fully *present* in any one group yet always *implied* in each such group' (Cohen 1979: 92, original emphasis). As narrative codes function at the level of implication or connotation, they are 'potentially comparable in a novel and a film . . . The analysis of adaptation then must point to the achievement of equivalent narrative units in the absolutely different semiotic systems of film and language' (Andrew 1992: 426).

This observation can be related to a central point argued in Christian Metz's *Film Language*: 'Film tells us continuous stories; it "says" things that could also be conveyed in the language of words, yet it says them differently. There is a reason for the possibility as well as for the necessity of adaptations' (Metz 1974: 44). There certainly is, and yet we need to remember that the 'dynamics of exchange', as Cohen suggestively calls it, go both ways between fiction and film. There is no doubt that a film such as John Huston's *The Dead* has made many spectators aware of Joyce's *Dubliners*, thus (sometimes if not always) turning a viewer into a reader.

Film-makers' relationships to the literary texts they adapt vary very considerably. For example, while Francis Ford Coppola nowhere in *Apocalypse Now* (1979) records his indebtedness to *Heart of Darkness* (Conrad's novella was not credited until the release of Eleanor Coppola's documentary *Hearts of Darkness* thirteen years later), Robert Altman's *Short Cuts* (1993) emphasizes the connection between the film and the nine short stories and one prose poem by Raymond Carver on which it is based. Carver's name features in the credits for the film, an edition of the stories and the poem has been published under the same title as the film and with an introduction by Altman, and the film's screenplay has been published with an introduction by Carver's widow, the writer Tess Gallagher. Although, presumably, this kind of explicit linking of film and literature has made many viewers interested in Carver's fiction, it does not follow that Carver is more important for Altman than, say, Conrad is for Coppola. If, employing Andrew's terminology, we ask whether *Short Cuts* is borrowing or intersecting, a tentative response could be that, while aspiring towards intersection, the film actually contains elements of both modes. In his introduction to the book *Short Cuts*, compiled after the film was made, Altman writes that he looks 'at all of Carver's work as just one story, for his stories are all occurrences, all about things that just happen to people and cause their lives to take a turn' (Carver 1995: 7). Thus, the film is based not just on Carver's short fiction but also on Altman's interpretation of Carver; and this interpretation, it could be argued, perhaps underestimates the ways in which Carver's short stories differ from one another structurally and thematically. To make this point, however, is not to suggest that the stories actually chosen by Altman do not provide a good basis for his innovative film. Although the film has been criticized for its tendency to melodrama in some sequences, it is a continually fascinating exploration of a variety of characters who lead ordinary lives and yet seem to be living on the edge, cut off from their social environments and struggling to communicate their emotions. In terms of film form, *Short Cuts* is notable for its extensive cross-cutting between one scene and another, thus activating, repeating, and modulating various facets of the Carver texts used as a vehicle for filmic presentation.

One interesting feature of Altman's *Short Cuts* is the manner in which Altman, ambitiously attempting to make nine separate short stories into one film, adapts not only third-person narratives but also stories in which Carver uses a first-person narrator. The most important of these is 'So Much Water So Close to Home'. If the thematic richness of this key text is generated in large part by the metaphor of water, it also depends on the female narrator's diverse functions. Now there is, as Brian McFarlane observes in *From Novel to Film*, 'only a precarious analogy between the attempts at first-person narration offered by films and the novel's first-person narration' (McFarlane 1996: 15). He finds that such attempts will usually be of two kinds, 'subjective cinema' and 'voice-over'. What Altman does is to explore the possibilities of subjective cinema, especially through cross-cutting and varied uses of camera angle. For example, the shots of the unidentified dead girl lying in the water while the men (including Stuart, the narrator's husband) are fishing activate film's voyeuristic aspect, accentuated by cross-cutting between the naked body and the fishing men. While in Carver's short story the reader's sympathy resides with the first-person narrator, in Altman's film one effect of the subjective camera is to dissociate the viewer's perspective from that of the fishing men, relocating it (unpleasantly but not morbidly) in the image of the dead body. This is a filmic achievement in its own right; it is also a filmic recreation of the short story's movement (on the level of plot as well as metaphor) towards identification of the narrator and the dead woman.

Before turning to Axel's *Babette's Feast* I shall briefly comment on the beginning of Andrzej Wajda's *The Shadow-Line* (1976), a film illustrative of some significant problems of adaptation not observable in Altman's *Short Cuts*. Wajda's film is an adaptation of Joseph Conrad's novella *The Shadow-Line* (1916). That the narrative of this text is first-person is consistent with the protagonist's 'compulsion to narrate' (Stanzel 1986: 93, cf. Lothe 1996a: 221). The narrative and thematic characteristics of the novella's beginning are closely associated with the kind of first-person narrative which Conrad employs. In Wajda's film, the narrator's identity is less clear, and his ontological status is consequently more uncertain. Wajda does, it is true, begin his film by focusing on the protagonist, whose first words are: 'This is not a marriage story. My action, such as it was, had more the quality of divorce, of desertion. For no good reason, I abandoned my ship. It was in an Eastern port, in Singapore.' Actually, the narrator does not (as we watch him on the screen) speak these words aloud, but comments—retrospectively, the viewer infers—on his own situation after having given up his berth. These voice-over comments, which correspond quite well with the relevant textual segment early in the novella, constitute only a small part of the film narration, however. If Conrad the author writes *The Shadow-Line* by making his first-person narrator speak, Wajda's film narrator is a heterogeneous, mechanical, and highly flexible instrument, constituted by a variety of techniques and performing diverse functions. The film narrator therefore needs to be distinguished from the voice-over Wajda uses at the beginning of the adaptation. Though important, such a technique is merely one component in a far more complex narrative communication.

Wajda's adaptation illustrates one of the most distinctive qualities of film: 'that every object that is reproduced appears simultaneously in two entirely different frames of reference, namely the two-dimensional and the three-dimensional, and that as one identical object it fulfills two different functions in the two contexts' (Arnheim 1957: 59). The viewer thus encounters two major frames of reference in film, 'the space and time of a *screen* as well as (a sample of) the space and time of a *story world*' (Branigan 1992: 33, original emphasis). In Wajda's *The Shadow-Line*, the protagonist's opening words (the voice-over commentary quoted above) intitiate the space and time of the story world (i.e. the film's plot), whereas the filmic segments preceding them foreground the frame of reference associated with the screen. It does not follow that there is no connection between these two frames of reference. 'Light and sound create two fundamental systems of space, time, and causal interaction: on screen and within a story world. One of the tasks of narrative is to reconcile these systems' (Branigan 1992: 34). Watching the phenomenal appearances on the screen, the viewer attempts to relate them to possible functions in the story world. This, as Branigan shows, is a complicated process during which major changes can occur; particularly at the beginning of a film, it is often difficult to identify and interpret the key functions of the story world. The beginning of Wajda's adaptation further complicates this process as the opening shots of the film do not refer to the story world directly but instead present a succession of pictorial frames which photographically reproduce scenes of historical reality: a picture of a sailing ship, another picture of officers and crew on the deck of such a ship, and further shots showing pictures of sailing ships at rest in what appears to be a major nineteenth-century port. Thus while reading that this film by Andrzej Wajda is 'from the novel *The Shadow-Line* by Joseph Conrad', the viewer also watches the photographs over which this information is projected, wondering about their significance and relevance for the story that unfolds. One essential function of the photographs, as it turns out, is to support the film's transition from fictional narrative to autobiography, identifying the first-person narrator as Conrad as he is looking at family photographs sent him from Poland. In no way impairing the film's quality, this kind of generic transition furthers a filmic exploration of the autobiographical elements in Conrad's novella (subtitled *A Confession*).

Gabriel Axel's *Babette's Feast*

One critical asset of Andrew's distinction between three modes of relation between film and literary text is its implicit demonstration that the most 'faithful' adaptation is not necessarily the 'best'. Adaptation is first and foremost *film*; it is not a 'second-hand version' of a literary text. This point also applies to those adaptations that, like *Babette's Feast*, seem unusually accurate in relation to their literary starting-point. A possible story version of this text, taken from the collection *Anecdotes of Destiny* (1958), looks thus:

> In a fishing hamlet in northern Norway lives a Dean with his two daughters Martine and Philippa. While the Dean is still living, his young and beautiful daughters are proposed to by two people 'from the great world outside Berlevaag' (p. 25), Lieutenant Loewenhielm and the singer Papin. Nevertheless they continue to live in the fishing hamlet, where after the death of their father they go on helping the poor and the infirm. Sixteen years later Babette Hersant comes to visit the sisters from Paris. Fourteen years again after this, in 1885, Babette is still living with them as a housekeeper and cook. That year Babette wins a large sum in a French lottery, but instead of going back to Paris she spends the money on arranging a feast to commemorate the priest's hundredth birthday on 15 December. Among the guests is Loewenhielm, now a general.

The fact that this story version is also valid for Axel's adaptation is a first indication that the film version's plot remains close to that of Blixen's text. The adaptation is precise not only in its presentation of the textual events but also in the filmic characterization of the text's main characters. Since the literary text in this case is a short story and not a novel, Axel can more easily transfer the plot's constituent elements to film. In the film as in the short story, moreover, the structure is symmetrical and the narrative method economical. The short story is in twelve parts or chapters. Combined with the content in each part and the short story's temporal anachronies, the chapter headings contribute to making the text fairy-tale-like and strangely mythical.

The narration in the short story is first-person. Blixen presents the plot through a distanced narrator who does not participate in the action. Omniscient in the sense that she can report the characters' thoughts, the narrator appears to be reliable (the text gives no indication that she is not). Overall, the narrator is soberly and precisely informative rather than critically evaluative.

The concentrated background information in the short story's first part confronts Axel with several challenges as film-maker. One example is the choice of place on Blixen's part. The topography of the small town Berlevaag in northern Norway is important for events, character portrayal, and thematics. As in, for example, Thomas Hardy's *The Return of the Native* (1878), the place lends support to the contrasts between the everyday aspect (the daily routine of life in Berlevaag and among the Dean's parishioners) and the intervention of the other: something unknown, exciting, and potentially threatening from the outside. This 'other' serves, as in many narrative texts, to initiate action. It is primarily linked to Babette, secondarily to Loewenhielm and Papin. It says something about Axel's respect for the literary text (and for Blixen as an author) that he had been planning to do the filming in Berlevaag, but for practical and financial reasons the film's location was instead transferred to West Jutland in Denmark. Thus Berlevaag becomes Nørre Vossborg, the dried cod becomes flatfish, and the snow (which falls on 15 December) turns into rain. Although the first change is probably the most important of these three, we cannot say that it turns out negatively for the film as an adaptation. As Axel portrays Nørre Vossborg in West Jutland, the place and milieu have in the main the same qualities as Berlevaag in the short story. The difference is one of degree which the film can live with as an adaptation, and which the viewer who knows the short story can tolerate.

The greatest challenge with which the beginning of the short story confronts Axel, however, is how to convey the background information that the first-person narrator provides in Blixen's text. Axel chooses to introduce the voice of an anonymous female narrator. Particularly in the opening sequence, but also throughout the film and especially in the transitions between different stages of the plot, this female voice-over (a voice outside the images on the screen) serves as a filmic equivalent to the short story's first-person narrator. As indicated in Chapter 2 above, it illustrates all three characteristics of voice-over identified by Sarah Kozloff in *Invisible Storytellers*.

Axel's use of an informative and commentating narrator in *Babette's Feast* is clearly inspired by literature. This aspect of *Babette's Feast* is reminiscent of several of François Truffaut's films—such as *Les Deux Anglaises et le Continent*

(1971) and *Jules et Jim* (1961)—in which the narrator's commentary is both more intrusive and has more diverse functions than in *Babette's Feast*. Some film theorists have tended to be sceptical about such use of a narrator's voice and have considered it to be a foreign element in film. That few have criticized Axel for using this technique is closely connected with the functions voice-over has in *Babette's Feast*: not only giving the viewer necessary information, but also creating an observant 'visual distance' that preserves something of the narrative distance of the short story. This said, it must be stressed that a filmic voice-over cannot be impersonal in the same way as the voice of a third-person narrator: we immediately identify the voice in *Babette's Feast* as female because we *hear* it. Yet paradoxically it may (for the same reason) be difficult to relate filmic voice-over to the different characters' perspectives.

The characterization of the two sisters begins as early as the second paragraph and is elegantly linked with the milieu in which the short story is placed. The naming of the two tends towards direct definition, linking the sisters' lives to the form of Protestant Christianity represented by their father: 'They were christened Martine and Philippa, after Martin Luther and his friend Philip Melanchton' (p. 23). In the film this sentence is uttered by the voice-over. The effect is like the one we experience in Blixen's text, especially if we suppose that the viewer has read the short story. The characterization of Martine and Philippa is carried further through the analepsis that ties together the first and second parts: 'But the true reason for Babette's presence in the two sisters' house was to be found further back in time and deeper down in the domain of human hearts' (p. 24). This analepsis, which takes the action back to 1854 before moving gradually forwards 'until the time of this tale' (p. 35), illustrates the connection between analepsis (as a variant on narrative anachrony) and character portrayal. Chapter 2 of the short story opens thus: 'As young girls, Martine and Philippa had been extraordinarily pretty . . .' (p. 24). How does the adaptation respond to this narrative statement? We note that the film too has a clearly marked analepsis, which Axel opens by combining voice-over (cf. the sentence just quoted) with dissolve. The moment when the two images blend in superimposition seems to transcend mechanical, repetitive time. Is the voice-over inviting us to regard all stages of the sisters' lives as equally significant? The effect of the dissolve is here dependent on the voice-over accompanying and supplementing the successive images—first of the sisters in their fifties, then of the sisters when they were young and so beautiful that 'the young men of Berlevaag went to church to watch them walk up the aisle' (pp. 24–5).

In the adaptation as in the short story, the introduction of Lorens Loewen-hielm and Achille Papin extends the characterization of the two sisters. The intensity of their adoration emphasizes how unusually beautiful Martine is and how wonderfully beautifully Philippa sings. When it comes to the filmic presentation of these two parts, we note three interesting variations.

Explaining Lieutenant Loewenhielm's visit to Berlevaag, the short story informs the reader that he 'had led a gay life in his garrison town and had run into debt' (p. 25). An interesting feature of the adaptation is that in order to visualize what in the short story is only *one* sentence, Axel presents a whole scene that gives a rather unflattering picture of the young Loewenhielm at the gaming table. More important, however, is the variation in the filmic presentation of the Dean's hold on his daughters. In the short story, the narrator reports that 'the Dean had declared that to him in his calling his daughters were his right and left hand. Who could want to bereave him of them?' (p. 25). Note how the last sentence modulates towards free indirect discourse. Axel goes a step further when he makes the Dean utter these words directly, as a refusal to another of Martine's admirers. Axel's adaptation thus advances a more severe criticism of the Dean than does the short story, and the film further distances itself from the Dean through the unmistakable element of *Schadenfreude* in the latter's behaviour just after he has sent the anonymous suitor packing. On the other hand, one could argue that the sentence quoted from the literary text *also* indirectly criticizes the Dean, thus responding indirectly to the power relations that form a significant aspect of the short story's thematics.

The third variation, which comes towards the end of the third chapter, occurs in Axel's presentation of the 'seduction duet' in Mozart's *Don Giovanni*. We note that here too, the adaptation has been *extended* in relation to the literary text. Such an extension—including a textual segment of the opera's libretto, which the literary text does not give us—considerably enriches the adaptation: activating various filmic devices, Axel can *show* us an excerpt from the opera—complete with music, song, and interplay between the two performers. Similarly, more clearly and more convincingly than the short story, the film can show Papin becoming one with the role of Don Juan and kissing Philippa as the conclusion to the duet. As we will recall, this kiss, which is part of a *role* (and which Papin cannot remember afterwards) has an effect he could not have anticipated: 'Philippa went home, told her father that she did not want any more singing lessons and asked him to write and tell Monsieur Papin so' (p. 31). Although this narrative comment in the short story becomes a reply from Philippa to the Dean in the film, the effect is comparable. A more important point, however, is that even if we exclude the filmic visualization, Mozart's *music* brings to life in this part of the adaptation qualities that the literary text can indicate only relatively weakly—most clearly in the tonal visual imagery (of the first two bars of the duet between Don Giovanni and Zerlina) with which Papin many years later concludes his letter to the sisters. Perhaps the reader ought to *play* these two bars to make the text complete?

The main function of the letter, which reopens the action after an ellipsis of sixteen years, is to introduce Babette: the third character from the outside that the story brings into the sisters' lives in Berlevaag. In the short story this is one of the most obvious variants on third-person narration. The gravity and disappointment apparent in the experiences the letter conveys are reinforced by the fact that Papin himself is the sender. Within the third-person narrative framework he thus functions in a way reminiscent of a first-person narrator, while the sisters for their part become narratees as they are reading the letter. In the film, voice-over presents parts of the letter, accompanied by shots of Papin writing it in Paris (while Babette is waiting in the same room) and cross-cutting to shots of the sisters reading it. The adaptation includes the end of the letter, in which Papin takes comfort in his feeling that

> In paradise I shall hear your voice again. There you will sing, without fears or scruples, as God meant you to sing. There you will be the great artist that God meant you to be. Ah! How you will enchant the angels.
>   Babette can cook.
>   Deign to receive, my ladies, the humble homage of the friend who was once
>
> Achille Papin
(p.34)

Since the dialogue in the film is here identical with the text of the short story, the adaptation not only brings out the understatement in the sentence 'Babette can cook'. It also invites us (albeit much more strongly on a second reading/viewing) to follow Philippa and Babette in parallel as great artists. In Axel's adaptation as in Blixen's short story, moreover, the conclusion of the letter anticipates the ending of the plot, thus drawing attention to the loneliness of the artist, the brevity of his career, and the vulnerability of his feelings.

The fourth and fifth chapters advance the plot to the date of the celebration dinner, 15 December 1885. Summary is a central narrative technique in this sequence, and it is most clearly indicated in the transition between the two parts: 'Babette remained in the house of the Dean's daughters for twelve years, until the time of this tale' (p. 35). We note that Blixen makes her third-person narrator limit the 'tale' to one day, Tuesday 15 December. Such a temporal limitation supports the title by marking the celebration dinner as the short story's main event, while also making the events in 'Still life', which constitutes the middle part of the short story, less central by contrasting them with the subsequent climax. Yet the chapter extends the characterization of both Babette and the sisters. That much of this information comes directly via the first-person narrator presents Axel with a challenge as director. His choice seems reasonable: he presents selected, representative events (such as Babette beating down the price of the fish she is buying) and invites the viewer to generalize on the basis of them. An effect of this technique is to make the distance between Babette and the sisters greater in the film's middle sequence than in the corresponding prose passage. One detail that reinforces this impression is that Axel lets Babette tell the shopkeeper, not the sisters as in the short story, that she gambles in the French lottery.

Axel's presentation of 'Babette's Good Luck' brings out many of the nuances in the literary original. Aspects of symmetrical structure are reinforced when something unexpected and exciting suddenly breaks into the sisters' sequestered and routine existence. Babette's win bursts asunder the limits of their experience. While the sisters' reaction to the win serves to characterize them ('They pressed Babette's hand, their own hands trembling a little', p. 41), the actual win is a kernel event in both the short story and the film. This letter number two, which for the sisters is notification of Babette's journey back to Paris, in a way repeats the first one which brought her to them. The adaptation of the next two chapters is based on selective but central textual passages. One relatively unsuccessful detail may be mentioned: the visualization of the dream Martine has after she has been horrified at the sight of the turtle and suspects Babette of wanting to poison all the guests at the feast. The main reason why the presentation of this dream is thematically unproductive is that the filmic devices employed appear to be at odds with the overall rhythm and considered distance so characteristic of both the short story and the film.

The significant contrast between everyday life and the feast presents a great challenge to Axel as director: would not any adaptation of this fabulous, miracle-like feast necessarily become trivial and simplistic? Nor is it any real alternative to make the dinner less central in the film—it is much too important for that both in the short story and in the adaptation as it reveals itself up to this kernel event. That Axel takes the challenge in his stride not only confirms his respect for Blixen's text, but also illustrates his high estimation of film's potential for adaptation. The director's success is essentially due to three interrelated factors: insightful editing, exceptional performances by the actors involved, and meticulous attention to detail. An example of the latter: the table service for the dinner is Haviland china from Limoges—in other words from France, as is reasonable, but in addition some of the best that can be purchased in Europe. (How the china reached Nørre Vossborg without a scratch is insignificant in this connection.)

The most difficult editing problem with which Axel is confronted becomes clear from the connection, established in the short story's narrative, between its third-person narration and General Loewenhielm's perspective. Earlier in the text, the voice-over has been generally distanced from the characters, sometimes cautiously approximating to the perspectives of the sisters, Lieutenant Loewenhielm, and Papin. In the dinner scene, however, narrative perspective is more clearly and more enduringly linked to the general. As we have seen, Axel also now uses a narrator's voice. Yet as we also have noted, this female voice-over (which in a way is first-person because we can hear it) has the more limited function of providing necessary background information that it is difficult for the film to convey. Thus Axel has to turn the general's

'The *convives* grew lighter in weight and lighter of heart the more they ate and drank' (Karen Blixen, 'Babette's Feast', 57–8).

'General Loewenhielm no longer wondered at anything . . .
"Beautiful grapes!" ' (Karen Blixen, 'Babette's Feast', 59).

thoughts, which the third-person narrator conveys in the short story, into character utterances. One example is the reflections on the meal at the Café Anglais a long time ago; in the film it becomes a monologue without any particular addressee.

That the general gets little response marks in itself a limit to how much Axel can let him speak without it seeming unnatural. Thus it makes sense that passages which in the short story relate the third-person narrator's reflections and attitudes to General Loewenhielm's perspective, are left out in the film. Some critics have expressed the view that while in the short story the general is a spokesman for the author, in the film he becomes a catalyst for the miracle. Although this view has something to support it, however, the thematic complexity of 'Babette's Feast' makes it impossible to reduce 'the author's opinion' (which I would regard as synonymous with textual intention) to what one character says and represents (furthermore, the general has a catalytic function in the literary text as well).

The actors in Axel's adaptation are all outstanding; yet the question may be raised whether Jarl Kulle as the general does not give the greatest performance. The way in which he portrays Loewenhielm is just as confidently achieved as it is faithful to Blixen's characterization in the short story. If there are significant aspects of the corresponding literary extract that Kulle does not bring out, this does not come from a lack of acting ability but rather from a limitation of his role in the film as an adaptation. Compensating in part for this limitation, Kulle's speech, which is relatively simple to adapt, has several functions: as the climax during the celebration dinner it is centrally placed in the film's kernel event; in rhetorically elegant form and enunciation it complements the fantastic dishes that are being served; and in content it repeats— mildly ironically through a contrastive character with 'his breast covered with decorations' (p. 60)—the Dean's key expressions on the hundredth anniversary of his birth.

If the general functions as a catalyst for the feast as a kernel event, it is Babette who realizes the kernel. Through Stéphane Audran as Babette, the adaptation makes effective use of cross-cutting to show that the dinner is her doing—and not just the dinner but also the reconciling and explanatory effects it has. The utterance she repeats to the sisters, 'I am a great artist, Mesdames' (p. 67), plays on both these dimensions of the dinner, in addition to establishing Babette more clearly as the main character of film and short story alike.

To these comments on Axel's *Babette's Feast* can be added some concluding points on intertextual patterns observable in the film. When Dudley Andrew introduces the concepts of borrowing and intersecting in order to describe two types of relation between literature and film, he implicitly raises the issue of intertextuality. Yet Andrew appears to suggest a more active (intentional) form of relationship to earlier texts than does Julia Kristeva, who, in an influential essay first published in 1969, defines intertextuality as 'a mosaic of quotations; any text is the absorption and transformation of another' (Kristeva 1980: 66). Seen thus, intertextuality is linked to different forms of textual change, influence, adapting, and restructuring. It is a complicated and special form of dialogue: 'Intertextual dialogue . . . [is] the phenomenon by which a given text echoes previous texts' (Eco 1990: 87). In relation to 'Babette's Feast'/*Babette's Feast* (i.e. the short story as well as the film) it is fruitful to link the concept of intertextuality to the Greek word *metamorphosis* and the Latin *transfigurare*, which can both (even if semantically not completely identical) be related to the Bible as the text's most important intertextual point of reference.

The relevance of these concepts is twofold. First, they can all be related to events, characters, and characterization; second, they can be related to both Blixen's story and Axel's adaptation. The feast actualizes three central events in the New Testament: the wedding at Cana in Galilee, at which Jesus turns water into wine (John 2: 1–11), the Last Supper with the twelve apostles just before he is crucified (Matt. 26: 17–29), and the day of Pentecost with the speaking in tongues and 'new' communication (Acts 2: 1–13). Blixen's integration of such different biblical events in one kernel event says in itself a good deal about the dinner scene's thematic complexity. The combination of intertextual echoes also gives the irony in the text a clearer polemical undertone: puncturing pietistic Protestant morality, it is humorous rather than sarcastic. It is a strength of the adaptation that, largely on account of the actors' performances, it succeeds in preserving this balance of attitudes.

The short story has approximately thirty intertextual references to the Bible. They range from direct references or quotations to more indirect echoes that must be brought out by analysis through repeated close reading. Although many of these naturally enough cannot be integrated in the film version, Axel has clearly made an effort to include as many as possible, for example the minor female character who, after having confused the glasses for water and wine, resolutely switches back to the exquisite Amontillado. The Dean and Babette, two *contrastive* characters in the short story as in the adaptation, are both given qualities characteristic of Jesus. While the short story characterizes the Dean as sympathetic, exemplary, and ascetic, Babette is portrayed as proud, unusually gifted, and imaginative. The New Testament relates *all* these qualities to Jesus (albeit in different contexts). The sisters in the short story are directly connected to Mary, and just as explicit is the connection between Martha and Babette: 'the dark Martha in the house of their two fair Marys' (p. 37). When it comes to Papin, it is striking that the prefiguration of Don Juan—in the film as in the short story—takes over and spoils things for Papin: 'Don Giovanni kissed Zerlina, and Achille Papin pays for it! Such is the fate of the artist!' (p. 32).

Now that these intertextual points have been briefly noted, it must be added that prefiguration in 'Babette's Feast' and *Babette's Feast* is predominantly ironic. An ironic function of this kind means that Blixen not only uses but also breaks with the historical intention of the concept of *figura*. Traditionally, 'figural interpretation establishes a connection between two events or persons, the first of which signifies not only itself but also the second, while the second encompasses or fulfills the first' (Auerbach 1959: 53). The classic example is the figural interpretation which (in the Christian theological tradition) transforms the Old Testament from a legal code and history book about the people of Israel to an integral part of the story of Jesus's salvation of mankind as the New Testament presents it.

As outlined above, Blixen establishes points of contact with this tradition through the many intertextual references to the Bible. She uses a tradition from which she at the same time distances herself; the effects of this double manoeuvre are among the most striking in the short story. This applies in particular to the combination, in the dinner scene, of intertextual references to the three events in the New Testament that we have noted. For example, the guests believe that the fantastic dinner is God's work, while in fact it is Babette's. Babette as an artist realizes what the guests believe only God can do. Another example is Philippa's words of comfort to Babette after the shocked sisters have learnt how much the dinner cost: 'Ah, how you will enchant the angels!' (p. 68). Closing the short story, these words repeat the ending of Papin's letter to Philippa (p. 34). Thus they acquire a touch of irony by being indirectly self-characterizing: in contrast to Philippa, Babette does not need any promise of becoming an artist in paradise—she has just shown that she is one here on earth.

Some film critics have said of *Babette's Feast* that the film is better as adaptation than as film. They find that 'as film' *Babette's Feast* is relatively traditional and cautious, and that filmatically Axel is hampered by his faithfulness to the literary text. Such an objection cannot be dismissed out of hand. Yet since adaptation is also film, it is not very helpful to judge filmic means and devices in isolation from the relationship the adaptation has to what it is adapting. As these selective comments have shown, this relationship is respectful and precise. Moreover, it is artistically creative since the adaptation manages to transfer so many of the short story's qualities to film, and since it compensates for what it cannot filmically achieve (e.g. presenting parts of the third-person narrator's comments) with what it can do just as well as, or better than, the literary text. One possible example of the latter is the 'seduction duet' between Philippa and Papin; another is the film's use of colour. Writing of Alfred Hitchcock's *Vertigo* (1958), Stanley Cavell finds that 'the film establishes the moment of moving from one color space into another as one of moving from one world into another' (Cavell 1979: 84). This is exactly what Axel achieves in his filmic presentation of Babette's feast.

This brief discussion of *Babette's Feast* constitutes a transition between Parts I and II of this book. The discussion has related events, characters, and characterization to both the adaptation and to the short story on which the film is based, and I have also linked these concepts to others introduced earlier in Part I. Since various narrative elements are interwoven in the shaping of the discourse, we need different and supplementary narrative concepts to be able to understand and discuss narrative texts. As indicated at the end of the introductory chapter (which should also be seen as an introduction to Part II), I relate narrative theory and narrative terms closely to (literary and filmic) fictional texts. A selection of such texts forms the basis for the analyses in Part II.

PART II

5

The Parable as Narrative Illustration:
From the Parable of the Sower to Franz Kafka's *The Trial* and Orson Welles's *The Trial*

I

The expression 'narrative short prose', which we usually associate with the genre of the short story, is actually an inclusive concept covering different sub-genres—folk-tales, fables, legends, essays, etc. One of the most interesting of these sub-genres is the *parable*. Like the folk-tale, the parable is an ancient literary form; it is a literary genre that is closely related to a fundamental human need to communicate our thoughts to others (first orally, subsequently also in writing) in an attempt to understand, explain, and structure our experiences. The parable's characteristic features make it well suited to illustrating linguistic and narrative communication.

The fact that the parable is a genre with a long tradition certainly does not make it irrelevant in a modern context. The works of Franz Kafka are a good example of this. Before we take a closer look at Kafka's narrative art, however, I want to comment on one of the most famous parables in world literature: Jesus's Parable of the Sower in Chapter 4 of St Mark's Gospel. The text runs as follows:

> And he began again to teach by the sea side: and there was gathered unto him a great multitude, so that he entered into a ship, and sat in the sea; and the whole multitude was by the sea on the land. And he taught them many things by parables, and said unto them in his doctrine, Hearken; Behold, there went out a sower to sow: And it came to pass, as he sowed, some fell by the way side, and the fowls of the air came and devoured it up. And some fell on stony ground, where it had not much earth; and immediately it sprang up, because it had no depth of earth: But when the sun was up, it was scorched; and because it had no root, it withered away. And some fell

Franz Kafka, *Der Process* [1914–15] (Frankfurt am Main: Fischer, 1998). *The Trial*, trans. Douglas Scott and Chris Walker (London: Picador, 1988). Orson Welles, *The Trial* (1962); video, Art House Productions. Biblical quotations are from the Authorized Version.

among thorns, and the thorns grew up, and choked it, and it yielded no fruit. And other fell on good ground, and did yield fruit that sprang up and increased; and brought forth, some thirty, and some sixty, and some an hundred. And he said unto them, He that hath ears to hear, let him hear.

And when he was alone, they that were about him with the twelve asked of him the parable. And he said unto them, Unto you it is given to know the mystery of the kingdom of God: but unto them that are without, all these things are done in parables: That seeing they may see, and not perceive; and hearing they may hear, and not understand; lest at any time they should be converted, and their sins should be forgiven them.

And he said unto them, Know ye not this parable? and how then will ye know all parables? The sower soweth the word. And these are they by the way side, where the word is sown; but when they have heard, Satan cometh immediately, and taketh away the word that was sown in their hearts. And these are they likewise which are sown on stony ground; who, when they have heard the word, immediately receive it with gladness; And have no root in themselves, and so endure but for a time: afterward, when affliction or persecution ariseth for the word's sake, immediately they are offended. And these are they which are sown among thorns; such as hear the word, And the cares of this world, and the deceitfulness of riches, and the lusts of other things entering in, choke the word, and it becometh unfruitful. And these are they which are sown on good ground; such as hear the word, and receive it, and bring forth fruit, some thirtyfold, some sixty, and some an hundred.

Even though the text can seem simple, it is narratively and thematically complicated. I specify that I am writing about it on the basis of literary research—in other words with the limitations that lie in a lack of competence in theology. The borderline between the two areas of research is blurred, and within theology there is increasing interest in the use of literary concepts and theories in the study of the Bible. Many of those engaged in literary research are also interested in Bible studies—three notable examples are Frank Kermode (whose *The Genesis of Secrecy* inspired the following analysis), Paul Ricoeur, and Northrop Frye. A mutual interest of this kind is not unnatural. The Bible is a unique collection of texts spanning all three main literary genres (one single text such as the book of Job even combines prose, drama, and lyric poetry) and representing several sub-genres—such as the parable in our case, love poetry in the Song of Solomon, and an early variant of the short story in the book of Ruth. In terms of theory as well there are several points of contact between the two fields of research, perhaps most clearly within interpretation studies (hermeneutics, or exegesis, as theologians say).

These introductory reservations actualize a problem we ought not to conceal. When I say that the Parable of the Sower is short, this is in one sense correct—but in another it is not. It is correct in the sense that Jesus's analysis or explanation of the parable stops at verse 20, which is the last one I quote, while verse 21 seems to mark a clear transition in content. On the other hand, this parable forms only the first part of Mark 4, which in fact contains two more parables. Mark 4 is furthermore a part of the Gospel according to St Mark, which completes the set with the other three gospels. Nor is the Parable of the Sower related only by Mark; it is also narrated in Matthew 13. The different versions in Mark 4 and Matthew 13 indicate how important this parable is as an element in the teachings of Jesus, but at the same time the complicating differences in the repetition of the parable make visible some of the genre's characteristics.

Short as it is, the parable in Mark 4 is related to other longer texts; thus it bears a structural resemblance to the placing of the parable 'Before the Law' towards the end of Kafka's *The Trial*. Here I shall be commenting on the Parable of the Sower in isolation, i.e. as a short text in the first part of Mark 4. However, even then we are confronted with a complex form of narrative communication in which the actual parable that Jesus relates forms part 2 in a structure divided into four. The text starts with an introduction, which on the basis of narrative theory we can say is communicated by a third-person narrator. This first part of the text ends with the sentence 'And he taught them many things by parables.' As part 2 follows the parable itself, or what we can call the parable's basis, which the third-person narrator quotes verbatim. Part 3 is the second paragraph plus the question Jesus puts to his disciples: 'Know ye not this parable? and how then will ye know all parables?' Then follows his explanation of the parable, which forms the fourth and final part of the text.

All these parts are important, and the way in which they are linked together is illustrative of the biblical parable as a narrative structure. Here the third-person narrator has a key function. After he has established (and introduced the reader to) the narrative situation and quoted the actual parable, he comments in part 3 on what happens afterwards. Finally, he reports the authoritative analysis Jesus gives of the parabolic narrative which the narrator has already related. The narrator is third-person in the sense that he does not identify himself as a character at the text's diegetic level: he is not a character involved in the plot as one of the 'multitude' or as one of the disciples (he says 'the twelve', not 'we twelve'). As a narrative instrument for the author (Mark), the narrator functions primarily as a communicator—he quotes and informs rather than interprets. This sober method of presentation contributes to making the narrator appear reliable.

Let us now place the narrator in a model of the narrative communication in this parable (see Fig. 5.1). We see that the narrative transmission of the text is complicated, especially in relation to how short it is. As the author of St Mark's Gospel, Mark is outside the textual universe he presents. His identity as a historical author is confirmed in the writings of the early Church Fathers (such as Papias and Clement of Alexandria). Although, in common with other authors, Mark wishes to present his text as effectively as possible, we must consider the

NARRATIVE TEXT

Figure 5.1

narrative strategies that this wish leads to in relation to the gospel's historical basis. Mark does not wish to present and dramatize what might happen, but what has happened: the life, death, and resurrection of Jesus. In a way reminiscent of the Norse sagas, the transition between historical facts on the one hand and organizational, narrative, and structural questions on the other thus becomes unclear. This fuzzy transition actualizes problems of interpretation that we cannot go into here. Still, it should be mentioned that even though the Gospel according to St Mark is the oldest of the four gospels, the relationship between its historical basis (the life of Jesus) and Mark's activity as an author is complicated by the oral transmission of the material up to the point when it was written down. The narrative was in other words involved in multifarious narrative activity even *before* it was given the form of a readable text. The functions of the third-person narrator can be linked to the two-way stretch that Mark experiences as an author: on the one hand, he is bound by historical material; on the other, his desire to communicate this material as effectively as possible carries over to his use of literary means.

The dominant character in the text, Jesus, is also a first-person narrator—both through the parable he relates and through his analysis of the parable to his disciples. The narrative dimension in the way Jesus is presented is reinforced as he successively turns to two different groups of narratees: first the 'multitude' (in which the disciples are included) and then 'they that were about him with the twelve', who are the delimited group who are allowed to hear his explanation of the parable. When it comes to the final link in the communication model (the historical reader), we note that at the same time as he or she may be anybody at all (cf. the sermonizing aspect of the New Testament), the text was written down in Rome around the year AD 60.

To be able to take this analysis further, we must now dwell for a moment on the parable as a genre. We can start with the literal meaning: placing two things beside each other to compare them. Seen thus, the parable is reminiscent of the allegory, which, for example in Dante's *Divine Comedy*, has an important narrative dimension. The use of parable is often related to the author's wish to illustrate a spiritual truth through a story from the earthly world. According to Aristotle, this is the intention of parable (in Classical Greek literature), and such an explanation may be applied to the New Testament as well.

However, the parable can have a further function and meaning corresponding to *mashal*, the Hebrew word often translated as 'parable' in the Septuagint (the most important Greek version of the Old Testament). *Mashal* means riddle or enigmatic narrative, and in a number of places in the Bible the meanings of riddle and parable appear to be extremely similar: 'Son of man, put forth a riddle, and speak a parable unto the house of Israel' (Ezekiel 17: 2). A parable may in other words be illustrative, but it may also be enigmatic and difficult in a way that requires interpretative activity: it is as if the reader's interpretation completes or adds the end to the parable. This need for interpretation that the parable creates is at the same time complicating and fascinating. The parable, notes J. Hillis Miller, has like allegory a 'tendency to keep secret in the act of making public' (Miller 1981: 357). When it comes to textual length, the parable may on the one hand tend towards an aphorism or pregnant proverb, but on the other hand it may take the form of a longer narrative structure reminiscent of the short story and even the novel. In *The Genesis of Secrecy* Frank Kermode points out that different combinations of these two main variants give the parable a huge potential for meaning. One point that Kermode emphasizes, and which is relevant in our connection, is how closely this potential for meaning and interpretation is linked to the narrative means of the parable.

Let us return to the Parable of the Sower in Mark 4. The chapter introduces Jesus's 'parabolic method'; it presents a new form of teaching that is correlated with a shift of focus from the multitude to the twelve disciples. The shift is reflected in the parable's structure since Jesus's explanation to the disciples differentiates the listeners into two contrastive categories: the privileged or chosen ones and 'them that are without'. This differentiation into separate groups of narratees presents a problem of interpretation in this text. The problem becomes conspicuous in Jesus's words to the disciples in part 3: 'Unto you it is given to know the mystery of the kingdom of God: but unto them that are without, all these things are done in parables: That seeing they may see, and not perceive; and hearing they may hear, and not understand; lest at any time they should be converted, and their sins should be forgiven them.' Within this statement, which the narrator quotes straight from Jesus's mouth, we can localize the interpretative problem in the Greek word *hina*, or 'that' as it is rendered in the Authorized Version. *Hina* relates to what Jesus wishes to achieve by telling parables. The literal meaning appears to be that the parable has a dichotomous function: first, to communicate the 'mystery of the kingdom of God' to the disciples; second, to conceal this truth from those who are not with Jesus. Yet such an interpretation conflicts with the narrator's introduction to the parable, in which he twice emphasizes that Jesus is not only teaching the disciples but also the people: 'And he taught them many things by parables.' Has the narrator misunderstood? Or have Jesus's words to the disciples perhaps a different meaning from the literal one? A third question prompted by the first two is whether the third-person narrator can be omniscient in relation to what he (*qua* omniscient narrator) quotes from Jesus's mouth. The opposition between teaching the multitude through parables and the motivation for telling parables (the one Jesus introduces with *hina*) thus makes visible a problem of narrative authority. Within theological exegesis some commentators have found the literal meaning of Jesus's words to his disciples to be such a complicating factor that they have been inclined to reject the authenticity of verse 12. However, as the verse stands as spoken by Jesus, commentators tend either to seek harmony of meaning or to admit that verse 12 complicates the sermonizing aspect of the New Testament. What is interesting is that the problem is made visible, although not solved, through the narrative strategies that constitute the parable.

A question we may ask is whether the problem of interpretation under consideration here indirectly reflects the parable's *mashal* dimension and thus sets a limit on attempts at rational explanation. For the listeners on the shore, the rhetoric of the parable is perhaps just as effective and important as its meaning, particularly when combined with the intensity of the actual experience of seeing and hearing the man who worked miracles and healed the sick. As a first-person narrator Jesus is also the speaker, and his rhetoric has a number of narrative components. For example, the ancient, mythical act of sowing (which is still a matter of solemnity loaded with symbolic significance in many cultures) is presented in a way that combines variation in the effects of the act with narrative intensification through repetition. On the other hand, the parable Jesus tells illustrates how strongly the genre invites interpretation. The first thing that happens when 'he was alone' is that 'they that were about him with the twelve asked of him the parable'. Jesus himself seems to point to this need for interpretation in the question that introduces his analysis: 'Know ye not this parable? and how then will ye know all parables?' The question reveals slight irritation at what slow learners the disciples are. Although such irritation is understandable, the question is strange since it appears to eliminate (or at any rate to make less absolute) the sharp distinction Jesus has just drawn between those who are with him and those who are 'without'. The reader may ask: if not even the disciples—who are those closest to Jesus and those to whom 'it is given to know the mystery of the kingdom of God'—can understand parables, then who on earth is supposed to be able to?

As the Parable of the Sower is presented in Mark 4, Jesus's interpretation is presented as final—as an authoritative version Mark asks us to trust. In terms of narrative, part 4 is closely related to part 2 because of Jesus's dominant position and because of the fact that he combines the functions of narrator and interpreter. In one way, therefore, this parable is incomplete for the multitude on the shore, as it would also have been for the disciples had they not had the opportunity to ask Jesus for an explanation. That the explanation they receive excludes those 'that are without' raises problems with the didactic aspect of the parable and makes it more ambiguous.

II

There are elements in the complicated relationship between narration and explanation in the Parable of the Sower that point forward to the functions this genre has in the prose texts of Franz Kafka. As with traditional parables, Kafka's parables also seem to invite the reader to participate in a narrative illustration of a principle or a moral point, but what is typical of Kafka's versions of parables is that the point they appear to be building up to becomes ambiguous—obscured in a way that frustrates the reader's attempts at interpretation. Variants of the problem and challenge of interpretation, which in the Parable of the Sower are actualized through the relationship between the text's four parts and through the conjunction *hina*, seem to be integrated in the structure of the Kafkaesque parable. Kafka's parables are similar to and yet different from the parables of the New Testament; they also owe something to other narrative forms such as the folk-tale and the fable. More recent variants of the parable can also be related to Kafka; as Jorge Luis Borges has shown (1979: 235), this applies not least to the religious parables of Kierkegaard.

Let us by way of illustration, and as a transition to the discussion of the parable in *The Trial*, return to the Kafka text presented in Chapter 1 (p. 4). As we will recall, the point there was to give an example of a fictional prose text and to outline what makes it narrative. If we now ask *what kind* of narrative text Kafka's version of the story of the cat and the mouse is, I may first mention that characteristically enough Kafka did not give this text any title. The title suggested by Max Brod—'Kleine Fabel' or 'Little Fable'—is only partly adequate, and it narrows down the interpretation. As Clayton Koelb notes in *Kafka's Rhetoric* (Koelb 1989: 163), at first sight the text reminds us more of an animal fable in the tradition of Aesop and La Fontaine than of a biblical parable. In La Fontaine's famous fable about the cat and the mouse too, we can see the main characters as representatives of two human types or two philosophical positions. The difference is that in Kafka's short narrative the text itself frustrates the interpretative directions it invites the reader to follow. At the same time as the text calls for interpretation (here lies the parabolic aspect), it greatly complicates the act of reading.

As Koelb writes, one possible interpretation might be that the text wants to warn the reader against taking advice from cats—or whatever cats might be supposed to represent. On the other hand, what the cat says does in a way seem sensible, since the mouse is now heading straight into the trap. The advice offered by the cat is *both* quite right and quite wrong (disastrous) for the mouse; it appears to be lost no matter what it does. Koelb is right in emphasizing how strongly this text focuses on and thematizes the actual process of understanding. It starts with the narrative trick that lies in using a talking mouse—and immediately this mouse discusses questions of great psychological complexity. It says of the world that 'it was so big that I was afraid', but just afterwards that 'there in the corner stands the trap I am running into'. Thus, as Koelb observes, it gives precise expression to an ambivalence between agoraphobia and claustrophobia. This ambivalence is reinforced narratively since in extremely concentrated form the text seems to present the course of a life, and since the experiences of life to which the mouse gives expression are of such a kind that they can be associated with the reader's life experiences (how much larger the world seemed when we were small!).

Short as it is, 'Kleine Fabel' thus reflects something of the opposition that makes the parable both alluring and difficult at the same time: on the one hand it invites interpretation, on the other hand it frustrates those attempts we make at interpretation. Koelb, who like Hillis Miller relates the parable to the allegory, speculates about whether this text may be read as 'an allegory on the unreliability of allegories' (Koelb 1989: 168). Perhaps this is so, but Koelb's reference to Nietzsche is more informative. In aphorism 381 of *The Gay Science*, Nietzsche observes that 'one does not only wish to be understood when one writes; one wishes just as surely *not* to be understood' (Nietzsche 1974: 343). This paradox is central to the genre of parable. In relation to the parables of the New Testament, it can be linked to narrative representations of what is mysterious, alien, and different—not of this world and therefore impossible to capture with the languages of this world. In relation to Kafka, this paradox can be related to a comment by Theodor Adorno about Kafka's narrative art: 'Each sentence says "interpret me", and none will permit it' (Adorno 1982: 246).

There are few places in which this point seems more apt than in the penultimate chapter of *The Trial*, 'Im Dom' or 'In the Cathedral'. The whole novel has in the opinion of many commentators a parabolic character, but in the chapter 'Im Dom' Kafka has inserted a separate, relatively independent parable—the story of the man from the country who comes to the door-keeper 'for admission to the Law'. This parable, which Kafka first wrote as a separate text, and which is usually called 'Before the Law', runs as follows in the English translation by Douglas Scott and Chris Walker:

> before the Law stands a door-keeper. A man from the country comes up to this door-keeper and begs for admission to the Law. But the door-keeper tells him that he cannot grant him admission now. The man ponders this and then asks if he will be allowed to enter later. 'Possibly,' the door-keeper says, 'but not now.' Since the door leading to the Law is standing open as always and the door-keeper steps aside, the man bends down to look inside through the door. Seeing this, the door-keeper laughs and says: 'If it attracts you so much, go on and try to get in without my permission. But you must realize that I am powerful. And I'm only the lowest door-keeper. At every hall there is another door-keeper, each one more powerful than the last. Even I cannot bear to look at the third one.' The man from the country had not expected difficulties like this, for, he thinks, the Law is surely supposed to be

accessible to everyone always, but when he looks more closely at the door-keeper in his fur coat, with his great sharp nose and long, thin black Tartar beard, he decides it is better to wait until he receives permission to enter. The door-keeper gives him a stool and allows him to sit down to one side of the door. There he sits, day after day, and year after year. Many times he tries to get in and wears the door-keeper out with his appeals. At times the door-keeper conducts little cross-examinations, asking him about his home and many other things, but they are impersonal questions, the sort great men ask, and the door-keeper always ends up by saying that he cannot let him in yet. The man from the country, who has equipped himself with many things for his journey, makes use of everything he has, however valuable, to bribe the door-keeper, who, it's true, accepts it all, saying as he takes each thing: 'I am only accepting this so that you won't believe you have left something untried.'

During all these long years, the man watches the door-keeper almost continuously. He forgets the other door-keepers; this first one seems to be the only obstacle between him and admission to the Law. In the first years he curses his piece of ill-luck aloud, and later when he gets old, he only grumbles to himself. He becomes childish and, since he has been scrutinizing the door-keeper so closely for years that he can identify even the fleas in the door-keeper's fur collar, he begs these fleas to help him to change the door-keeper's mind. In the end his eyes grow dim and he cannot tell whether it is really getting darker around him or whether it is just his eyes deceiving him. But now he glimpses in the darkness a radiance glowing inextinguishably from the door of the Law. He is not going to live much longer now. Before he dies all his experiences during the whole period of waiting merge in his head into one single question, which he has not yet asked the door-keeper. As he can no longer raise his stiffening body, he beckons the man over. The door-keeper has to bend down low to him, for the difference in size between them has changed very much to the man's disadvantage.

'What is it you want to know now then?' asks the door-keeper. 'You're insatiable.' 'All men are intent on the Law,' says the man, 'but why is it that in all these many years no one other than myself has asked to enter?' The door-keeper realizes that the man is nearing his end and that his hearing is fading, and in order to make himself heard he bellows at him: 'No one else could gain admission here, because this door was intended only for you. I shall now go and close it.' (pp. 239–40)

As a short prose text placed inside a larger one, this parable structurally resembles part 2 of the Parable of the Sower. Kafka's parable is also difficult to understand, while it too provokes interpretation. My commentary on this parable is divided into three: first, we shall look briefly at the narrative presentation of the parable itself, then at the introduction to it, and finally at the interpretations which it inspires.

As we have seen, the parable can function partly as an illustration, partly as a *mashal*-like riddle that makes understanding difficult, and perhaps impossible—especially for those who are 'without'. Both of these functions can be attributed to the parable 'Before the Law', though it is probably the parable's enigmatic and strange aspect that strikes us most. The text resists attempts at interpretation: 'the ability of the one who would penetrate the text falls far short of the text's ability to resist penetration' (Koelb 1989: 176). For example, the man from the country believes that 'the Law is surely supposed to be accessible to everyone always' (p. 239), and in a certain sense it *is*. The door is open and the door-keeper is not blocking it. Yet although he does not directly prevent the man from going in, he does not *allow* him to, and this refusal is sufficient for the man to sit and wait. If we ask what this Law actually is, the parable does not appear to provide any answer. But if we ask what the Law means to the man, the answer appears to be: everything. One striking feature of this text is the soberly reported communication of how weirdly consistent and enduring the man from the country is in his passive waiting: 'During all these long years, the man watches the door-keeper almost continuously' (p. 240). This is how the parable presents a deadlocked situation that seems more and more absurd measured by 'realistic' standards: not only does the man sit for an unbelievably long time on the chair, but of the two characters he is the only one who grows old!

If the story of the man from the country grips us in spite of such improbable or fantastic elements, a partial explanation of our empathy is provided by its parabolic function. Thus the story can have, and does in fact have here, elements of legend and folk-tale—with the folk-tale's characteristic mixture of everyday realism and fantastic happenings. Reading the story as a parable, we also more easily accept that the text may be improbable on some points: we reckon that it has an illustrative function. Furthermore, the parable's textual brevity and swift temporal progression cause the reader's interpretative energy to be concentrated on the peculiar end—the final reply from the door-keeper to the dying man. This effect is reinforced as the parable carries straight over into K.'s response, which is already interpretative. For Ritchie Robertson this parable is

> perhaps the supreme moment in Kafka's writing, thanks to its Old Testament plainness and economy, and to the final peripeteia, which wholly transforms the reader's understanding of it. This peripeteia—the doorkeeper's information to the dying man that the door was all along intended for him and for him only—is an essential part of the story's meaning, for the story embodies, for the reader, precisely that transformation of consciousness, that escape from one's mental set into a new understanding of the world, which Josef K. needs in order to escape from his trial but which he cannot achieve. Nor can the man from the country achieve it: the information is the very last thing he hears before his death. (Robertson 1985: 122–3)

Like the Parable of the Sower in Mark 4, the parable of the man from the country in *The Trial* is communicated through a combination of third- and first-person narration, but in such a way that the first-person narrator is secondary in relation to the third-person one. In order to comment on this narrative technique I must say a little about the sequences before the parable (i.e. the first part of the chapter 'In the Cathedral'), also outlining how this chapter is placed structurally.

However difficult, labyrinthine, hermetically sealed, and enigmatic it may be, *The Trial* can seem narratively simple in the sense that it presents the main character's life, development or 'process', between two specified events. These two events—K.'s arrest and his execution—are placed right at the beginning and right at the end of the novel. The opening is one of the most famous in world literature: 'Jemand musste Josef K. verleumdet haben, denn ohne dass er etwas Böses getan hätte, wurde er eines Morgens verhaftet' (*Der Process*, 9). In our English translation this first sentence reads as follows: 'Someone must have been spreading lies about Josef K. for without having done anything wrong he was arrested one morning' (p. 17). We can see that the hypothetical subjunctive in 'hätte' has not been rendered in the English version. 'Hätte' implies that, although K. was not aware that he had done anything wrong, he perhaps nevertheless might have done. Thus the subjunctive form makes the text ambiguous in a way that creates suspense. This ambiguity, which is linked to K. as the main character, is thematically very significant in *The Trial*. Indeed it is also crucial to the narrative communication of K.'s thoughts, self-awareness, and situation in life. Since no account has been taken of the subjunctive form in the English translation (which broadly speaking is accurate), the narration appears here as more traditionally third-person than it actually is. That K. was arrested 'without having done anything wrong' indicates that the narrator knows he is innocent and invites the reader to consider the narrator as omniscient. An alternative English translation such as 'without being aware of having done anything wrong' makes us see that Kafka's use of the subjunctive works the other way: the subjunctive form implies that although the narrator informs us that K. was arrested, he lets it remain open whether this was with good reason or on thin evidence—perhaps he does not know the reason at all. Combined with the verb form 'musste' in the first sentence of the German text, 'hätte' indicates a perspective closely associated with that of K. The thematic (and interpretative) implications of this narrative variation are far-reaching. As Beatrice Sandberg and Ronald Speirs put it, 'we are not reading the story of a man who is arrested despite the *fact* that he is innocent, but rather the story of a man who *maintains* that he has been wrongfully arrested' (Sandberg and Speirs 1997: 68).

In this way the first sentence in *The Trial* signals the characteristic variant on third-person narrative that Kafka explores in many of his fictional texts, including the novel *The Castle* which in many ways supplements *The Trial*. It is a narrative method in which the narrative perspective is closely related to the main character's perspective, but without the two coinciding completely. Since the narrator's perspective influences and in part steers the reader's perspective, this creates what Roy Pascal in *Kafka's Narrators* calls 'that intense enclosedness of Kafka's stories. There is no escape from the spell they weave, scarcely an opportunity for reflection, contemplation, for a relaxation of tension, until the spell is broken by the death of the narrator's chief medium, the chief character' (Pascal 1982: 57).

Yet it is crucial to the structure and thematics of *The Trial* that the narration is not first-person. For even if the narrative perspective is linked to K.'s perceptual perspective, it is not *limited* to one character in the way that first-person narrative entails—for instance, in Hamsun's *Hunger*, Charlotte Brontë's *Jane Eyre*, or Dostoevsky's *Notes from the Underground*. Repeatedly associating himself with the main character, the third-person narrator can also distance himself from him—among other things through observations of K., through placing him in relation to the other characters, and through the way in which he structures and links the narrative sequences. The use of the past tense also comes in here. The past tense is in itself implicitly a structural device since it implies a completed action viewed retrospectively. As the narrator does not seem to have any personal identity, it seems consistent that he should give the reader little help in the form of authoritative evaluations of the characters. The narrator functions as a narrative instrument who on the one hand communicates what happens to the main character by associating himself with his thoughts and feelings, and on the other hand distances himself from him by structuring the narration and localizing it at an unspecified point in time after the action is over.

The structure of *The Trial* can be read as a series of variations on this basic narrative pattern. This also applies to 'Im Dom', the penultimate chapter which includes 'Before the Law'. This parable is integrated in *The Trial* through a combination of narrative devices (which together constitute the third-person narrative technique), and I shall point to some of the most important ones. At the beginning of the chapter, we read that K. is given the task of showing an Italian around the city. Although he feels insecure and would rather not be away from the office (where he is still working even though he is under arrest), he arranges to meet the Italian outside the cathedral. While he is waiting, K. goes into the church: here he meets the priest who tells him the parable of the man and the door-keeper. This plot sequence makes visible a number of features of the novel's narrative method. On the one hand, K. is observed and presented by the narrator; on the other hand, he serves as a consciousness that experiences, reflects, and guides the narrator's communication. The transitions between these two aspects of the narrator's function are characteristically blurred. For example, the narration is characterized by precise and realistic observations, but the narrator also lets *K.* observe and remember exactly:

> The cathedral square was completely empty, and K. remembered how it had struck him, even as a small child, that almost all the houses in this narrow square always had their blinds drawn. With the weather as it was today, though, that was more understandable than usual. The cathedral seemed to be empty too, for naturally no one thought of coming there now. (p. 229)

Such realistic details and observations contribute to establishing Kafka's fictional universe as strangely, not to say ominously, present. The reason for this does not only lie in the detail of the observations, but is to be found just as much in the way in which they are linked together. One effect Kafka achieves by connecting the presentation so strongly to K. is that a sentence often appears as an attempt logically to carry forward the reasoning in, or associations from, the previous sentence. Thus those sentences (or paragraphs) where this is *not* successful become particularly important in that they give the narrative a new and potentially crucial change of direction:

> K. felt a little forlorn as he went on alone between the empty pews, perhaps with the priest watching, and the vastness of the cathedral seemed to him to lie on the very limits of what a man could bear . . . He had almost got clear of the pews, and was nearing the empty space between them and the door, when for the first time he heard the priest's voice. A powerful, well-trained voice. How it rang through the expectant cathedral! But the priest was not addressing the congregation; what he said was quite unambiguous and there was no escaping his call of:
> 'Josef K!'
> K. came to a halt and stared at the ground in front of him. For the moment he was still free . . . (p. 234)

The way in which the priest uses his authority to stop K.'s planned action (of leaving the church) is structurally reminiscent of his arrest right at the beginning of the novel. That the priest should know K.'s name is of course improbable, but this becomes *less* improbable through K.'s reaction, for he immediately connects the priest with the trial, and the priest for his part confirms such a connection when he informs K. that 'for the moment at least, your guilt is taken as proven' (p. 236). We note the use of free indirect thought in the example above. Here the free indirect thoughts clearly communicate K.'s impression of the priest's voice: 'How it rang through the expectant cathedral!' That the voice is strong and inviting contributes to the fact that K. stops.

Immediately the priest mentions that K. is held to be guilty, K. goes on the defensive by protesting his innocence. A crucial point here is that the only way he can protest is by claiming that the court made a mistake in arresting him. Yet how can K. claim this when he does not know the court and thus cannot know the criteria for right and wrong according to which the court works? Stanley Corngold formulates this problem thus:

> Joseph K. is inculpated by his very impatience to find himself innocent; it prevents him from taking on the question: What, apart from my need to find myself innocent, is the nature and authority of the court that has arrested me?
> Since personal experiences end precisely where what one is afraid of begins and hence cannot survey what one is guilty of, they are very likely able to offer only the worst road to this reflection. (Corngold 1988: 238–9)

K. puts himself in an impossible situation by claiming that he is innocent: it means claiming something for which his limited experience provides no basis. The priest, who seems willing to help K. out of this impasse, becomes so exasperated at how little K. understands that he yells at him: 'Can't you see what is just in front of your nose?' The narrator comments that 'It was a howl of anger, but at the same time it sounded like the cry of someone who sees another person fall and, because he is frightened himself, screams unwarily, involuntarily' (p. 237). Since the reader relates 'another' to K., this comment is an example of the fact that the third-person narrator can distance himself from the main character. It is as if he distances himself from the priest as well, with the result that the priest and K. are as it were placed on the same level: they are both afraid.

' "You're deluding yourself about the Court," the priest said. "In the writings which preface the Law it says about this delusion: before the Law stands a door-keeper . . ." ' (p. 239). This is how the priest introduces the parable 'Before the Law', which we have already quoted. Part of the motivation for telling the parable is, in other words, to help K. to a better understanding of the court (and the Law on which the court bases its judgments). We see that the parable is not taken directly from the Law itself, but from 'the writings which preface the Law'. Is it perhaps more a comment on how difficult the Law is to understand than a contribution to the provision of insight into it? If so, this would give the parable a *mashal*-like function. It is also striking that what has hitherto been presented as K.'s problem (his confusion or delusion concerning the Law) has already been commented on in writing. Since this seems to imply that others must have made the same mistake before K., his problem becomes generalized—and its relevance made greater for the reader.

By introducing the parable the priest at the same time brings in a new narrative level in *The Trial*, the hypodiegetic level that the parable forms. The priest, who communicates the parable as a first-person narrator, is the central link between the two levels. As a narrator the priest reveals thorough knowledge of the writings of the Law. As he afterwards informs K., he tells the parable 'im Wortlaut der Schrift' (*Der Process*, 227), i.e. verbatim from the writings. That he is at the same time something quite different from simply a reliable quoter becomes clear in the discussion that the parable provokes between him and K. This transition from the communication of the parable to the interpretation of it is narratively just as interesting as the way in which Kafka introduces the parable.

> 'Der Türhüter hat also den Mann getäuscht', sagte K. sofort, von der Geschichte sehr stark angezogen. 'Sei nicht übereilt', sagte der Geistliche, 'übernimm nicht die fremde Meinung ungeprüft. Ich habe Dir die Geschichte im Wortlaut der Schrift erzählt. Von Täuschung steht darin nichts.' (*Der Process*, 227)

> 'Then the door-keeper deceived the man', said K. immediately, very strongly attracted by the story. 'Don't be too hasty', said the priest, 'Don't accept someone else's opinion without testing it. I've told you the story exactly as it's written. It doesn't say anything about deception.' (*The Trial*, 240)

In a study of Kafka's language, Jörgen Kobs points out how important the rhythm of the language and syntax is in his texts, not only stylistically but also semantically. The example above illustrates this point already in the first sentence. For it is important that K.'s response to the parable follows 'immediately' after its telling has been completed. This makes the transition from the communication of the parable to the interpretation of it as direct as possible, something which both increases its relevance in relation to the main action on the diegetic level and further supports the parable's in-built invitation to interpretation. The ending of the first sentence is masterly. After a brief pause marked by a comma, we read that K. is 'very strongly attracted by the story'.

The most probable reason that the story makes such a strong impression on K. is that he draws a parallel between the situation of the man from the country and his own. The narrator, however, further invites us to understand K.'s strong interest as a response to the parable *as a story* ('Geschichte'), i.e. as a narrative structure. Narratives have always fascinated human beings, and the enigmatic aspect of the parable serves to increase this fascination rather than to reduce it. Yet one condition appears to be that, even if the parable is enigmatic and difficult to understand, it contains elements that not only invite an attempt at interpretation but also signal that such an attempt is important—even existentially important. When K. immediately says that the man has been deluded, it is because he believes he has been deluded himself. By seeking to understand the parable he hopes to find out about his own frustrated situation in life.

If the man from the country in the parable represents K., who then is the door-keeper? Arguing that he is the priest, Heinz Politzer refers to the discussion between the priest and K. after the parable has been told. Here the priest and K. interpret the parable differently. While K. believes that the door-keeper deceived the man, the priest claims the opposite. First, he says, there is no mention of 'deception' in the writings from which the parable is taken (that the priest himself introduced the parable by saying that it deals with 'delusion', he now seems to have forgotten). Second, if anybody is deluded, it is the door-keeper and not the man, for while the door-keeper must stand on guard in front of the door to the Law all these years, the man is free to go whenever he wishes. At the same time as he rapidly gets the upper hand in the discussion, the priest assumes an air of modesty. 'I'm only telling you the different opinions there are about it,' he says. 'You mustn't pay too much attention to them. The scripture is unalterable, and the opinions are often merely an expression of despair on the part of the commentators' (p. 243).

The parable that the priest tells K. to help him to understand the Law and his own position in relation to the Law has instead the effect of making K. even more tired: 'He was too weary to be able to grasp all the implications of the story' (p. 246). Yet even if the story does not give K. the insight into the Law he had been hoping for, it is at least a good demonstration of how difficult reading and interpretation are—and of how strong counter-arguments can be, even against an interpretation that at first seemed obvious. The parable, which starts off as an illustration of K.'s situation, finally becomes incomprehensible to K. Yet in this incomprehensibility lies a paradoxical hope of something true and authentic: 'If Kafka the reader believes in an inaccessible truth concealed within the texts he is unable to decipher, Kafka the writer produced parables whose indecipherability is their only hope of authenticity' (Koelb 1989: 178). A critic such as Politzer reads the parable 'Before the Law' as a nihilist feature in *The Trial*, and in Kafka's fiction altogether, but Koelb has a point when he claims that the force of this parable presupposes an attitude to the man from the country that is *not* nihilist. This is an important reason why Kafka presents the priest as an authoritative and reliable narrator: the reader must not doubt that the Law exists for the man and that he really wishes to gain admission to the Law. In spite of the inconceivably long time he waits to be allowed to slip in, the parable does not give any signal that the man does not have confidence in the Law. Nor, writes Koelb, 'is there any hint in Kafka's writings that Kafka doubted the existence of the absolute truth that he himself could never grasp' (Koelb 1989: 178).

For Kafka, the parable is a narrative means of expressing this absolute truth, a truth concealed and apparently lost. What this truth is, is unclear, but the emphasis on the Law suggests that it has to do with fundamental principles of justice. It also appears to have a religious component, probably most strongly of Judaism. Walter Benjamin has this connection in mind when, in a letter to Gershom Scholem, he finds that 'the writings of Kafka are by their nature parables. But what makes them tragic and beautiful is that at the same time they had to become *more* than parables' (Benjamin 1979b: 201, my translation).

Parable and yet more than parable. The parable 'Before the Law' in *The Trial* resembles the Parable of the Sower in several ways: it has an introduction by a third-person narrator, a story or a 'parabolic basis' by a first-person narrator, and finally an interpretative part. The meaning of the actual parabolic story is in both cases unclear and difficult. However, while Jesus's disciples admit that they do not understand the parable, K. immediately claims that he does. The discussion with the priest nevertheless creates doubt as to whether this understanding is the right one. The greatest difference between the two texts lies precisely here, in the interpretative part. As I have tried to show in the first part of this chapter, the problematic aspect of Jesus's explanation lies perhaps less in the actual analysis (with absolute authority he explains to his disciples what he himself is doing on earth) than in the selection process preceding the analysis. In *The Trial*, rather, this analysis takes the form of a problem-oriented discussion. Although the priest refers to several interpretations, he withholds the right one—perhaps he does not know it either. However, he is indeed inspired by his own story, and he shares this fascination not only with K. but also with the reader. This is a fascination created partly by the parable's function as a narrative, partly by its strange ability to suggest a possible meaning inside (and through) a closed text that complicates any attempt at understanding.

III

Is it possible to film *The Trial* as a parabolic text? The differences in media between film and parable (as a variant of literary prose) are so great that presenting this kind of problem must perhaps be dismissed as mistaken. Among the adaptations of *The Trial*, however, there is one that is strongly inspired not only by the parabolic character of the whole text but also more specifically by the parable 'Before the Law'. This film is Orson Welles's *The Trial* from 1962, and some comments on it will conclude this chapter.

When a literary text is adapted, Robert Scholes writes in his essay 'Narration and Narrativity in Film', the spectator discovers that 'the achieved fiction is *there* with a specificity which the printed text alone can never hope to match. The price for this intensity is a reduction in the interpretive richness of the written text . . . When the story is filmed, all choices are final' (Scholes 1985: 392). An adaptation visualizes *selectively*; it generalizes *one* interpretation of a literary text. The screen versions of *The Trial* illustrate this constituent aspect of adaptation: as one might expect, they are very different. However, the fact that an adaptation thus implies an interpretation that reduces 'the interpretive richness of the written text' does not necessarily mean that it is simple, one-dimensional, or unambiguous (see my comments on adaptation and on Axel's *Babette's Feast* in Chapter 4 above). I emphasize once again how different the two media are, and how differently they function for the person who reads the book on the one hand, and for the viewer who at the same time both sees and hears the film on the other. Thus Scholes is right to point out 'the different kinds of interpretation that verbal and cinematic texts entail' (Scholes 1985: 392). Although an adaptation is basically a process of narrowing down, in the sense that it visually presents a single interpretation of many possible ones, this interpretation (i.e. the film) can in its turn be interpreted differently and evaluated as more or less successful. We are confronted with a pattern of reaction that is basically dichotomous. A film which is also an adaptation may be understood and interpreted differently by all those who see it—whether they know the literary original or not. For anybody who does know it, however, the response to the film will have an inevitable element of evaluative comparison with the literary starting-point. Such a comparison is understandable, but since it can easily become too direct (in relation to the great differences between the media), the screen version often comes off worse than it deserves.

Orson Welles's adaptation of *The Trial* is to a high degree a subjective interpretation. It is a controversial screen version critics have disagreed about. Partly this comes from the way in which Welles presents K., but most of all perhaps from the fact that the literary starting-point for the film is in this case so well known—and also known as being unusually ambiguous. As Welles presents K. through Anthony Perkins, the main character appears as being more active and apparently stronger than does Kafka's in *The Trial*. Welles compensates for some of this difference, however, by presenting both K. and the other characters as small and vulnerable in overwhelmingly large interior and exterior landscapes. This aspect of the film suggests an influence from German expressionist film of the 1920s, such as F. W. Murnau's *Nosferatu* (1922) and Fritz Lang's *Metropolis* (1926). One image in particular has become a classic: a long shot of an enormous open-plan office with hundreds of clerks all sitting bent over their typewriters at completely identical desks, all looking grave and working mechanically. Avoiding close-ups, Welles presents the characters as small, both in relation to their physical surroundings and in relation to the tiny majority who have power. Overall, the problem of power, which is of course also part of the thematics of *The Trial*, is presented more explicitly as social criticism by Welles. The viewer is reminded of Lang's *Metropolis*, and of novels such as Arthur Koestler's *Darkness at Noon* (1940) and George Orwell's *Nineteen Eighty-four* (1949).

The emphasis on the parabolic aspects of *The Trial* does on the other hand contribute to generalizing those questions that Welles dramatizes in his screen

Josef K. (Anthony Perkins) wandering through labyrinthine interior spaces in Orson Welles's *The Trial*.

version. Here the beginning of the film has a key function. As we will recall, the novel opens one morning with the unexpected arrest of K. The first thing the adaptation presents, however, is the parable 'Before the Law'. Welles takes a text section from the novel's penultimate chapter, condenses it, and places it right at the beginning of the film. Such a change is in itself significant, not only structurally but also thematically. By being placed right at the beginning, the parable becomes at one and the same time a prologue to the film's plot and an illustration of it. This impression is reinforced when later in the film the parable is presented for the second time. This underlining repetition of the parable comes at a point in the film's plot corresponding to the penultimate chapter of the novel.

Presenting the parable 'Before the Law' twice, first as an illustrative prologue and then as an integral part of the plot, implies in itself a strong emphasis on it. Let us take a closer look at the two presentations. Welles's most original device is to present the parable as a succession of images which look like stylized drawings. Asked about these illustrations, Welles explained that 'All those pictures were made by the shadows of pins. Thousands of pins. These two deliriously lunatic, highly civilized, elegant, and charming old Russians—a man and his wife [Alexandre Alexeieff and Clarie Parker]—sit and on huge boards they place pins. And the shadow of the pins is what makes the chiaroscuro on the picture' (Welles and Bogdanovich 1998: 273).

The camera remains focused on these illustrations of the man from the country and the door-keeper in front of the door into the Law. As a radically condensed visual presentation of the parable's most important stages, these pictures made by Alexeieff and Parker change as the voice of a narrator communicates the content to the viewer. Suggestively illustrating the parable of the man from the country, the pictures also show Welles's respect for and insight into the parable as a genre. As we have seen, the parable in *The Trial* is characterized by the way in which it is integrated into the structure of the novel, though it also appears as a peculiarly independent short text. This double structural function is reinforced thematically since the parable at one and the same time presents and complicates a possible thematic centre or core in the novel (cf. the discussion between K. and the priest about what the parable means). By placing the parable first in the film, Welles removes it from its surrounding textual context. Thus the parable appears more as an illustration of the subsequent action as it evolves through the plot, but it is crucial that Welles does not attempt to explain the action. When the presentation of the drawings is over, the narrator comments that 'This tale is told during the story called *The Trial*. It has been said that the logic of this story is the logic of a dream, of a nightmare.'

Who the narrator is we are not told until the very end of the film: 'This film was based on a novel by Franz Kafka . . . I played the advocate and wrote and directed this film. My name is Orson Welles.' When we add the role of narrator to the others that Welles himself mentions, we can state that he is just as central in *The Trial* as in *Citizen Kane*. True enough, such a combination of functions does not make Welles an author in a literary sense (like other films *The Trial* is also the result of a technically complicated production process with many players). Yet the fact that he is active on so many levels in the film— and not only successively but also in parallel—clearly contributes to giving the film a character of subjective, interpretative response.

If Welles's presentation of the parable at the beginning of *The Trial* shows insight into the parable as a genre, it also indicates how difficult it is to adapt the parable. The parabolic genre enlarges one of the most difficult problems in the transformation from verbal story to screen story. Simply but effectively, the parable usually presents a general, typified train of action in a way that activates interpretation. Since the adaptation of a parable must necessarily be concrete and specific, it will quickly remove the genre's characteristics and reduce its interpretative potential. The pictures by Alexeieff and Parker, however, illustrate characteristic features of the parable, thus capturing some of its monumental simplicity. Accompanied by Welles's narrative voice, these illustrations serve to provoke a variety of responses to the parable rather than damagingly reducing its meaning. This effect is reinforced through the thought-provoking stability a picture can have, a quality exploited by Welles as the camera dwells on each individual illustration.

Welles, then, answers the question of whether Kafka's parabolic text can be filmed by experimentally encapsulating another art form in his own. It is as if out of respect for the parable he does not wish to go further than illustrating it with some simple pictures. Yet since the incorporation of these is structurally and thematically productive in the film, Welles succeeds precisely through his insight into what a film *cannot* do, in extending the limits to what a film *can* represent. This last comment applies particularly to the beginning of *The Trial*. When at a quite advanced stage of the film's plot Welles presents the parable again, the repetitive aspect of this scene contributes to underlining how important the parable is. And yet the parabolic features of this scene (as Kafka presents it in the novel) become unclear in the screen version. Partly this comes from the speed of the action and the film's swift tempo, but Welles also introduces an unnecessary complication: he lets K. first talk to the priest, but when the priest tells K. 'your case is going badly', K. becomes irritated and wants to go back to his work in the bank. On his way out he meets the lawyer, and it is *he*, not the priest, who in the screen version tells K. fragments of the parable of the man from the country. The idea seems to be that the viewer will link these excerpts from the parable with the presentation of it right at the beginning of the film. To a certain extent we probably do so, particularly since Welles again makes use of the same pictures to illustrate the story the lawyer tells K. However, the tempo of the presentation and its textual positioning combine to reduce the parabolic dimension here compared to the opening. What this sequence best brings out is how confused K. is and how threatened he feels. The last picture it shows is the closed door into the Law. This image marks a transition to the film's final sequence in which K. is executed, with a stick of dynamite instead of a knife.

Welles's interpretative adaptation involves a screen presentation of Josef K. which partly gives him other personal characteristics than those he has in the novel, among other things by making him an American anti-hero who is 'brought back' to a European environment. Yet as John Orr has pointed out, this is not necessarily a weakness in the adaptation:

> When the film was premiered in Paris in December, 1962, some critics deplored what they saw to be Perkins' aggressive and inappropriate posture towards the authorities who eventually destroy him. Yet the tone of defiance is clearly there in Kafka's text and Welles evokes this aggression not only as defiance but also as unexplained guilt. In his view, Joseph K. is guilty, sharing prior complicity in the system which persecutes him. (Orr and Nicholson 1992: 14–15)

What does Orr understand by 'guilt' in this connection? After having stated that guilt involves a form of joint responsibility, he relates this concept to another aspect on which Welles places great weight in his adaptation: the cinematic parallel thread between the intelligence system and K.'s relationship with women. As Welles designs this kind of parallel, it emphasizes the paranoid aspect of K.'s nervous and hyperactive pattern of reacting both to the apparatus of power and to women, while also stressing the nightmarish aspect of the situation in which he finds himself.

In the film as in the novel, the ending serves to pose questions rather than to provide an answer. Thus in a way it repeats the parable, which forms a paradox formulated by Jacques Derrida: 'The text is intended to be the door, the entrance (*Eingang*), that the doorkeeper closes' (Derrida 1985: 130). As a narrative text *The Trial* invites the reader to attempt to create meaning, but at the same time the novel systematically frustrates our attempts to understand. This applies not least to the representation of the Law as mighty and unapproachable; it is like a hidden thematic core that manifests itself as a continuous series of varying power relations. It is a strength of Welles's adaptation that, as Gilles Deleuze points out in *Cinema 2*, it brings out some of this quality of the novel. In Deleuze's opinion, 'the system of judgement becomes definitively impossible' in Welles, 'even and especially for the viewer' (Deleuze 1989: 139). This effect is created partly by the tempo in many of Welles's films, not least *The Trial*; it is as if K.'s failure to understand his own situation accelerates his trial towards his execution.

If Welles's adaptation of *The Trial* is controversial, there can be no doubt that as a subjective response it is both *engagé* and engaging. The question may be asked whether a fictional literary text such as *The Trial* can in fact ever be understood 'correctly' or 'completely', but this does not mean that what we think we understand is necessarily wrong. In the discussion with K. about the parable, the priest refers to the commentators on the Scriptures, who, when commenting on a difficult point in the Law, say that 'The correct interpretation of a certain subject and misunderstanding of the same subject do not wholly exclude each other' (p. 242). Response is already a form of understanding, and our response to *The Trial* as a literary text is also a response to this text *as difficult*—closed, enigmatic, and mysterious. 'The mysterious', says Wilhelm Emrich in his influential study of Kafka, 'is an element in all great poetry' (Emrich 1981: 11, my translation). It attracts us, but since it also frightens us we read on for a possible explanation of what we do not understand. Thus our activity as readers becomes in a certain sense directed at the parable, as is the energy of the narrator, since he links the perceptual perspective so closely to that of K. The final narrative effect of *The Trial* is that when K. dies it is also the end of the narrator's attempt at understanding.

6
James Joyce's 'The Dead' and John Huston's *The Dead*

'The Dead' is the final text in James Joyce's *Dubliners*, a collection of short stories from 1914. Like Kafka's *The Trial* 'The Dead' has become a classic modernist text; it is a short story written on the threshold of the period that produced Joyce's next three major works: *A Portrait of the Artist as a Young Man* (1916), *Ulysses* (1922), and *Finnegans Wake* (1939).

The reasons why 'The Dead' has achieved the status of a classic in world literature are many, and the short story's narrative technique is clearly one of them. This chapter will comment on and analyse this technique, which I shall relate to both narrative theory and to the kind of thematics Joyce develops through his writing. A pedagogic advantage of 'The Dead' is that this text is relatively easily accessible; it is not so demanding as *Ulysses* or so provocatively difficult as *Finnegans Wake*. A further relevant point for my purposes is that John Huston's adaptation of the short story indirectly illuminates several of its narrative devices and characteristics.

I

A leading Joyce scholar, Florence Walzl, has formulated a plot summary which may serve to open our discussion of the short story. According to Walzl, 'The Dead' has 'a plot of oscillation and reversal' (Walzl 1975: 429) that reflects the mental changes in the protagonist. She then summarizes the main action as follows:

> The protagonist is Gabriel Conroy, a Dublin school teacher, who, with his wife, Gretta, attends a Christmas party given by his two aunts, the Miss Morkans. During the evening a series of small events makes him alternate between emotions of confidence and inferiority. His self-esteem is undermined by the remarks of a bitter maid, Lily, by the criticisms of a fellow teacher, Molly Ivors, and by the doubts he secretly feels. On the other hand, his ego is bolstered by his aunts' dependence on him, his presiding at the carving, and his making the after-dinner speech. The

James Joyce, *Dubliners* [1914] (Harmondsworth: Penguin, 1992). John Huston, *The Dead* (1987); video, First Rate.

attention, the festivities, and the prospect of an unaccustomed night at a hotel arouse in Gabriel romantic emotions and memories of his wife that have long lain dormant. When later at the hotel he approaches her amorously, he finds that she too is remembering a past love, but it is a different love from his. It is for a boy of her youth, Michael Furey, now dead. The sudden realization that for his wife the memory of a long dead lover has greater reality than does the physical presence of her living husband precipitates a crisis of self-evaluation in Gabriel. For the first time he gains an insight into his own identity and that of his society. In imagination he has a confrontation with his long dead rival, and from this meeting evolves the snow vision which ends the story and the book. (Walzl 1975: 429–30)

As this plot summary shows, the combination of third-person narration and few chronological breaks makes it relatively easy to present a story version of 'The Dead'. Visible breaks between third-person and first-person narration, or between different first-person narrators (as in Conrad's *Heart of Darkness*) are not to be found here. It does not follow, however, that this short story is without narrative variations. For Joyce's narrative method is flexible and sophisticated—perhaps particularly in its combination of sympathy and distance in the presentation of Gabriel.

A story version like this one of 'The Dead' is a paraphrase, a summarizing and chronologically ordered retelling. This summary by Walzl may be good and relatively precise, yet it is also much more than a story version that simply states the facts. Particularly towards the end the summary becomes clearly interpretative: to say that the protagonist 'for the first time gains an insight into his own identity and that of his society' is interpretation rather than reporting. Although many critics would agree with such a reading, we shall see that there are also alternative interpretations of the ending and that these different interpretations partly depend on whether one reads this short story as an independent text or as the final part of *Dubliners*.

Richard Ellmann has aptly said of 'The Dead' that the story 'begins with a party and ends with a corpse' (Ellmann 1982: 245). In a little more detail Kenneth Burke (1975: 410–12) has divided this short story into three parts or stages: 'expectancy', 'a catalogue of superficial socialities', and 'events following the party'. The 'antithetical moment' (Burke 1975: 412) in the final part is broken up by Burke into several smaller parts, which are all structured around the mental process of revelation that Gabriel goes through. As Burke sees it, Joyce perfects his narrative technique in 'The Dead', developing a kind of narrative equivalent to a Platonic dialogue.

If, following Burke, we say that the short story has a tripartite structure, then in a narrative analysis it is important to point to techniques and variations in the three parts. Furthermore, the *transitions* between the stages will be interesting from a narrative perspective: how does Joyce link the parts together, and what thematic effects does the narrative technique have? Such questions are important, even though the answers may not be absolutely clear.

The first part, which Burke calls 'expectancy', I see as extending up to and including the brief paragraph which states that the aunts 'both kissed Gabriel frankly. He was their favourite nephew, the son of their dead elder sister, Ellen, who had married T. J. Conroy of the Port and Docks' (p. 179). With the conversation that follows between the aunts, Gretta, and Gabriel, the party must be said to be in progress. The transition to the third and final part is much more clearly marked in the text: it lies in the narrative ellipsis between the community singing that ends the description of the dinner, and the parting scene. In the Penguin edition of *Dubliners* this transition is even marked typographically by dots before the sentence that begins as follows: 'The piercing morning air came into the hall . . .' (p. 207). It is clearly important to Joyce to separate the final part out from the two preceding ones: the parting scene after the party moves into the narrative presentation of the parting-like, dramatic distancing between Gretta and Gabriel at the end of the short story. When in the opening of the third part Gabriel asks: 'Gretta not down yet?' this distancing process, with an ever stronger narrative focusing on Gabriel, has already begun. In Huston's adaptation as well the transition to the final part of the short story is clearly marked as the camera moves from a close-up of the dinner to a more distanced shot of the house, the snow in the street and guests coming out of the front door on their way home.

Let us now comment on narrative means and variations in each of these parts of 'The Dead'. We can start by referring to some relevant points in Allen Tate's analysis of the short story. 'The Dead', says Tate, 'brings to the highest pitch of perfection in English the naturalism of Flaubert' (Tate 1975: 404)— the short story repeats and accumulates naturalistic details and thus lays the foundation for some complex symbolism in the final part, centred on the symbol of the snow. 'Joyce's method', Tate further claims,

> is that of the roving narrator; that is to say, the author suppresses himself but does not allow the hero to tell his own story, for the reason that 'psychic distance' is necessary to the end in view . . . Joyce must establish his central intelligence through Gabriel's eyes, but a little above and outside him at the same time, so that we shall know him at a given moment only through what he sees and feels in terms of that moment. (Tate 1975: 404–5)

These points in Tate's analysis have been emphasized and developed by subsequent Joyce studies. What Tate calls a 'roving narrator' means in our terminology a third-person narrator with great narrative flexibility and varying perspective. The most important narrative orientation is towards Gabriel, yet precisely for this reason Tate's point about the need for 'psychic distance' from this character is central. In 'The Dead' as a literary text, the thematically important 'psychic distance' from Gabriel must be presented *narratively*: through a third-person narrative Joyce combines narrative distance and sympathy in a way that is closely related both to the characterization of Gabriel and to the portrayal of a specific social milieu in Dublin at the turn of the century.

As we saw in Part I, a third-person narrator often functions more as a narrative instrument than as a character. This is particularly clear if the narrator is omniscient, with knowledge of the thoughts and feelings of several characters, something which it is difficult for an individualized character to have. It does not follow that a third-person narrator is without human qualities, but it may be unclear to what extent these qualities are related to the author, to a given character, to the narrative instance itself, or to a combination of all three elements. The latter is not uncommon and may in part explain why narrative theory is uncertain on this point: it must constantly be qualified and modified, not only in relation to countless narrative variations but also in relation to the different thematic effects these have.

For example, the presentation of the party as an annual event prompts a narrative variation which has both an analeptic and a proleptic function. The analeptic element is particularly clear in the marking of how long the sisters have lived in the house. The third-person narrator implies that the aunts are old, but we notice that when their old age is confirmed, it is also modified: 'Old as they were, her aunts also did their share' (p. 176). That this analeptic qualification is short does not mean that it is unimportant. Since the short story is structured around the party, it is reasonable that we have here analeptic flashes rather than a fully realized narrative analepsis (which could more easily have been integrated in a novel). The brief analeptic elements in the first part of 'The Dead' do not simply place the coming party in a context; this context—a temporal sequence that we associate with continuity and tradition—is so strongly emphasized that for the reader it can easily be linked with the more negative alternatives, rebellion (against tradition), and change. The reference to the fact that their brother Pat died much too long ago seems to invite the reader to make such a connection.

On a second reading, this form of thematic linking is reinforced since the difficult, frustrating relationship between tradition on the one hand and protest/rebellion/change on the other is a theme central to the tension in 'The Dead', indeed in much of everything that Joyce wrote. Thus the analeptic variation on which I have commented also carries a proleptic function: it points forwards towards the thematics developed through the presentation of the party (particularly the dinner speech) and in the concluding third part. To sum up we can say that the first part *narratively* contains analeptic elements and that these elements *thematically* function both analeptically and proleptically. By pointing backwards—and even to the title, which is the first thing we read—they also point forwards towards the two main events of the plot: the dinner speech and the scene in the hotel room with the imagined confrontation between Gabriel and Michael.

The distinction between narrative voice and narrative perspective proves necessary for the analysis of 'The Dead'. In the first part the third-person narrative perspective is fairly stable, while the narrator's voice can cautiously tone down people's opinions about the party or about the aunts who are 'dreadfully afraid that Freddy Malins might turn up screwed' (p. 176). They are relieved that Gabriel and Gretta have at last arrived, and here the narration concentrates on the brief scene with Gabriel and Lily. As I have divided up the short story, this scene concludes the first part. Since the scene is complex, I shall limit myself to commenting on the introduction of the snow metaphor and the increasing narrative focus on Gabriel. First, however, a couple of comments on the concepts of 'metaphor' and 'symbol'.

In a metaphor a word that stands for something, A, is replaced by or identified with another word that stands for something else, B, so that qualities/characteristics of A are ascribed to B. In other words a metaphor involves a form of *transference* (as for instance in the sentence 'A woman is a rose', in which 'rose' is identified with 'woman'). Now in one sense such transference is a general characteristic of language since language refers to or 'represents' something that itself it is not. Seen this way *literary* language is a kind of double transference as it refers the reader to a fictional universe in place of the external world of reality. At the same time, through its special language system, literature can establish metaphors within its own register. This happens in the final scene of the first part of 'The Dead'. When we read that Gabriel scrapes the snow from his goloshes on the doormat, we register this as a completely natural thing; the fact that it is snowing is not unnatural either in Dublin in early January. Yet when reference is made to the snow four times on the same page— twice by the narrator, once by Lily, and finally by Gabriel—something happens to our attitude to the snow as a semantic element in the action. The repetitions invite us to activate the metaphorical potential the snow has—it is white and connotes what is pure and innocent, but we may also associate it with death and perhaps with the eternal.

The constellation snow/snowing (noun and verb) constitutes in 'The Dead' a condensed verbal relationship in relation to other textual elements. As soon as we read the snow not only as snow but also as an expression of (for example) something pure and innocent, we turn it into a metaphor. What then is the difference between a metaphor and a symbol? To this question there is no simple answer. The boundary between these concepts is unclear; many interpret metaphor so inclusively that the concept also covers symbol. In relation to narrative texts such as 'The Dead' and *To the Lighthouse*, though, it is meaningful to see a symbol as an *extended* metaphor that establishes itself through repetition in important textual passages. The questions that a symbol actualizes can be very complex and difficult to delimit; the 'darkness' symbol in *Heart of Darkness*, for instance, enters into a complex of problems relating to power and violence; the symbol of light in *To the Lighthouse* is closely related to Mrs Ramsay's qualities as the novel's main character. This characteristic of symbols tends to provoke interpretation. A symbol, says Umberto Eco, may be understood as a '*textual modality*, a way of producing and of interpreting the aspects of a text' (Eco 1984: 162, original emphasis).

This aspect of the symbol is linked together with the reading process, and not least *re*reading. When we read 'The Dead' again, the second narrative reference to snow appears particularly important in the symbol-creating process: 'A light fringe of snow lay like a cape on the shoulders of his overcoat . . .' (p. 177). The apparent limitation of the snow to 'a light fringe' is counteracted not only by the comparison with a shoulder cape, but also by the coupling with 'cold fragrant air' just below. Both the reference to the cold winter air and Gabriel's reply to Lily's question whether it is snowing again ('I think we're in for a night of it') function proleptically, most clearly in relation to the beginning of the third part ('The piercing morning air . . .', p. 207) and in relation to the short story's concluding paragraph. The gradual development of the snow symbol is linked to the characterization of Gabriel. The qualities that the narrator links to the snow are coupled with characteristics of the protagonist, and these characteristics are formed through a series of narrative means. This applies in a high degree to the introductory characterization, which is centred around three paragraphs (pp. 178–9) dealing only with Gabriel. The narrative narrowing down that started in the scene with Gabriel and Lily is thus carried further here.

Narrative concentration on one character will as a rule make that character more important, although not necessarily the main character. The effect of associating the narrative perspective with Gabriel is then reinforced as Joyce activates a greater part of the story's narrative register. It is particularly important that the narrator reveals more knowledge of Gabriel as a character. That this happens cautiously and gradually is consistent with the distinctive linking of narrative distance and sympathy in relation to Gabriel—a combination Joyce uses the third-person narrator to develop. There are several links in this rather complex development of attitude, which turns out to be closely related to the text's thematic ambivalence. When Lily spontaneously reacts to his unfortunate utterance, we read that 'Gabriel coloured as if he felt he had made a mistake . . .' (p. 178). His reason for blushing is only tentatively formulated; the characterizing effect lies primarily in the way his uncontrolled reaction to an embarrassing situation that has arisen of itself is conveyed.

This diverges from the longest and most important paragraph that characterizes Gabriel in the first part. The mid-section runs as follows:

> He was still discomposed by the girl's bitter and sudden retort. It had cast a gloom over him which he tried to dispel by arranging his cuffs and the bows of his tie. Then he took from his waistcoat pocket a little paper and glanced at the headings he had made for his speech. He was undecided about the lines from Robert Browning for he feared they would be above the heads of his hearers. (pp. 178–9)

The first thing we notice here is the sharp profiling of Gabriel as a character. Joyce exploits the well-established convention according to which a third-person narrator can be 'omniscient' in the sense that he has knowledge of Gabriel's thoughts and feelings. We shall now proceed to explore some of the complexities behind the expression 'third-person narrator' in relation to the theoretical presentation of this term in Chapter 2. In narrative analysis it does not necessarily imply that the narrator knows 'everything' about a character, but more often that she or he conveys the thoughts, feelings, plans, or memories a character has in a way that a first-person narrator cannot do. The fact that a first-person narrator presents the action (and her or his response to the action) from her or his own perspective may serve to give the narrative presentation greater intensity and enhance its rhetorical power (cf. Hamsun's *Hunger*). In a text such as 'The Dead', however, the third-person narration opens the way for a perspectival variation that makes it possible to combine narrative distance (and irony) with sympathy.

Characteristically enough Joyce uses this narrative technique precisely and in a thematically productive manner. An important nuance lies in the combination of the words 'discomposed', 'gloom', 'try', and 'fear'. They are all connected with Gabriel but with varying and complementary thematic effects. To say that he is 'discomposed' after Lily's reaction has mainly the effect of a narrative statement. That he is anxious we need not doubt in any case, since the narrator's authority is well established at this stage of the short story. The noun 'gloom' in the next sentence both reinforces and specifies this anxiety, an anxiety which his mechanical attempt at correcting his tie does little to dispel. Then, in a sentence which again is more externally informative, we for the first time get to hear of the dinner speech Gabriel is to make (as the conclusion of the second part). On the diegetic level, this reference to the speech is clearly proleptic. In relation to the interpretation of the text this prolepsis becomes more interesting if we link it to the next sentence: not only does the narrator let us know that Gabriel is thinking of quoting the English poet Browning in his speech, he also reveals that Gabriel is afraid the quotation may be too advanced for his listeners. The narrator's ability to convey this kind of information enables the reader to see how concerned Gabriel is about what impression he makes, and wants to make, on others. This gradually turns out to be an important element in the self-centredness which characterizes him, and which is a problem for him—not only in relation to other people in general but in relation to Gretta in particular.

I have commented on this extract partly because it illustrates the economy of Joyce's narrative technique, partly because it exemplifies one of many possible ways in which the author combines narrative distance and sympathy. Distancing is marked through Gabriel's slightly trivial and mildly comical reactions. Signs of sympathy lie in the concentration on Gabriel as a character and in the narrative variation at the end of the paragraph, on which I have not yet commented. For if we consider the whole paragraph as a unit, we can see that it gradually glides from reported discourse to free indirect discourse. Just look at how the reflections on the speech are concluded:

> He would only make himself ridiculous by quoting poetry to them which they could not understand. They would think that he was airing his superior education. He would fail with them just as he had failed with the girl in the pantry. He had taken up a wrong tone. His whole speech was a mistake from first to last, an utter failure. (p. 179)

This indirect discourse takes the form of free indirect thought. If we rewrote the final sentence as reported discourse, the natural introduction would be: 'He thought that his whole speech . . .'. Thus we have mentioned one of the linguistic characteristics of free indirect discourse. The other two requirements for this form of discourse have also been satisfied here: the use of the past form of the verb and of the third person. In 'The Dead' free indirect discourse constitutes a thematically important variation on the narrator's speech presentation. The discourse enters not only into the task of forming Gabriel as the main character but also (especially in the third part) into the development of the short story's thematics.

In this paragraph there is a connection between the gradual, almost unnoticeable glide from third-person narration to free indirect discourse and the ambivalent attitude the narrator has to Gabriel. One effect of this ambivalence is to make Gabriel more complex as a character. This paragraph also contributes to establishing the transition between the first and second parts of the short story. We will recall that Kenneth Burke describes the second part— i.e. the actual party, which the first part introduces and the third part is an appendix to and consequence of—as a catalogue of superficial conversation. Adequate as far it goes, such a description is so brief that there are necessarily things it does not include. One such aspect is Gabriel's own attitude to the conversation: since he also experiences parts of the conversation as superficial, the alliance is strengthened between him and the narrator on the one hand and between him and the reader on the other. Another aspect is the proleptic elements which, partly in interplay with the snow metaphor and references to death, give parts of the conversation an undertone of melancholy, uneasiness, and resignation.

II

With the transition to the second part Joyce has established a third-person narrative technique that is precise yet selectively observant. The narrator seems to be in sympathy with the characters and the party that brings them together, but the narrative variations we have noted make us suspect that the narrative flexibility also implies a certain distance. The result is an attitudinal ambivalence which becomes particularly clear in the presentation of Gabriel. It is as if the ambivalence between distance and sympathy is duplicated, and thereby also complicated, through the narrator's relationship to Gabriel. For that too becomes gradually more complex. In a deconstructive analysis of 'The Dead' Vincent Pecora sees a characteristic of Joyce's fiction here. 'In learning to read him', says Pecora, 'one learns all the more effectively how to adjust one's own ironic self-detachment' (Pecora 1989: 215). It is indeed characteristic of Joyce that the narrator's position is constantly changed and complicated so that, for instance, if we read a given situation ironically on the basis of previous models in the same text, we are often surprised and compelled to adjust our reading. Towards the end of the chapter we shall return to this point, which actualizes questions discussed in reception theory.

Burke links the conversation catalogue to the functions different characters have in the presentation of the party. It is characteristic, thinks Burke, that the piano piece Mary Jane plays wins the most vigorous applause 'from the four young men in the doorway who had gone away to the refreshment-room at the beginning of the piece but had come back when the piano had stopped' (p. 187). For Burke, this is one of many superficial social events in the second part. Other examples he mentions are Miss Ivors's nationalistic commitment to Ireland (she prominently takes her leave with the words '*Beannacht libh*'—an old Gaelic greeting that means 'goodbye'), the disconnected dinner conversation about the opera, the obligatory conversation Gabriel has with the mother of Freddy Malins, and Gabriel's half-hearted dinner speech.

Burke's discussion of the second part is convincing as far as it goes, but he does not bring out how closely the 'superficial' conversation and events are related to the thematic dynamics up to the third part and the end of the short story. In order to emphasize this connection I want to comment on three points in the dinner conversation which are not only important as constituent elements in the second part, but which by preparing the end of the short story also become thematically significant. The first two points concern opera and politics, the third deals with Gabriel's dinner speech.

Opera, as the third-person narrator comments via the diplomatic Mary Jane, is the permitted and presumptively safe conversation topic during the dinner. Yet precisely by emphasizing that one subject is 'legitimate' (p. 199), the narrator indicates that other, more important themes become intrusively present, even though (and because) they are suppressed in the conversation. This shows itself most clearly when the conversational convention that one should express oneself 'legitimately' begins to crack, as when Joyce lets the befuddled and slightly comical Freddy Malins claim with some force that he has heard a Negro sing in 'a grand voice' (p. 199). Irritated at not being believed, he asks: 'And why couldn't he have a voice too? . . . Is it because he's only a black?' The fact that nobody answers the question approaches an answer in the affirmative. The question is embarrassing because it is a good one; it brings out racial prejudices and uncertain attitudes to what is foreign, and furthermore profiles the political dimension that practically always constitutes part of the thematics in Joyce. In this connection we can consider 'opera' as a trope, a picture of 'civilized' art talked about by people who also like to appear civilized and cultured. Just before Freddy's utterance the word 'vulgar' is used in a way that reveals such an attitude—true enough about another singer, but it can also be linked to the Negro Freddy mentions.

Two aspects of the suppressed political dimension in 'The Dead' must be briefly commented upon. The first concerns the presentation of the question of equality. If as a rough categorization we say that three aspects of this question concern the relationship between the sexes, races, and social classes, then it is striking how Joyce—in concentrated, dramatized form—is able to integrate all these aspects in the thematics he gradually develops. This thematic integration in the text's structuring process means that individual comments on each of the elements easily have a simplifying effect. This applies in particular to the question of the equality of the sexes, which is closely related to the relationship between Gabriel and Gretta. We shall be coming back to the presentation of this relationship in our discussion of the short story's ending, but we must not overlook the fact that Joyce also emphasizes the question of equality through the use of minor characters such as Miss Ivors and Aunt Kate.

Miss Ivors's independent and self-assured appearance in the conversation with Gabriel functions proleptically in relation to the traumatic experience Gretta causes him in the third part. This effective linking is in a way surprising, since Gretta is not presented as politically involved as is Miss Ivors. In John Huston's adaptation of 'The Dead', this side of Miss Ivors is made clear by the fact that she does not leave the party to go home, but instead accords a political meeting priority over the Christmas party. When one of the guests (in the adaptation) comments that she will probably be the only woman at the gathering, her jocular response is that 'It won't be the first time!' This could not have been said by Kate, but precisely because as a representative of the older generation she is more cautious, her strong commitment on behalf of Julia makes an impression on the reader. This episode, which comes immediately after Julia has sung the song for which she wins exaggerated applause, concerns the Church's attitude to, and exploitation of, a faithful servant like Julia. This also very much concerns equal status and actualizes the religious dimension of politics in Catholic Ireland. Yet having said this, I hasten to add that perhaps the most important effect of this episode is to bring out the futility, the apparent uselessness, of Kate's protest. Inhibited by the dinner in progress this protest enters into the series of frustrations that the characters partly display and partly attempt to give incomplete vent to through words.

This latter point is also related to the second point I want to mention concerning the political dimension in this short story. It can briefly be presented thus: one reason why the political dimension forms an important part of the thematics is that it is correlated with another dimension, which is also suppressed in the conversation: the references to, not to say the intervention of, the dead and death. A good example of the presentation of this thematic aspect (which is linked to the snow symbol, to the title, and to several other elements in a way that makes it one of the most important of all in the short story) is the point in the conversation about the monks in the Trappist monastery of Mount Melleray. In one sense it is ironic that this textual segment (roughly a page long and the last before Gabriel's speech) again demonstrates that the conversation cannot be confined to 'legitimate' topics of conversation. Yet even if there is a touch of irony here (as there is in much of what Joyce wrote) it is at the same time modified by the serious direction the conversation gradually takes. Typically enough it is once again Freddy who, perhaps unintentionally and because he is less concerned with middle-class etiquette, 'twists' the conversation in an unfortunate direction, although he gets good help from Mr Browne.

This textual segment illustrates a form of narrative technique that combines characterization through conversation with the development of an important thematic element. The effect of this combination is reinforced by the way in which the conversation is framed by two narrative comments—an introductory one placed immediately before Mr Browne expresses scepticism about the ascetic life-style of the monks, and a concluding one, after Mary Jane tries to explain to him why the monks sleep in their coffins:

> 'The coffin', said Mary Jane, 'is to remind them of their last end.'
>   As the subject had grown lugubrious it was buried in a silence of the table . . .
> (p. 202)

It is as if the constellation 'grown lugubrious' reflects how the conversation gradually, via Freddy's intended visit to the monastery and Mr Browne's sceptical reactions, more or less inevitably approaches the questions of which it is basically trying to steer clear. Thus the narrative variations, to which this segment contributes, gradually form a thematic pattern of repetition in which this short story constantly tends towards, circles around, or returns to its own title. The relevance of the title in relation to the text thus becomes ever clearer, at the same time as its thematic implications are extended.

The many references and allusions to death and the dead do not deprive the political dimension of a thematic value of its own, but integrate it in other, equally important existential and religious semantic structures. The result is a more open and more complex thematics. And yet this integration contributes to the short story's presentation of an elementary yet significant insight into Irish history: if there is one thing that characterizes it, it is the interweaving of politics (including nationalism and British domination) and religion (including the relationship between Catholicism in the south and Protestantism in the north). The most important connecting link between this historical aspect and the motif of death is the *past*, which more and more strongly imposes on the short story's plot development. Across the genre boundaries this dimension of 'The Dead' shows something of the influence of Henrik Ibsen, Joyce's literary hero. A number of structural and thematic elements in Ibsen's last plays, including metaphorical patterns and the titles of plays such as *Ghosts* (1881) and *When We Dead Awaken* (1899), are interestingly related to 'The Dead'. In an essay on Thomas Hardy, I have noted that 'if Ibsen's rejuvenation of dramatic form is inseparable from his incorporation of "genre-alien" narrative elements, Hardy's achievement . . . is also closely related to, though not solely dependent on, experiments in genre' (Lothe 1999: 112). Although Hardy and Joyce are very different writers, this point could also be made about the latter's fiction.

The narrative comment that concludes the extract at which we have just been looking also introduces the dinner speech made by Gabriel. Structurally this speech constitutes a mid-point in the short story. Thematically it forms an important basis for, and furthermore a contrast to, the imagined confrontation between Gabriel and Michael (who on one level represents the power the past has over the characters) towards the end of the third part. The dinner speech strengthens Gabriel's position as main character. The speech is more affirmative than surprising; it confirms through words—in a realized speech act influenced by a set of social expectations and conventions—features of Gabriel that the characterization has already drawn in outline.

This characterization is formed partly through Gabriel's previous utterances and reactions, and partly through narrative comments and free indirect discourse. Yet although Joyce uses narrative techniques in this way to confirm the reader's impression of Gabriel in the dinner speech, we cannot for this reason ignore other narrative variations that make the picture more nuanced. A key element in the production of such nuances is repetition. As we will recall, it is a characteristic of repetition that it may have—often at the same time, in the same narrative device—both narrative and thematic functions. Such a combined function is present in 'The Dead', even though the thematic aspect reasonably enough becomes clearer when the reader knows the end of the short story.

The concept of repetition is actualized by the expression 'as in years past' (p. 203) which Gabriel uses in the opening of his speech. It shows that this speech will be one of a series of speeches Gabriel has given at these annual parties, 'as long as anyone could remember' (p. 175). Furthermore, the listeners' expectations indicate that these speeches have resembled one another and that the listeners reckon that this one will follow an earlier pattern. This gives the speech the character of play-acting—in which the role of speaker has been given to Gabriel, and in which the boundaries become unclear between what Gabriel really means and what he says because it is expected of him. Yet even if this characteristic of the speech leads to clichés, this alone does not mean that the speech is uninteresting. The element of monotonous repetition makes the careful narrative variations Joyce puts into the speech more visible and thematically more important. The mid-part of the speech illustrates this. After having referred to the 'new ideas' that the 'new generation' has, Gabriel is on his guard against them:

> But we are living in a sceptical and, if I may use the phrase, a thought-tormented age: and sometimes I fear that this new generation, educated or hypereducated as it is, will lack those qualities of humanity, of hospitality, of kindly humour which belonged to an older day. Listening tonight to the names of all those great singers of the past it seemed to me, I must confess, that we were living in a less spacious age. (p. 204)

The fact that here Gabriel sees his own times—modern times, we might say—as 'thought-tormented' and 'less spacious' than the past accentuates again the dimension of the past in the short story's narrative discourse. One reason why we perceive the speech as important and relatively original (i.e. in relation to what we believe about the content of Gabriel's previous speeches) is paradoxically enough that he repeats and extends a paragraph earlier in the text: the sentence in italics (p. 192) in which the third-person narrator omnisciently reports Gabriel's thoughts about possible formulations he can use in his speech. Thus we have an element of analepsis here, and we can see the two sentences in the quotation as provoked by Miss Ivors. This reveals an ironic aspect since the listener at whom Gabriel's words are specially directed has already left the party. This irony modifies the effect of attitudinal sympathy the narrator seems to have with Gabriel in the quotation.

The speech Gabriel makes is narrative in the sense that it fits into (and marks an important stage of) a narrative sequence, but it does not form any self-supporting narrative on a par with for instance the hypodiegetic elements in *Don Quixote*. With Genette we can say that the narrative presentation here is scenic, with coalescence of narrative time and narrated time. (For a film director such coalescence eliminates some difficult choices she or he would otherwise have to make in the transfer from verbal to filmic fiction. In the sequence that covers Gabriel's speech in 'The Dead', Huston uses Joyce's text almost as a screenplay.) In a similar way as in the sequence about the monks at Mount Melleray, the scenic aspect is here emphasized by the third-person narrator's sparse commentary on what he is reporting. The few comments he allows himself are soberly informative and are limited to briefly commenting on the performance of the speech and the listeners' reactions.

There is one exception, though, which we can situate right at the beginning of the speech. This narrative variation constitutes a move beyond the scenic presentation. The fact that it comes so early in this sequence means that it does not establish itself as an important narrative variation until a second reading takes place. Gabriel has stood up, the conversation at table has faded into silence:

> Gabriel leaned his ten trembling fingers on the tablecloth and smiled nervously at the company . . . People, perhaps, were standing in the snow on the quay outside, gazing up at the lighted windows and listening to the waltz music. The air was pure there. In the distance lay the park where the trees were weighted with snow. The Wellington Monument wore a gleaming cap of snow that flashed westward over the white field of Fifteen Acres. (pp. 202–3)

Although the narrative discourse here too has on one level the character of a report, these sentences stand out from the subsequent presentation of the speech. The difference constitutes a significant variation that Joyce achieves by combining different narrative techniques. We can note the element of free indirect discourse in the third-person narrative. The perspective is linked to Gabriel from the very first sentence, and the use of 'perhaps' in the next one reinforces the narrative move towards free indirect speech. Yet what about the last couple of sentences? Here the anchoring of the perspective is more unclear: the impression of free indirect thought holds to a certain extent, but at the same time the discourse again becomes more neutrally report-like. It is as if the narration makes a crescent-shaped movement here. First it is obser-vant, even a little revealing, in referring to the fact that Gabriel's hands were trembling and that he smiled nervously at the listeners. Then the narration modulates to Gabriel's perspective only to distance itself from the protagonist again towards the end. I emphasize that particularly this final point includes an element of interpretation on my part. When I say that the narrator's dis-tance from Gabriel increases towards the end of the quotation, it is primarily for two reasons. First, the last two sentences seem authoritatively affirmative in a way that becomes constantly more difficult to reconcile with the more limited perspective of Gabriel, whose gaze is nervously directed at the dinner party. More importantly, however, the word 'snow' crops up again: first we read that the trees were weighted with snow and then that the Wellington Monument was covered in 'snow that flashed westward over the white field of Fifteen Acres'. What we have here is not only the opening of Gabriel's speech but also a proleptic device, an incipient transition, in relation to the third part and the short story's ending. As I read 'The Dead', this sentence is more closely related to the third part than is the end of the second part. Thus this sentence qualifies the social harmony (and Gabriel's success as a speaker) that seen in isolation characterizes the end of the dinner party. By proleptically linking up with the third part the sentence confirms the contrast and sharp transition that are marked narratively by the use of dots in the text.

III

The first four words of this final part of the short story are 'the piercing morning air' (p. 207). The Dublin air is cold and heavy with snow; the snow 'flashed westward' it says in the sentence which we have just discussed. In this final part 'The Dead' takes a 'westward' turn, if not on the realized level of action, at least metaphorically. It does not really help much that Gabriel and Gretta spend the night in a hotel in Dublin after the party. For they are both involved in a 'journey westward', which the narrator lets Gabriel imagine in the final paragraph. Yet they are on their own, and not together as Miss Ivors imagines when in the second part she invites them both to the Aran Isles off the west coast of Ireland. Gabriel's negative response to her proposal is primarily important seen in relation to the strong desire Gretta has to visit the islands. Here it is her enthusiasm which, coupled with her disappointment that Gabriel turns down the invitation without even asking what she wants, is most important in relation to the third part.

The sharp transition from the second part to the third signals the dramatic course the action takes. In a consolidating and complicating manner the narrative technique in this final part builds further on devices that have already been introduced, but this does not mean that the third part is without narrative variations. Reasonably enough, they are centred on Gabriel's relationship with Gretta and around what Walzl calls his 'crisis of self-evaluation'.

A possible approach to the first variation is to go back to the key comment the narrator makes right at the beginning of Gabriel's speech in the second part. Why is Gabriel so nervous about the speech, why are his hands trembling? Is it because he has an instinctive feeling that this party will be different from the preceding ones, even if everything is apparently just as before? The latter question indicates an interpretative direction with emphasis on the concept of repetition, to which I shall be returning at the conclusion of this chapter. We note that even though the third-person narrator may be omniscient, he does not give any direct answer to why Gabriel is nervous. Indirectly this links his nervousness more closely to the final part and in particular to the section that dramatizes his uncertain relationship with Gretta.

One function the third-person narration has in the third part is to 'upgrade' Gretta from a minor character to main character number two after Gabriel. The question from Gabriel, 'Gretta not down yet?' (p. 208) has perhaps an undertone of nervousness; a line runs from this question and on to the narrative statement 'She was fast asleep' (p. 223). That she falls asleep confirms the distancing process between her and Gabriel. A turning-point in this process comes early in the third part:

> Gabriel had not gone to the door with the others. He was in a dark part of the hall gazing up the staircase. A woman was standing near the top of the first flight, in the shadow also. He could not see her face but he could see the terracotta and

salmonpink panels of her skirt which the shadow made appear black and white. It was his wife. (pp. 210–11)

What makes this paragraph important both narratively and thematically is the presentation of Gretta as 'a woman'—a stranger, another, an unknown person. There is a peculiar opposition between the two words 'woman' and 'wife' in the quotation. The latter, which reports that Gabriel finally identifies the woman as Gretta, functions affirmatively for Gabriel and confirms the relationship between the two as husband and wife. On a second reading, however, 'woman' becomes the most semantically charged word. It signals the increasing distance, the gap that is opening up between Gabriel and Gretta. 'It was his wife' thus takes on an additional meaning: it is his wife Gabriel sees but he does not see that she has already become distant from him *beyond* the spatial distance. Ironically enough the first visual impression of 'a woman' is therefore more correct than the latter; the identification is illusory.

The presentation of Gabriel in this paragraph combines narrative sympathy and distance. The distance in insight is most striking. Since the narrator here presents the relationship between the two in a manner that points forwards towards the end, an 'alliance of understanding' is established between the narrator and the reader who knows the outcome of the short story. If we bring in D. C. Muecke's conception of irony as a 'two-storey phenomenon' in which the irony's victim is so to speak 'downstairs' (Muecke 1969: 19), we might say that in addition to being 'in a dark part of the hall' in a physical sense, Gabriel is here 'in the dark' in a figurative sense too; he does not yet know what is to happen, even if he perhaps vaguely suspects it.

Yet if the narrator so clearly marks distance from Gabriel, does this not undercut the narrator's sympathy? Not completely, and for two reasons. In the first place Gabriel's ignorance of what is in store for him in itself arouses a certain amount of sympathy. This narrative sympathy is, at any rate in part, created by the second reason, which lies in the strangely unstable and 'infiltrating' quality that the irony has in 'The Dead'. If a relatively simple form of irony presupposes a difference (in insight, knowledge, or attitude) between the ironist and the irony's victim, it is complicated here by virtue of the fact that both positions—the positions on both levels, so to speak—become peculiarly unstable. This destabilizing of distance and irony goes right into the reader's understanding of the text. Thus the narrative technique manipulates us into adjusting our way of reading, perhaps in particular our judgement of Gabriel. This does not mean that as readers we will all judge Gabriel in the same way—some people find few redeeming features in the portrait Joyce draws of him. Yet this part of the narration makes Gabriel more complex as a character.

On this point the film version is significantly different from the literary text. In the part of the adaptation that corresponds to this textual paragraph, the perspective (i.e. the film camera) is placed near Gabriel's perspective. Thus far there is good correspondence with the text, since after the third-person narrator in the first two sentences observes Gabriel in the dark in the hall, the word 'woman' indicates that the perspective is now limited to Gabriel's. In an interpretative context this limitation of perspective is closely related to Gabriel's lack of knowledge of his own wife; indirectly Joyce sketches here yet another variant of the theme of loneliness that permeates *Dubliners*. Since the camera in the film immediately identifies the woman as Gretta, the film appears to miss the literary meaning—the great potential for interpretation—that is linked to the distance between 'woman' and 'wife' in Joyce's text. By this I do not wish to say that the film version is 'bad' here. The two media are too different for us to be able to draw such hasty conclusions. Having noted how effective and thematically productive Joyce's third-person narrative is in this paragraph, primarily through the constellation of two words ('woman' and 'wife') and through perspectival variation, we can ask how Huston could have achieved something of the same effect by filmic means. One possibility would be to supplement the relevant sequence of images with voice-over narration, which would have reduced the difference between the text and film versions on this point. Yet such a voice-over would not have eliminated the difference, and it would furthermore have broken markedly with the film narration thus far. Huston is right to wait until the final sequence before putting in the voice of a narrator.

What Huston does instead is to exploit the interpretative potential associated with the camera. Lesley Brill has observed that Gabriel, the main focus of the third-person narrator's attention in Joyce's story and 'the most frequent object of Huston's camera' in the adaptation, sometimes establishes the camera's perspective 'and occasionally serves as the source of subjective shots' (Brill 1997: 222). In this scene the camera, closely associated with Gabriel's perspective, remains stably focused on Gretta in a manner which peculiarly combines objective and subjective qualities. The filmic presentation is objective in the sense that it immediately identifies the woman as Gretta. This kind of filmic objectivity is in large part conventional: film, to adapt the title of Seymour Chatman's book on the Italian film director Michelangelo Antonioni, focuses on 'the surface of the world', it places its stars (and Anjelica Huston clearly is one) in the light. And yet the camera is also 'subjective' as Gretta is made into a madonna. The characters' angle of gaze is upwards here—Gabriel is looking up at Gretta, who is also looking up. This kind of upward movement via Gretta (the main actor in this segment) has perhaps, with its religious— and Victorian—connotations, an interpretative potential comparable to that of the corresponding literary passage.

The paragraph just considered shows the direction of Gabriel's development in the third part: every time he believes he is on top of the situation

'There was grace and mystery in her attitude as if she were a symbol of something' (James Joyce, 'The Dead', 211). Positioned in the hall and thus associated with Gabriel's perspective, the camera focuses on Gretta (Anjelica Huston), who is listening to Mr D'Arcy singing the song Michael used to sing, 'The Lass of Aughrim'.

(especially in relation to Gretta), new complications arise, which finally provoke the crisis in his estimation of himself. That this process takes such a long time for Gabriel is perhaps decisive for the outcome. On several occasions when Gabriel believes he understands Gretta's feelings, the narrator reveals that his insight is an illusory form of understanding which in fact marks increasing distance. For example, we read that when Gabriel sees Gretta with 'colour on her cheeks and that her eyes were shining', he feels that 'a sudden tide of joy went leaping out of his heart' (p. 213). Here the third-person narrator omnisciently reports the protagonist's feelings—his happiness at being married to Gretta and his expectations of the night they are to have to themselves at the hotel. More interesting, however, is the distancing, irony-revealing and proleptic element in the sentence. For Gabriel does not know that Gretta's eyes are shining because of Michael Furey, whose memory is brought back to her by Mr D'Arcy's song. By thus indirectly referring to an unknown man in addition to the unknown 'woman', the text indicates that Gabriel has only partly identified Gretta.

That the party itself is terminated with the guests saying 'Good night' to one another as many as thirteen times shows something of the span in the use of repetition—from single words to complex thematic patterns. Yet if the distance may seem great from 'Good night' to the form of repetition which Gabriel experiences at the hotel, it is characteristic of Joyce's narrative technique that he relates variants of the concept of repetition to one another. All the repetitions of 'Good night' cause the parting to have something strangely definitive about it. When we read the short story again, we associate the parting with Gabriel's thoughts right at the end of the text: that the next time he comes here to the sisters' house, the occasion may well be a death. The most important intertextual echo in 'Good night' supports such a reading. One of the last things Ophelia says before she goes mad and drowns is 'Good night, ladies, good night. Sweet ladies, good night, good night' (*Hamlet*, IV. v).

By breaking up the party so definitively all the wishing of 'Good night' further marks the fact that Gabriel and Gretta now want to be alone. Even these wishes take on an element of irony: they form a transition to the subsequent paragraphs, in which the narration conveys Gabriel's feelings for Gretta while also revealing how the two of them distance themselves from each other. This does not imply that Gabriel is presented as particularly naïve in the third part. Although here too he seems self-centred, the characterization of him is still to a certain extent sympathetic. Yet if we ask the reasons for this sympathy, the answers will quickly touch on factors that are concerned with the narrator's distancing himself from Gabriel. Again Joyce combines narrative means in a paradoxical and effective way. One example is the narrator's reference to Gabriel's memory of the 'secret life' he has had with Gretta. The reference is dichotomous; it is emphasized through repetition. First we read that 'Moments of their secret life together burst like stars upon his memory' (p. 214), and in the next paragraph that 'Like the tender fires of stars moments of their life together, that no one knew of or would ever know of, broke upon and illumined his memory' (p. 215). If the reference precisely characterizes Gabriel's memory, it refers just as precisely to Gretta's memory of Michael Furey. A dead intruder means that they are not alone. Yet Michael Furey's intrusion increases their loneliness, separating them from each other by evoking memories in Gretta that depart radically from Gabriel's.

As Gabriel's attempts at approaching Gretta meet unexpected resistance, free indirect thought conveys some of his frustration: 'Why did she seem so abstracted? . . . If she would only turn to him or come to him of her own accord!' (p. 218). When he finally gets round to asking what she is thinking about, her account of her thoughts connected with 'The Lass of Aughrim' precipitates a crisis in their relationship. The gradual progression of the crisis contributes to giving it the character of a climax that is correlated with the ending of 'The Dead'. By linking up with Burke's division of the short story into different stages, we can identify four stages in the midsection of the third part where the crisis between Gabriel and Gretta is made visible.

At first, when Gretta says that she is thinking of the song Mr D'Arcy sang, Gabriel reacts with 'astonishment'. When Gretta then links the song to 'a person I used to know in Galway', he feels 'dull anger'—an incipient jealousy of someone he does not know but who he suspects has made a great impression on Gretta. This jealousy turns into 'a shameful consciousness' when Gretta, in the third part of the quadripartite information chain says that Michael is dead. It is nevertheless the fourth and final piece of information that makes the greatest impression on Gabriel by surprisingly and dramatically relating the unknown Michael's premature death to Gretta:

> 'I think he died for me,' she answered.
>   A vague terror seized Gabriel at this answer as if, at that hour when he had hoped to triumph, some impalpable and vindictive being was coming against him, gathering forces against him in its vague world. (pp. 221–2)

The story of Michael that follows may remind us of an inserted piece of hypodiegetic narration, with Gretta as the strongly committed first-person narrator. In the narrative structure of 'The Dead' this story is a complementary appendix to the dramatic, economically tailored dialogue between Gabriel and Gretta. This dialogue, which is more important than the supplementary story about Michael, is a good example of what Burke calls Joyce's 'narrative equivalent of a Platonic dialogue' (Burke 1975: 413): Gabriel must realize that every step he has taken to get closer to Gretta—including his response to the information about Michael—has actually contributed to an opposite, distancing movement. He has tried reacting understandingly and generously to what Gretta tells; he has also tried being ironic. Both have failed. As an example of narrative precision we note how the dialogue, in the presentation of Gabriel's reaction number two, links back to the episode with Miss Ivors in the story's second part: '"Perhaps that was why you wanted to go to Galway with that Ivors girl?" he said coldly' (p. 220). As we will recall, Joyce uses just this distance-marking adverb to comment on the negative attitude Gabriel has to this invitation: '"You can go if you like", said Gabriel coldly' (p. 191). Gretta's reaction here confirms the adverb the narrator uses, and this reaction is also relevant in relation to the dialogue she has with Gabriel in the third part.

After Gabriel's feeling of 'vague terror' has been confirmed by the story Gretta tells him about Michael, it modulates in the final sequence of the short story to an intense, epiphany-like experience of resignation, loneliness, and self-knowledge. In this final sequence, which begins with the affirmative statement 'She was fast asleep' (p. 223), the third-person narration is focused on Gabriel. The narration is concentrated and suggestive; it provides material for the interpretation of Gabriel, of the relationship between him and Gretta, of 'The Dead', and of *Dubliners*. Since an analysis of this sequence would require a chapter of its own, I can here comment on only a few central points.

We asked above why Gabriel is so nervous about the speech he is to make in the second part. The omniscient narrative discourse in the final sequence provides some of the answer: he is a weaker and more insecure person than he has pretended to be. At the same time it is characteristic of Gabriel that he cannot admit the weak sides of himself to others. Therefore it is crucial that the third-person narrator has insight into his thoughts, as in this central paragraph which forms the basis for Gabriel's concluding vision of the snow:

> Generous tears filled Gabriel's eyes. He had never felt like that himself towards any woman but he knew that such a feeling must be love. The tears gathered more thickly in his eyes and in the partial darkness he imagined he saw the form of a young man standing under a dripping tree. Other forms were near. His soul had approached that region where dwell the vast hosts of the dead. He was conscious of, but could not apprehend, their wayward and flickering existence. (p. 224)

As Florence Walzl puts it, 'Gabriel's sudden realization that he has never experienced a love like this brings with it the discovery that he has never lived to the full depth of being' (Walzl 1975: 436). Such an interpretation seems reasonable and so does Walzl's next point: 'Hence to his wife he is less real than Michael Furey, this shade of her youth.' Paradoxically, the short story's most dramatic confrontation occurs so to speak at the extremities of the text: not only presented in thought (imagined by Gabriel), it is also a confrontation with a dead person. A further paradox is that in the imagined confrontation Michael appears as stronger, more youthfully vital than Gabriel. The latter paradox has an ironic element, but it will vary from reader to reader how much irony we see in the relationship between the narrator and Gabriel at this late stage of the text. In my reading the narrator's marked distance from Gabriel clearly implies an ironic attitude, but the irony (to bring in a point in Pecora's analysis) is modified by the process towards disillusioned self-knowledge that Gabriel undergoes.

The short story's narrative economy is in the final sequence closely related to the symbolism of the snow and death, and furthermore to several contrasting pairs such as light–darkness, warmth–cold, and east–west. The naming of Gabriel and Michael is also significant; it has a characterizing function both through associations with the actual names and through qualities the third-person narrator attaches to each of them. In both the Jewish and the Christian occult traditions the four principal angels—Michael, Gabriel, Raphael, and Uriel—correspond with the four elements, seasons, and wind directions. Michael symbolically represents the element water: he is called the 'snow prince' and is associated with silver; Gabriel represents fire: he is called the 'prince of fire' and is associated with gold (cf. *Encyclopaedia Judaica*, xi. 1491). Another polarity between the two is that, as an archangel, Michael ranks above Gabriel as an angel, and as a third contrast we may add that in the New

Testament tradition Michael is primarily associated with the day of the Last Judgement and Gabriel with the announcement of the birth of Jesus. The text which in addition to the Bible is most clearly alluded to here is Dante's *The Divine Comedy*. That region 'where dwell the vast hosts of the dead' is practically synonymous with Dante's universe, and Joyce's contrasting of light–darkness and fire–cold also seems inspired by *The Divine Comedy*. This applies in particular to the epic's first part, *Inferno*, although the intense light which in *Paradiso* is linked to the colour white stands in an intertextual relation to the meaning-charged use of this colour in 'The Dead'. To say that the colour white is charged with meaning is not to connect it with *one* meaning; rather, it is characterized by semantic ambiguity. Through an elegant combination of dialogue and third-person comment, the colour white is related to innocence, to love and intense feelings, to snow, to death and the dead, and to Gabriel's 'journey westward'.

The qualitative contrasts we have identified are interesting in relation to 'The Dead' because the narrative discourse is so designed that several of them are constantly actualized. Michael Furey, for example, is associated with the cold, sometimes in connection with rain, sometimes with snow. This observation also applies to the imaginary confrontation which Gabriel has with Michael in the hotel room, a confrontation which culminates in the beginning of the next paragraph as 'a few light taps upon the pane made him turn to the window' (p. 225). When the two words 'light taps' are linked to the snow in the following sentence, the reader has already associated them with the gravel Michael threw up against Gretta's window. Thus the narration draws Gabriel's confrontation with Michael over into the final paragraph of the short story.

The way in which Joyce combines reporting narrative statement and commentary makes the structural east–west contrast thematically productive. Here too we are confronted with a thematic opening move that is characterized by ambiguity and provides the basis for different interpretations. On the diegetic level, there is a contrast between the main action in the east (the Christmas party in Dublin) and the west of Ireland with the Aran Isles and the waves of the Shannon. On this level, east is associated with the relatively urbane (or less provincial) and west with the more primitive—which true enough is qualified in the vision of death and the churchyard that Gabriel has right at the end. However, as this narrative analysis has shown, such a contrast comes to seem simplistic and partly wrong—among other things because the third-person narrative not only communicates but also questions the 'positive' values linked to the east. Joyce develops this narrative problematizing through another east–west contrast which both supplements and deconstructs the first. This second contrast, which is closely related to characterization through dialogue and third-person comment, establishes east as old, fossilized, and paralysed, while west appears as vital and strong. The relationship between these two contrasting pairs is not stable, but neither does the lat-ter pair completely oust the first. In any event the evaluation of these contrasts (and the relationship between them) is intimately connected with how we interpret the concluding vision Gabriel has.

In Joyce studies this vision, as it is narratively designed in the last paragraph of 'The Dead', is usually called an 'epiphany'. The word is Greek and is generally used of gods who show themselves, manifest themselves. More par-ticularly, in classical Greek drama it may refer to the climax that arises when a god reveals himself on the stage and clears up its conflicts. Joyce uses the con-cept in a special but related way: in his case it refers to situations in which things or people show their true character or essence. To evaluate Gabriel's concluding vision as an epiphany does not necessarily entail seeing the final sequence as a synthesizing movement that forms the basis for an overall theme. The epiphany is also too complex and too polysemous for that, among other things since it is based on a movement beyond *both* the east–west con-trasts we have been discussing, while also reaching back to content structures and symbols (particularly the snow) that have already been established as important.

The interpretation of the epiphany Gabriel has right at the end of 'The Dead' quickly becomes the determining factor for the direction of the inter-pretation of the text as a whole—whether by 'text' one means this short story or the collection of stories called *Dubliners*. Many believe that the epiphany reveals a new insight on the part of Gabriel, that it reflects the final point of the painful process of maturation that the third part in particular dramatizes. Against this interpretation others (such as Pecora) argue that the 'essence' in Gabriel's epiphany becomes problematized, perhaps even eliminated, as soon as one attempts to determine what he actually gets insight into. My own view is that Gabriel does no doubt go through a process of maturation but that it is qualified by marked elements of disillusion and resignation.

Such a view may gain support from further consideration of the concept of repetition as we have been using it until now in this analysis. As we will recall from Chapter 3, one distinctive feature of repetition is to combine narrative and thematic functions. In relation to 'The Dead', this theoretical point may be related to how the different variants of repetition contribute both to establish-ing and characterizing the crucial but polysemous process through which Gabriel goes. Hélène Cixous notes that 'Joyce's work is crossed right through by a subject-waiting-for-itself which assumes the formal appearance of a quest, an apprenticeship, a journey, of all those literary genres where the advent of the self finds its niche and is proclaimed . . . with never a definitive way out, with no conclusion' (Cixous 1984: 15–16). This point is most apt for the early Joyce. Cixous shows that the narrative presentation of what she calls 'discrediting the subject' in Joyce is to a high degree based on repetition. Her main example is 'The Sisters'—the short story that opens the collection of short stories that 'The Dead' concludes. In 'The Sisters' Joyce uses a first-person narrator to create repetition even in the first sentence: 'There was no hope for him this time: it was the third stroke' (p. 1). What we have here, believes Cixous, is 'anaphora, the sign of repetition from the very first sentence: there has been a series, *involution*, closing up of repetition in identity . . . instead of evolution' (Cixous 1984: 23).

In 'The Dead' too the text brings in repetition at an early stage. A relatively simple example is to be found at the beginning of the second paragraph: 'It was always a great affair, the Misses Morkan's annual dance' (p. 175); and when the third-person narrator repeats the word snow, this is a narrative act that contributes to making the snow into a symbol. Parallel with this move the word 'snow' becomes semantically loaded in a way that extends the meaning thematically. This is most clear in the final paragraph, where there is reference to the snow—Gabriel's observation of the fact that it is snowing—in every single sentence but one: 'The time had come for him to set out on his journey westward.' Indeed, when we read on, we see that the key word 'westward' closely links the snow to this sentence too:

> Yes, the newspapers were right: snow was general all over Ireland. It was falling on every part of the dark central plain, on the treeless hills, falling softly upon the Bog of Allen and, farther westward, softly falling into the dark mutinous Shannon waves. It was falling, too, upon every part of the lonely churchyard on the hill where Michael Furey lay buried. (p. 225)

If the numerous references to the snow modulate the narration towards Gabriel's perspective, we can relate another variant of the concept of repetition to the speech Gabriel makes at the dinner. Here we can bring in Hillis Miller's distinction between two forms of repetition. As in Blixen's 'Babette's Feast', the dinner is a kernel event in the text. It is linked to different catalysts (such as Miss Ivors's provocative questions to Gabriel), and it forms both an endpoint and a basis for a new development. As an endpoint the dinner can be related to Miller's first form of repetition: it enters into an annual series of such dinners, integrated in a long tradition and with a well-established pattern, in which the speech by Gabriel has a set place and a harmonizing function.

One of the first textual signals that this dinner may nevertheless break the established, safe pattern is conveyed to us by the unexpected nervousness Gabriel displays before the speech. Indeed, as the action develops, he really *has* reason to be nervous. The dinner conversation contributes to the fact that Mr D'Arcy sings 'The Lass of Aughrim', with the dramatic consequences this has for the main characters. A party and a dinner speech that are ostensibly like many previous ones become fundamentally different. The way is opened for the second form of repetition by revealing a destabilizing, phantasmal world in which Gretta—the one person Gabriel ought to know best of all—appears as a stranger, and in which an unknown, dead person appears as the stronger in an imaginary confrontation. However, it would be oversimplifying to conclude that 'The Dead' unambiguously dramatizes a movement from the first to the second form of repetition. For Gabriel's epiphany also qualifies the *second* form of repetition. Further, even if we do not read the ending as conciliatory, it is a thought-provoking paradox that those qualities the text associates with the destabilizing and menacing Michael Furey perhaps characterize the first form of repetition more than the second. The narrative technique in 'The Dead' creates a thematic ambiguity that opens the way for different interpretations. Yet in addition it provides a necessary basis for interpretation; and it may provide a point of reference against which we can assess different interpretations.

IV

The references so far to John Huston's adaptation of 'The Dead' indicate that I judge it positively. It remains to justify such an evaluation better and to comment on some important aspects of the film that we have so far not touched upon. From Chapter 4 we will recall that adapting a literary prose text for the screen will as a rule, in addition to the radical changes connected with the transition from a literary medium to a visual one, entail a series of choices between textual elements in the literary original, since far from all of them can be included in the film. This in itself simple fact—which Stuart McDougal in *Made into Movies* calls 'contraction' (McDougal 1985: 4)—is to a high degree determined by differences of medium, something which often makes it irrelevant to criticize a film for not containing this or that textual element from the text it is inspired by or based on.

Yet there is a difference between texts considered as a basis for filming. Clearly, since 'The Dead' is a short story and not a novel, the director can 'transfer' a greater part of the discourse to the screen than it is possible to do with *Ulysses* for instance. On the other hand, a short text may well be thematically complex because 'discourse' refers not only to the action but also to narrative comments, imagery, and other literary devices. When it comes to Joyce, we can safely state that it is extremely difficult to adapt his texts, and it does not become any less demanding if the director chooses to attempt a relatively 'direct' transfer from literary to filmic text. It is precisely this that John Huston has done—unusually successfully. True enough, there will as a rule be some degree of variation in how different people judge an adaptation; it depends for example on the attitude one adopts to the question of 'media transfer'. Still, the main reason why criticism of Huston's *The Dead* has been broadly positive is suggested by the meticulous respect for the literary original the film shows. Now of course such respect can manifest itself in different ways—I do not mean that Francis Ford Coppola, for instance, has less respect for Joseph Conrad than Huston has for Joyce. As films *The Dead* and *Apocalypse Now* exemplify the range in the way in which an adaptation may be done. While Coppola is strongly inspired by Conrad and selectively draws in narrative and thematic elements from *Heart of Darkness*, the most striking indication of respect on the part of Huston lies perhaps in what he does *not* do: the film's plot is so similar to that of Joyce's short story that parts of the literary text approximate to a screenplay. This said, Huston's *The Dead* is a work of art in its own right; to draw attention to Huston's respect for Joyce is certainly not to suggest that the film's effects (and meaning) are identical with those of the literary text.

Since Huston has chosen to add so little, the few additions there are become all the more interesting. I shall comment on the two most important ones, which are both integrated into the main part though they show different sides of the relationship between verbal and filmic fiction. The tripartite action structure in the short story can also be used of the film. While the first part follows the text closely, the most important (actually the only important) addition in the second part is connected with the introduction of a new character. His name is Mr Grace, an older colleague of Gabriel's. Mr Grace participates in the dinner conversation in a way that partly replaces Browne's utterances in the short story, but his most important function is to recite a poem. This poem, which in other words is not to be found in the literary text, is interpolated between the piano piece played by Mary Jane and the conversation Gabriel has with Miss Ivors. It is a poem about 'broken vows', and Mr Grace apologizes for its seriousness. This is how the last eight lines of 'Broken Vows' appear as written text:

> You have taken the east from me.
> You have taken the west from me.
> You have taken what is before me,
> and what is behind me.
> You have taken the moon,
> you have taken the sun from me.
> And my fear is great:
> you have taken God from me.

Among the elements in the poem are dream and longing, but most strongly it expresses disillusion, disappointment, and criticism of the person addressed by the speaker. Mr Grace explains that the poem has been translated from Irish (Gaelic) by Lady Gregory, and it is presented as an anonymous poem from the Irish poetic tradition. Born in County Galway, Lady Gregory (1852–1932) was a central figure in the Irish literary revival; her interest in Celtic mythology led her to study Gaelic and pursue manuscript research.

In the film the poem is related to the conflict which awaits Gabriel and Gretta, but which neither of them is at this stage prepared for. This proleptic

Why is Gabriel so nervous before giving his speech? Donal McGann as Gabriel in John Huston's *The Dead*.

'Ladies and Gentlemen. It is not the first time that we have gathered together under this hospitable roof, around this hospitable board . . .' (James Joyce, 'The Dead', 203). Gabriel (Donal McGann) gives the dinner speech in John Huston's *The Dead*.

function is made clear through three of the comments on the song. The variation in these comments is interesting. The first response comes when one of the female guests exclaims: 'Imagine being in love like that!'—an utterance that points forward to the intense love relationship between Gretta and

Michael. Then we have D'Arcy's comment, 'It would have made a lovely song', thus linking the poem to 'The Lass of Aughrim', which he sings later and which we have discussed above. The last comment diverges from the first two by being more exclusively filmic: when the listeners give Mr Grace a round of applause for his recitation of the poem, the camera focuses on the face of Gretta, who seems strangely confused and upset. Thus the adaptation invites us to draw a parallel between Gretta's reaction to the poem and her reaction to 'The Lass of Aughrim'. All these comments invite interpretation and are variously proleptic, but in a way that conforms well with the text on which the film is based. Who is speaking in the poem? The most obvious choice is to relate the person speaking to Gretta and 'you' to Gabriel, but other combinations are also possible—such as that Michael addresses Gretta or she Michael. I do not say that the latter possibilities are probable, but surely the lack of identification of the two speakers makes the viewer wonder about their identity. Thus, in one of the additions he permits himself, Huston preserves something of the thematic ambiguity that characterizes Joyce's short story.

The adaptation of the final sequence confronts a director with great challenges, particularly when it comes to conveying filmically Gabriel's epiphany. The attempt Huston makes is supported by the performances of the actors Donal McCann and Anjelica Huston as Gretta. In a narrative context it is nevertheless the way in which Huston conveys Gabriel's thoughts that is most interesting. Joyce here confronts the director Huston with a problem that can be formulated simply but which is far from simple to solve: how to show and communicate filmically the powerful experience of existential crisis and new insight concentrated in Gabriel's epiphany. For even though film can combine images and words (the visual element, which a camera mercilessly reveals, and the auditive, which a microphone exactly records) into effective narration, it has no instrument corresponding to the third-person narrator's nuanced presentation of a character's thoughts and feelings.

The solution Huston chooses is perhaps the best he has at his disposal. He does not let Gabriel speak, something which would have seemed artificial and improbable, given the situation (with Gretta sleeping in the same room) and the character the epiphany has, but instead inserts a voice-over which fairly exactly communicates the same thoughts as the third-person narrator does in the short story. It is difficult to see that the ending of the adaptation could have been conveyed without such a voice. And yet the way in which the voice is used here reveals an important difference between verbal and filmic fiction. For although the camera shows that Gabriel is not speaking, his voice in the film sounds personal, something which marks a break with the short story's third-person narrative. The important elements of distancing and ambiguity, which in Joyce's text are linked to the third-person narration (with its character-oriented modulations), Huston preserves mainly through the way in which he uses the camera. In an interview he gave in 1982, Huston said that 'the things the camera does are what the eye does also' (Brill 1997: 223). The images the camera shows are related to Gabriel's vision, yet they are affirmative in a way that, even though the form is different, conveys something of the same narrative authority as the third-person narrator.

The filmic communication of the short story's final paragraph produces— through the combination of voice (personally conveying Gabriel's thoughts) and images of what this voice is thinking about—thematic effects that in part correspond to those we find in the final passage of the literary text. Both cinematography and cutting follow the text relatively exactly, and it seems reasonable to end the film by letting the camera dwell on the snow that is falling over Ireland. *How* similar (or different) the final thematic effects in the literary text and its adaptation appear will vary from reader to reader and from viewer to viewer. For Franz Stanzel, the personal voice-over gives the adaptation a completely different ending from Joyce's text:

> This shift from third to first person reduces the dimension of meaning from near-universal validity to Gabriel's subjectively limited personal view. Such a procedure, probably induced by the necessities of the camera art, throws light on the difficulty, if not the impossibility, of rendering in the medium of film the precarious equilibrium between figural and narrative voices achieved in the story through free indirect style. (Stanzel 1992: 121)

A 'figural' voice in Stanzel's terminology is a voice that 'reflects' what a character thinks and perceives (cf. Stanzel 1986: 5). His point is that in the short story Joyce filters such a recording voice through the third-person narrator. Thus Gabriel's subjectively experienced thoughts are placed in a larger narrative frame, something which is crucial to the complexity in the symbolism of the snow. In the adaptation's presentation of the final section, on the other hand, Gabriel's subjective reflections dominate over the more distanced narrative presentation in the short story. Stanzel is perhaps right that this difference contributes to making the end of the film less thematically pregnant than the short story's ending. If the difference is not so striking as Stanzel believes, it is because (by concentrating on the voice) he places too little weight on the distancing effects of Huston's use of the camera.

Another difference between the film and the literary text is to be found a little earlier in the story. Towards the end of the second long paragraph in the final sequence, different impressions from the party pass through Gabriel's mind. This narrative variation, which starts as an explicit internal analepsis, tends towards an external prolepsis when the narrator reports Gabriel thinking that 'soon, perhaps, he would be sitting in that same drawing-room, dressed in black, his silk hat on his knees' (p. 224). Even if Gabriel, in the depressed mood he is in, feels in his bones that a death in the Morkan family may be imminent, this is something he *thinks*. When the film *shows* a brief but clear glimpse of Gabriel placed in the situation of mourning he imagines, the actual visualization has the effect of confirming what Gabriel is thinking about, although in the short story this has not yet happened. Still, viewed as a whole the film, as a relatively direct adaptation of a complex literary text, is unusually perceptive and tactfully made. In spite of the partly media-governed limitations of which Stanzel provides examples, the film presents the short story's plot in a manner which confirms, and extends, the reading experience of many viewers. Through the aesthetic structure of the narrative fiction film, Huston's adaptation accentuates, qualifies, and further explores thematic and formal aspects of the literary text.

It is difficult to conclude a discussion of Joyce. 'It is always too late with Joyce,' comments Jacques Derrida (1984: 145). His title announces 'Two words for Joyce', yet his discussion of 'HE WAR' fills fifteen densely printed pages. It is true that these two words are from *Finnegans Wake*—Joyce's last literary text and a much more difficult one than 'The Dead'. If, as Umberto Eco believes in *The Aesthetics of Chaosmos*, Joyce here 'bend[s] language to express "everything"' (Eco 1989: 83–4), this chapter has attempted to show how already in 'The Dead' Joyce uses literary language in a narratively effective and thematically productive manner. Thus this short story—in addition to having a great value of its own—forms part of the basis for both *Ulysses* and *Finnegans Wake*, at the same time as, inspired by Ibsen's drama, it builds further on Flaubert's precisely observant realism.

7

Joseph Conrad's *Heart of Darkness* and Francis Ford Coppola's *Apocalypse Now*

If 'The Dead' is short story tending towards becoming a short novel, Joseph Conrad's *Heart of Darkness* is a short novel (or 'novella') that is more complex than many full-length novels. This kind of literary complexity implies that there are significant aspects of Conrad's text that cannot be properly considered in a narrative analysis. Yet it also signals that this enigmatic, multi-layered tale cannot be adequately understood without close attention being paid to its narrative strategies. Moreover, at a different yet related level, the novella's complexity implies that we read *Heart of Darkness* differently depending on how well acquainted we are with the author and the text itself, what questions we ask about the text and how we put them, what critical terms we use, and what interests influence us in our critical activity.

Jürgen Habermas's concept of human *interest*, which can be related to all the analyses presented in Part II, is perhaps especially relevant to readings of *Heart of Darkness* and *To the Lighthouse*. To summarize his position, we can say that Habermas regards 'interest' as a concept that supplements what Hans-Georg Gadamer refers to as the critic's 'horizon' or 'horizon of understanding' (Gadamer 1975). The way in which we read and understand literature, Habermas claims, is not solely governed by the horizon of understanding within which we are working—and which is variable in space and time and from reader to reader. Our reading is also influenced by how interested we are in the subject-matter of our reading; and this interest is further shaped by language and by the exercise of power in its diverse manifestations (Habermas 1973: 54). We may further relate the components of language and power to other concepts such as gender, race, and social class. Significant aspects of the problems associated with these concepts are explored in *Heart of Darkness*. Concomitantly, issues related to the

Joseph Conrad, *Heart of Darkness* [1899/1902], Oxford World's Classics, ed. Cedric Watts (Oxford: Oxford University Press, 1998). Francis Ford Coppola, *Apocalypse Now* (1979); video, Zoetrope Studios.

concepts of language, power, gender, race, and class are variously observable in the many different interpretations Conrad's novella has provoked—and continues to provoke.

The essential point to be made here is that, more insistently than most narratives, *Heart of Darkness* actualizes what Anthony Fothergill, in a helpful introductory book on this novella, calls 'the process of orientation' by which we approach the text:

> By 'orientation' I mean the largely unconscious give and take, the processes of assimilation of information, ordering, judgement, and imaginative reconstruction, and all the other delicate forms of readerly activity by which we negotiate the text. It is as if we are in dialogue with the text, with another voice. We are one half of a conversation (unspeaking but by no means passive) through which its material, language, comes to meaning. (Fothergill 1989: 13–14)

Although, obviously, such a comment on the process of reading is applicable not only to *Heart of Darkness*, Conrad's novella illustrates exceptionally well the connections between the critic's starting-point, perspective, and approach on the one hand, and his or her interpretation on the other. It follows that no analysis, including one concerned with the novella's narrative, is 'neutral' in relation to the text. A narrative analysis represents a type of sustained textual focus—a critical attention to language and form that presupposes an appreciation of the literary text as an aesthetic structure but that may entail improper, or insufficient, consideration of other important issues such as, for instance, the question of textual ideology. And yet again, all literary interpretation assumes a selective method of questioning (cf. the quotation from Paul Armstrong's *Conflicting Readings* in Chapter 1), and most critics agree that in *Heart of Darkness* Conrad's narrative method constitutes a decisive link between narrative and thematic structure. J. Hillis Miller relates this aspect of the novella to what he regards as a parabolic feature of *Heart of Darkness*: in a manner reminiscent of the parable, Conrad's novella dramatizes (through narrative form) a 'simple' and 'realistic' plot. Yet the meaning and implications of the characters' actions are ambiguous, tending like the parable to provoke interpretation while at the same time complicating the reader's interpretative activity.

As *Heart of Darkness* is our main example of first-person narrative, this chapter will discuss this narrative variant as it is moulded in this work. First, I shall be commenting on two non-fictional texts that Conrad wrote in Africa prior to *Heart of Darkness*. The second section of the chapter will focus on important aspects of the novella's narrative method, paying particular attention to those aspects that bear a relevance to Francis Ford Coppola's film *Apocalypse Now*. The final section then proceeds to discuss *Apocalypse Now*, the classic film on the Vietnam War released in 1979 and strongly inspired by Conrad's novella.

I

Born in the Russian-held part of Poland in 1857, Joseph Conrad was a conservative Polish anti-Russian nationalist who, after leaving Poland for France in 1874, became a sailor and later qualified as a master mariner in the British merchant navy. He became a British citizen in 1886 and settled permanently in England in the 1890s, embarking on a new career as a writer of fiction. Conrad is the author of a number of works whose originality and influence on later generations of writers are remarkable. His most impressive achievement ('my largest canvas', as he himself commented) is perhaps the novel *Nostromo* (1904)—an unusually complex literary work that at one level incorporates a prophetic, fictional vision of the effects of imperialist forces in Latin America during the twentieth century.

The thematic, ideological relevance of novels such as *Nostromo* and *Under Western Eyes* (1911) has contributed to Conrad's being canonized as a modern classic. Even so, the world-wide interest in his works cannot just be explained by a sense of thematic and political urgency: equally important is the way in which the author generates, shapes, and intensifies his thematics through a variety of literary devices, means, and variations. We cannot, for instance, isolate the critique of imperialism in *Nostromo* from the narrative strategies used by Conrad to formulate that critique. If we do, we reduce the novel's rhetorical persuasiveness, humane appeal, and sense of urgency forged through a combination of personal experience, intellectual insight, and imaginative power.

In Conrad's fiction the motif of imperialism is associated with, and tends to provoke, imperialist critique. That this critique can be implicit rather than explicit, covert as well as overt, certainly does not make it less powerful. Reading the early short story 'An Outpost of Progress' (1897), for example, we infer that the main characters are two Belgians in Africa. Yet their nationality is not actually mentioned, and, as Cedric Watts has pointed out, the short story's 'degree of reticence encourages us to consider how far the tale's criticisms may apply to colonialism in general' (Watts 1998: p. ix). A similar point could be made about *Heart of Darkness*—and indeed Watts does so in his study (1977) of this novella. If in the former short story 'progress', the key word of the title, needs to be read ironically in order to be understood, in the later novella the critique of imperialism is inseparable from, and largely dependent on, the irony with which all of the narrative (again, including its title) is infused. To stress the interplay of irony (as a formal element) and imperialist critique (as an aspect of content) is to draw attention to the ways in which *Heart of Darkness* operates as literature, as a work of fiction. (Whether irony is a suitable way of expressing this kind of critique is another matter.)

As in *Nostromo*, the plot of *Heart of Darkness* unfolds for the most part outside Europe. Writing the novella, however, Conrad seems to have drawn to a greater extent upon his own experiences than when working with *Nostromo*. I stress the word *seems* because, in Conrad as in fiction generally, the links between personal experience and the literary text produced by a person are subtle and indirect. Still, to say that the relationship is indirect does not mean that it is unimportant or uninteresting. In spite of Conrad's claim in his 'Author's Note' to *Heart of Darkness* that the novella is 'experience pushed a little (and only very little) beyond the actual facts of the case' (Kimbrough 1988: 4), this text is a fascinating example of the complex relationship between personal experience and literary presentation.

Early in 1890 Conrad signed a three-year contract as officer on a river boat operated by the Belgian concern for trading in the Congo, the Société Anonyme Belge pour le Commerce du Haut-Congo. When he left for the Congo, Conrad was unavoidably, for all his deap-seated scepticism, influenced by contemporary ideas of Europe's civilizing mission in Africa. On his return to Britain half a year later, not only was he ill physically and mentally, his scepticism about human nature seems to have been reinforced by the shocking experiences the trip to Africa led to. Furthermore, it is as though the journey to Africa curiously converges with Conrad's childhood experiences in Poland and with later experiences during his life as a sailor. As Zdzisław Najder (1983, 1997) has shown in convincing detail, Conrad's Polish background was fundamentally marked by a series of events and traumas variously related to imperialist oppression. The title of Norman Davies's history of Poland, *God's Playground*, succinctly indicates something of this experience. Conrad's country had vanished from the map of Europe after being annexed by Russia from the east, Prussia from the west, and Austria from the south-west, and his own family had suffered deeply as a result. Nor was Conrad in a position to identify with the victims of colonialism and imperialism: partly because his background was that of the Polish ruling class (the *szlachta*), partly because he, as an officer in the British merchant marine, was an integral part of an enormous imperialist system towards which his attitudes were mixed (that is, neither unambiguously supportive nor wholly critical), and last but not least because as a writer he was dependent on the interest and sympathy of his readers in order to survive and support his family.

Conrad wrote *Heart of Darkness* unusually swiftly. The text was composed immediately before another work, the novel *Lord Jim* (1900), where Conrad also uses Marlow as a narrator. To the extent that formal and thematic fragmentation is characteristic of European modernism, *Heart of Darkness* complies with an important constituent aspect of modernist literature. Yet even though the novella is fragmentary in a number of ways, it is remarkable how the different fragments are joined together, thus curiously destabilizing the text and making the narrative discourse more dynamic and engrossing. *Heart of Darkness* is a fragmentary text not just narratively and thematically, but also intertextually through allusions to writers ranging from Virgil through Dante down to more recent travel literature. The text is fragmentary in another way too, as it reflects Conrad's need for distance from his personal experiences in the Congo in order to give those experiences a literary, fictional form. In an essay on *Heart of Darkness*, Peter Madsen writes:

> Language is more than a dictionary and a grammar, but this 'more' is not, as the formalist-structuralist poetics would have it, like a specifically literary grammar which is neutral in relation to experience. Literary forms are formulations of experience—they are, as Adorno puts it, sedimentation of experience (*Erfahrung*). The narrative forms are of this kind. Any new story is related to earlier stories to the extent that these have interfered with the author's formulation of experience . . . But the word 'narrative' is ambiguous. Pointing beyond the text itself, it refers not only to the chain of events (the 'story'), but also the act of narration. The narrator narrates something (the 'narrative'); this 'narration' is a linguistic act, an act of discourse—and as such an uttering (*énonciation*) bringing forth a statement (*énoncé*). The 'discourse' (the linguistic chain) is a multidimensional phenomenon of which the 'story' (the chain of events) is just one dimension. Yet it has a specific role to play: it is the thread that holds the discursive web together, but the pattern that emerges from the web is not only governed by the story's sequence of events. (Madsen 1995: 131–2)

Madsen gives here a nuanced view of the complex relationship between personal experience and literary presentation. As indicated above, one of the reasons why *Heart of Darkness* provides such a telling fictional illustration of the issues Madsen raises is suggested by the intricate and indirect ways in which the novella is related to, and draws on, Conrad's Congo experience.

Now Conrad is actually the author of two non-fictional texts that may be situated in the space or distance between the individual experience of his journey on the river Congo and *Heart of Darkness* as 'sedimentation of experience' (Adorno). The two texts are like pieces from a large but incomplete jigsaw, providing fascinating glimpses of the raw material which constituted an experiential and epistemological basis for the writing of *Heart of Darkness*. And yet, as Najder reminds us, 'the finished product should not be treated in the same way as raw material' (Najder 1983: 493).

The first text is directly related to, in fact the result of, Conrad's duties as an officer on the *Roi des Belges*. Conrad commenced the 'Up-river Book' on 3 August 1890. The text takes the form of factual notes, all related to the traffic on the Congo river and taken by Conrad in his professional capacity as captain: 'On leaving—from A after passing the two islands steer for clump—high tree. two is[land] points. Sandy beach. [Two sketches with contours of land and islands, marked: No 1, trees, sandy, point, bay, foul, and stones]' (Conrad 1978: 17). The two sketches, none of which are included in Najder's edition of 'Up-river Book', are characteristic of this kind of discourse. For the reader, and one is led to think of Conrad's professional colleagues here, the sketches would be charged with relevant and possibly invaluable information. Pertaining directly to the traffic on the river, this kind of information serves to define and delimit the discourse of the 'Up-river Book': another captain would probably have taken much the same notes as Conrad did.

Having said this, we must be careful not to oversimplify this kind of non-fictional discourse: neither the selective criteria nor the discourse in which they are embedded are as neutral or ideologically innocent as they may appear at first glance. Thus the way in which the passage provides topographical information is reminiscent of travel narratives from and about Africa in the nineteenth century. Like David Livingstone's *Narrative of an Expedition to the Zambesi* (1866), for example, Conrad's 'Up-river Book' privileges a form of information whose assumed significance is indicated by its usefulness for other travellers. I employ the term 'usefulness' advisedly, suggesting that the landscape—be it the river on which Conrad is manoeuvring or the plain Livingstone is traversing—is being mapped for the benefit of later European travellers. The implied reader is a European rather than a 'native'; in one sense the 'Up-river Book' affirms an imperialist position and perspective in the nautical vocabulary it employs and in the careful cataloguing of observable objects. Implied in the overall discourse, these assumptions sometimes become more explicit. That the text's only indication of human activity ashore takes the form of a reference to the Catholic Mission lends support to a generalized point Mary Louise Pratt makes: landscape descriptions in European nineteenth-century travel narrative from and about Africa (the two non-fictional texts by Conrad we are considering can be seen as variants on this genre) tend towards eliminating current inhabitants from the environment (Pratt 1994: 204). If, as far as landscape description is concerned, the 'Up-river Book' is also possessed of qualities untypical of the predominant contemporary travel literature, the reasons for this discrepancy are partly explained by the codified language of professional seamanship: had Conrad been travelling up the Thames rather than the Congo, references to human beings would still have been largely eliminated from his discourse. Yet I venture to posit a subtle kind of link between the auditively registering and visually observant accuracy which characterizes 'Up-river Book' and the series of more personal observations which inform the discourse of Conrad's 'Congo Diary'.

The 'Congo Diary' is the only journal known to have been kept by Conrad—possibly because, at this geographical spot and at this point in time, he felt a need for a kind of writing which could supplement the rather mechanical exercise of the 'Up-river Book' and his habitual letter-writing. In spite of significant differences between these two texts, however, the discourse of 'Congo Diary' is closer to that of the 'Up-river Book' than to the literary discourse of *Heart of Darkness*. Predictably, the diary's discourse is marked by generic conventions associated with diaries. Maurice Blanchot has observed of Kafka's diaries that they 'foreground someone who has lived rather than one who has written' (Blanchot 1995: 2). Signalling the inescapably autobiographical element in any diary entry, such a foregrounding of personal experience is noticeable in Conrad's 'Congo Diary' too: 'Feel considerably in doubt about the future. Think just now that my life amongst the people (white) around here cannot be very comfortable. Intend avoid acquaintances as much as possible' (Conrad 1978: 7). We notice the combination of personal impression and reflection in these sentences. But we also note that a connection is established between the factual and highly selective information of the 'Up-river Book' and the reflections serving to characterize the diary. To put this another way, Conrad is led to think like this by the setting and situation in which he is placed. If I go on to suggest that part of the literary quality of *Heart of Darkness* resides in the indirect yet strong linkage established between Marlow's experiences in the Congo and the scepticism about the imperialist enterprise, then I have also indicated a kind of literary potential or signal in Conrad's diary.

The reader's knowledge of *Heart of Darkness* discloses other such signals as well: '24th. Gosse and R. C. gone with a large lot of ivory down to Boma. On G.['s] return to start up the river. Have been myself busy packing ivory in casks. Idiotic employment. Health good up to now' ('Congo Diary', 7). 'Ivory' is an example of a specific physical object that makes an impression on Conrad at the time of the experience; eight years later, it is transformed into a powerful literary symbol in *Heart of Darkness*. As we have seen in Chapter 6, two distinctive features of the symbol are its elusiveness and its interpretative suggestiveness: once we specify what a symbol means, its symbolic quality is reduced. What the reference to ivory in the 'Congo Diary' reminds the reader of *Heart of Darkness* of is this particular symbol's presence as a physical object. Metonymically representing the elephant, and symbolically in one sense representing all of Africa, its great market value was one of the reasons for the struggle with competitors for natural resources which Conrad witnessed in the Congo. The Belgians' exploitation was as ruthless as that of Mobutu has been in recent years, and the violence associated with it is indicated in a sentence further on in the diary: 'Saw another dead body lying by the path in an attitude of meditative repose' (p. 9). The word 'another' is curiously meaningful in the sentence, suggesting that death accompanies the Europeans' presence in Africa as a matter of course. The sentence presents, in remarkably condensed form, the particular combination of qualities so characteristic of the diary as a whole: factual information based on visual impression on the one hand, and reflections provoked by these impressions on the other.

Now, although these two non-fictional texts constitute no autobiography of Conrad in the Congo they could certainly provide material for one, in which case they would have served—combined with and as a supplement to Conrad's letters from the Congo—as constituent aspects of an autobiography proper. John Sturrock has observed that autobiography suggests the idea of a 'thought whole . . . a life storied is a life made meaningful, and any life, however vapid, is at least storiable' (Sturrock 1993: 20). The paradigm of autobiographical stories in Western culture is St Augustine's *Confessions*. The tone of this introspective story of Augustine's conversion is deliberate and reflective. Augustine was baptized as a Christian in Milan in 387; his *Confessions* were not published in North Africa until ten years later. Such a strategy of deferment is also observable in Conrad: compare the temporal distance of eight years between the 'Up-river Book'/'Congo Journal' and *Heart of Darkness*. Having said this, the narrative and thematic difference between the former two texts and the literary discourse of *Heart of Darkness* needs to be emphasized: contrasting with Augustine, the temporal distance between the central experience and the extended writing it provokes is in Conrad correlated with a movement from autobiographical entry to fictional account. To underline such a difference between the two former texts and *Heart of Darkness*, however, is not to disregard the important issue of how, and to what extent, literature refers to an 'outer reality', and how it can represent, through the dynamics of verbal fiction, individual and collective experience.

The autobiographical elements observable in the 'Congo Diary' indicate how, to use Walter Benjamin's concepts, in simple narrative forms *Erzählung* (narrative) becomes an agent of *Erfahrung* (experience) (Benjamin 1979a: 84–5). Returning home, the traveller imparts his experience of distant places; thus, for Benjamin, the traveller becomes a narrator whose compulsion to narrate is complemented by the listeners' desire to serve as an audience. As the diary approximates to a fragmented autobiography, its narrative features are highlighted, thus obliquely supporting Benjamin's notion that the act of travel can be formative in the sense of generating experience, as well as Sturrock's understanding of the genre of autobiography as self-storying, and retrospectively selected and organized, life experience. To draw attention to the diary as a narrative is to say that, as a narrative, it is highly fragmented and disconnected; indeed the diary's literary potential is more strikingly indicated by the indeterminate gaps between the textual instalments than by the text itself. As dissimilar forms of discourse, the 'Congo Diary' and *Heart of Darkness* both illustrate Benjamin's idea that narrative is fundamentally connected with the production of knowledge. Briefly hinted at in the 'Congo Diary', the effects of knowledge, power, and desire associated with narrative are assiduously explored in *Heart of Darkness*. Uneasily combining the genres of diary, autobiography, and travel narrative, the 'Congo Diary' is a personal non-fictional document which, bearing witness to Conrad's presence in Africa, serves to give the fiction of *Heart of Darkness* a rare authenticity.

II

A biographically inclined literary critic might well have used these two non-fictional texts in order to construe an expressive and relatively direct connection between Conrad's experiences in the Congo and *Heart of Darkness* as a literary expression of those experiences. The main point of my argument is rather to emphasize the narrative and thematic *difference* between the two texts Conrad wrote in Africa and *Heart of Darkness*. Although, as we have seen, there is an indirect connection between all three of them, *Heart of Darkness* appears as a text that is radically different from the first two. This difference derives in part from the ways in which, in *Heart of Darkness*, Conrad's experience, insight, and imagination are blended and generalized as literary form.

If we accept that the production of literature involves such a process of generalization, this may partly explain the temporal distance between the two non-fictional texts and *Heart of Darkness*. We recall Edward Bullough's definition of distance (see p. 35 above) as the quality of an expression that makes it aesthetically valid. As regards Conrad, this point can be related to his lasting need for distance both from his own experiences and, in a complicated and complicating manner, from his readers, in order to produce fiction at all. For Conrad, the need for distance from personal experience seems to converge with several of the means serving to constitute the genre of narrative fiction. In Conrad's fiction, distance in time, space, and attitude are the most important variants. In *Heart of Darkness* the temporal distance of eight years is linked with the spatial distance between London/Europe and the Congo, and they are both related to variations of attitudinal distance. This last variant of distance is the most complex of the three because it is joined to the narrators' and characters' varying levels of insight, and because the concept of distance here functions more metaphorically and is more closely related to literary interpretation.

Before proceeding further it may be helpful to summarize the action of *Heart of Darkness*. This can be done in a number of ways; the version that follows is virtually identical with that given in *The Oxford Companion to English Literature*:

> On board a yawl anchored peacefully on the Thames the narrator, Marlow, tells the story of his journey on another river. Travelling to Africa to join a cargo boat, he grows disgusted by what he sees of the greed of the ivory traders and their exploitation of the natives. At a company station he hears of the remarkable Mr Kurtz who is stationed in the very heart of the ivory country and is the company's most successful agent. Leaving the river,

Marlow makes a long and arduous cross-country trek to join the steamboat which he will command on an ivory-collecting journey into the interior, but at the central station he finds that his boat has been mysteriously wrecked. He learns that Kurtz has dismissed his assistant and is seriously ill. The other agents, jealous of Kurtz's success and possible promotion, hope that he will not recover and it becomes clear that Marlow's arrival at the inner station is being deliberately delayed. With repairs fully completed Marlow sets off on the two-month journey towards Kurtz. The river passage through the heavy motionless forest fills Marlow with a growing sense of dread. The journey is 'like travelling back to the earliest beginnings of the world' (p. 182). Ominous drumming is heard and dark forms glimpsed among the trees. Nearing its destination the boat is attacked by tribesmen and a helmsman is killed. At the Inner Station Marlow is met by a naïve Russian sailor who tells him of Kurtz's brilliance and the semi-divine power he exercises over the natives. A row of severed heads on stakes round the hut give an intimation of the barbaric rites by which Kurtz has achieved his ascendancy. Ritual dancing has been followed with human sacrifice and, without the restraints imposed by his society, Kurtz, an educated and civilized man, has used his knowledge and his gun to reign over this dark kingdom. While Marlow attempts to get Kurtz back down the river Kurtz tries to justify his actions and his motives: he has seen into the very heart of things. But, dying, his last words are: 'The horror! The horror!' (p. 239). Marlow is left with two packages to deliver, Kurtz's report for the Society for Suppression of Savage Customs, and some letters for his Intended. Faced with the girl's grief Marlow tells her that 'the last word he pronounced was—your name' (p. 251).

If this summary, as a paraphrasing and ordered story version, is less accurate than that Walzl gives of Joyce's 'The Dead', the main reason is suggested by the differences in narrative technique between these two texts. For example, Marlow's trip to Brussels is not mentioned and, although the first sentence of the summary informs us that Marlow is both the text's main character and its principal narrator, the significance of the narrative situation is (as typically happens in summaries of action) toned down. In actual fact this narrative situation, which establishes a strangely static frame round the main plot of *Heart of Darkness*, has a decisive function both narratively and thematically. We are introduced to a group of five persons on a sailing-boat that is lying anchored waiting for the tide to turn:

> The sea-reach of the Thames stretched before us like the beginning of an interminable waterway. In the offing the sea and the sky were welded together without a joint, and in the luminous space the tanned sails of the barges drifting up with the tide seemed to stand still in red clusters of canvas sharply peaked, with gleams of varnished sprits. A haze rested on the low shores that ran out to sea in vanishing flatness. The air was dark above Gravesend, and farther back still seemed condensed

into a mournful gloom, brooding motionless over the biggest, and the greatest, town on earth. (p. 135)

The visual qualities of this description resemble those often referred to in discussions of Conrad's literary impressionism. The pronoun 'us' refers to the five characters aboard the *Nellie*. One of them is Marlow, who is to perform crucial functions both as narrator and as character. However, as I have noted in 'Conradian Narrative' (Lothe 1996b: 167), it is significant that not Marlow but an anonymous first-person narrator is narrating here. This frame narrator introduces us both to the narrative situation and to Marlow as the main narrator. When Marlow is introduced and begins to tell his story, the function of the frame narrator becomes more complex, since he also becomes a narratee in the group Marlow addresses. To put this another way: in accordance with the narrative conventions employed, once Marlow has started telling his story the frame narrator functions first as a narratee, and then as a first-person narrator relaying Marlow's story to us as readers. The phrase 'narrative convention' is necessary because the time of traditional, simple narratives is over in *Heart of Darkness*. At first sight, the novella's narrative situation seems to resemble the epic 'proto-situation' that we discussed in Chapter 2. The resemblance is none the less superficial—not only because the concept of the epic proto-situation excludes the device of the frame narrator but, more importantly, because in *Heart of Darkness* both the narrative act, its motivations, and its thematic implications are much more problematic.

In the classic frame narrative the frame narrator is often the most authoritative and knowledgeable of the narrators. This is not so in *Heart of Darkness*. For although the frame narrator passes on Marlow's story and appears to be reliable, his insights are distinctly inferior to Marlow's. A second example will illustrate this point. Having finished his introductory description, the narrator exclaims: 'What greatness had not floated on the ebb of that river into the mystery of an unknown earth! . . . The dreams of men, the seed of commonwealths, the germs of empires' (p. 137). Considered in isolation from its context, the exclamation sounds like a piece of imperialist rhetoric. The narrator has just been referring to explorers such as Sir Francis Drake and Sir John Franklin, 'the great knights-errant of the sea' (p. 137). Signalling that for the frame narrator history is heroic and progressive, such references 'imply a certain sort of reader, one whose competence enables the correct decoding of the historical referents and more importantly one who endorses the positive judgements made on these "heroic" figures' (Fothergill 1989: 15). References and allusions of this kind remind us of the connections between Marlow's audience (of which the frame narrator is a member) and Conrad's readers, on whose interest and goodwill he was dependent as an author. It is worth remembering that *Heart of Darkness* was first published in *Blackwood's Magazine* (February–April 1899); considering the fact that it appeared in this conservative journal, the novella's critique of imperialism is all the more striking.

The frame narrator's exclamation increases the impact and suggestiveness of Marlow's first words: 'And this also . . . has been one of the dark places of the earth' (p. 138). This narrative variation is one of the most effective in all of Conrad's fiction. Marlow's remark exposes the relative naïvety and limited insight of the frame narrator and prefigures the sombre implications of the tale he is about to tell. The comment anticipates his later reflections on the arrival of the Romans in Britain, 'nineteen hundred years ago—the other day' (p. 139). For the Romans, Marlow plausibly goes on to suggest, Britain must have seemed an inhospitable wilderness at 'the very end of the world'. Moreover, it is indicative of the extraordinary narrative economy of *Heart of Darkness* that Marlow's opening words are also a prolepsis of 'darkness', the text's central metaphor which (like ivory) becomes a powerful symbol. Although the Romans 'were men enough to face the darkness . . . They were conquerors, and for that you want only brute force—nothing to boast of, when you have it, since your strength is just an accident arising from the weakness of others' (pp. 139–40). This generalizing statement obviously refers to the Romans, but also includes a proleptic reference to the narrative Marlow is just starting. Suggesting that Marlow's level of insight is superior to that of the frame narrator, these brief observations also indicate some key characteristics of Marlow's first-person narrative: a reflective rhetoric designed to impress and persuade, a peculiar blend of personal and intellectual curiosity, and a tendency to generalize on the basis of individual experience. Conrad thus uses two narrators in *Heart of Darkness*, and the effect of Marlow's narrative is inseparable from the function of the frame narrator.

As we have seen in Part I, the use of a narrator is a distancing device. *Heart of Darkness* accentuates this distancing process by the use of two narrators rather than one. At the same time, the novella is also a good example of a fictional text where distancing devices paradoxically increase the reader's attention and interest. Conrad effectively exploits the conventional or common character of the frame narrator to make Marlow's story more plausible. The frame narrative manipulates the reader into a position resembling that of the frame narrator as narratee, a position distinguished by a meditative and broadly sympathetic response to the disillusioned insights of Marlow's story. This effect is particularly evident in the novella's last paragraph, which is uttered by the frame narrator. Echoing the numerous references to 'darkness', its concluding words—'immense darkness' (p. 252)—repeat Marlow's last words in the paragraph above.

In *Heart of Darkness* there is a productive correlation between Marlow's first-person narration, which takes the form of an ordering and existentially motivated re-experience, and that of the frame narrator, which proceeds

A Map of the Congo Free State 1890

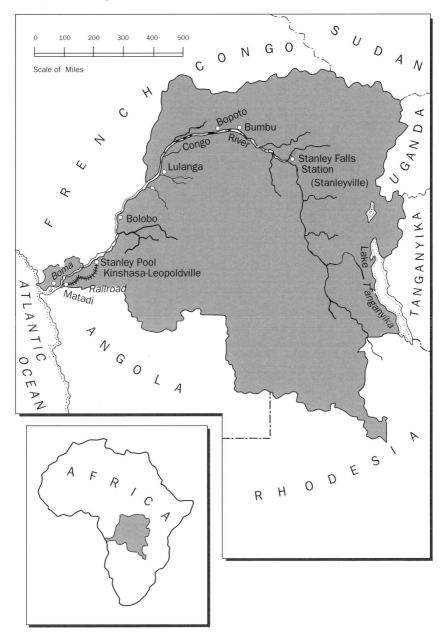

Seen in the light of Conrad's *Heart of Darkness*, the title of this map of the Congo in 1890 acquires an additional, ironic meaning: the territories (76 times the size of Belgium) were not 'free' but under King Leopold II's control.

from an unexpected involvement and surprising understanding. The frame narrator's insight appears to increase as a result of the impressionist narrative he himself transmits, thus suggesting that in this text not just the plot but also its narrative presentation are peculiarly unstable. An early indication of the frame narrator's insight occurs in his introductory comments on Marlow:

> The yarns of seamen have a direct simplicity, the whole meaning of which lies within the shell of a cracked nut. But Marlow was not typical (if his propensity to spin yarns be excepted), and to him the meaning of an episode was not inside like a kernel but outside, enveloping the tale which brought it out only as a glow brings out a haze, in the likeness of one of these misty halos that sometimes are made visible by the spectral illumination of moonshine. (p. 138)

This passage tells us something important not only about the narrative and thematic characteristics of Marlow's tale, but also about the frame narrator's surprising understanding of Marlow's narrative presentation. If, as in the earlier example we have considered, the frame narrator's naïvety makes him more reliable as a narrator, his increased insight here has a comparable effect. For Marlow, the frame narrator seems to indicate in this passage, meaning is not unproblematically located in the centre of an episode or a story; it is rather part of the narrative process, which implies that it is also related (as challenge and/or possibility) to the process of reading.

Moreover, this view of Marlow is linked to the thematics of *Heart of Darkness*. It is as though the frame narrator's characterization of Marlow is influenced by the impression Marlow's tale has made on him. The frame narrator's comments may be related to Tzvetan Todorov's conception of the novella's thematic centre as one of vacuity or emptiness. Kurtz, notes Todorov in *Les Genres du discours*, 'is certainly the centre of the narrative, and his knowledge, the driving force of the plot . . . Kurtz is the heart of darkness but this heart is empty' (Todorov 1978: 167, 169, my translation). In order to substantiate this point Todorov puts emphasis on the novella's discourse and on Marlow's growing fascination with Kurtz. Kurtz's knowledge assumes a predominantly negative form; his is a disillusioned insight expressed metaphorically through words such as 'darkness' and 'horror'.

Todorov stresses the productive interplay of narrative and thematics in *Heart of Darkness*. So does Peter Brooks, who in *Reading for the Plot* illustrates the novella's narration as shown in Fig. 7.2. The diagram illustrates that what Todorov calls the novella's thematic vacuity, which he links directly to Kurtz, is also a *narrative* emptiness. Thus it provides a simplified illustration of the text's narrative structure. However, it also raises a question Brooks is aware of: the static impression such an illustration gives has a tendency to suppress those textual elements that contribute to its dynamism, progressive development, and plot formation. It therefore needs to be stressed that the dynamic aspects of the novella's narrative (such as

Figure 7.1

the frame narrator's learning process, provoked by Marlow's tale) are fundamentally important for the thematics which the narrative serves to generate and shape. Hillis Miller's notion of the narration of *Heart of Darkness* as a 'process of unveiling' (Miller 1985: 43) is relevant here. This process includes both paradoxical and ironic elements, the combined effects of which support the kind of thematic conclusion reached by Todorov. The novella's structure as a relay of narrators establishes what Cedric Watts has called its 'principle of entanglement' (Watts 1977: 33)—a characteristically 'tentacular effect' which enhances the moral complexity of the tale and the reader's involvement in it.

I have said that the frame narrator transmits an impressionist narrative told him by Marlow. As Ian Watt has observed, 'Marlow's emphasis on the difficulty of understanding and communicating his own individual experience aligns *Heart of Darkness* with the subjective relativism of the impressionist attitude' (Watt 1980: 179). One of the main characteristics of Marlow's narrative is the way in which he repeatedly puts the reader into sensory contact with the events as they unfold through the act of narration. As Watt puts it, this means that 'the physical impression must precede the understanding of cause. Literary impressionism implies a field of vision which is not merely limited to the individual observer, but is also controlled by whatever conditions—internal and external—prevail at the moment of observation' (Watt 1980: 178). Watt has coined the term 'delayed decoding' to describe one important aspect of this narrative method: through delayed decoding Conrad attempts 'to present a sense impression and to withhold naming it or explaining its meaning until later . . . This takes us directly into the observer's consciousness at the very moment of the perception, before it has been translated into its cause' (Watt 1980: 175). One of the notable manifestations of this device in *Heart of Darkness* is Marlow's confusion when his boat is attacked just below Kurtz's station. Only later does he discover the cause of the various odd changes he observes: 'Arrows, by Jove! We were being shot at!' (p. 200). The concept of delayed decoding is probably most helpful in describing relatively simple instances of temporarily inexplicable impressions and occurrences. A larger problem—Marlow's impression of Kurtz, for instance—is not decoded for us, but it does not follow that Marlow's encounter with the novella's other protagonist may not be meaningful.

As a first-person narrator Marlow characterizes himself both by communicating his African experiences and through his comments on these experiences. Broadly, both variants on characterization are indirect rather than direct. As far as characterization of Kurtz is concerned, a notable example of direct characterization occurs when Marlow finally meets him, lying diseased on an improvised stretcher in the heart of the jungle:

> Kurtz—Kurtz—that means short in German—don't it? Well, the name was as true as everything else in his life—and death. He looked at least seven feet long. His covering had fallen off, and his body emerged from it pitiful and appalling as from a winding-sheet. I could see the cage of his ribs all astir, the bones of his arm waving. It was as though an animated image of death carved out of old ivory had been shaking its hand with menaces at a motionless crowd of men made of dark and glittering bronze. (p. 224)

Kurtz appears to Marlow as 'an animated image of death carved out of old ivory'. This is an example of direct characterization. And yet its interpretative suggestiveness is enhanced because of the manner in which it is related to, and extends, the *indirect* characterization of Kurtz that we have already received from Marlow and from those he meets on his up-river journey. The characterization of Kurtz is further related to the text's elaborate pattern of metaphors; and it bears a relation to Conrad's original use of the journey motif in *Heart of Darkness*.

The motif of travel is constantly present throughout Marlow's narration. Conrad uses it to create a structure that is both linear and circular. The structure is linear in its narrative, impressionist presentation of the up-river journey on the dilapidated steamer, 'a sluggish beetle crawling . . . towards Kurtz' (p. 185). This journey is progressive inasmuch as it penetrates deeper and deeper into the African continent, but at the same time Marlow increasingly has an impression of a regressive movement: 'Going up that river was like travelling back to the earliest beginnings of the world' (p. 182). Both the progressive and regressive aspects are linked to the diegetic level of action, yet they also serve to characterize Kurtz indirectly. One of the agents Marlow meets speaks highly of Kurtz as 'an emissary of pity, and science, and progress' (p. 169). This characterization is in sharp contrast to the self-characterization implicit in Kurtz's final words, 'The horror! The horror!' Somewhere between these two extreme positions, closer to the last than to the first, we can situate Marlow's attempt at characterizing Kurtz.

If the up-river journey towards Kurtz creates a linear structure, the frame narrative places this structure within a circular one. An integral part of Conrad's narrative method in *Heart of Darkness*, this combination of two fundamental structural forms is vital for the novella's thematics. Through such a combination the horrible acts of brutality committed deep in the African jungle are linked to, indeed presented as the consequence of, decisions and priorities made in European centres of power such as Brussels, Berlin,—and London.

It is not just the frame narrative that creates this circular structure, however. It is supported by two other structural components, and both are constituted through Marlow's narration. The first component is what we may call Marlow's return, the journey down the river with Kurtz aboard the steamer. The fact that Kurtz is present on this journey, where he dies uttering the final words that we have quoted, proves decisive for Marlow's experience both of Kurtz and of the European activites he represents. The return with Kurtz is closely related to the second component which serves to give *Heart of Darkness* a circular structure: the two visits Marlow pays to 'the sepulchral city' (p. 242; cf. p. 145). As it is clear from the context that the city is Brussels, why does Marlow avoid calling it by its familiar name? And why does the city remind him of a whited sepulchre? A partial answer to the first question may be to draw attention to Conrad's tendency to avoid geographical names in his fiction, while at the same time conveying topographical details specifically and precisely (the reader is never in the slightest doubt that we are in Africa on the river Congo). Whereas the 'Congo Diary' is littered with geographical names, Conrad avoids using them in the novella as this would make the discourse too explicit, something he, in a letter to Richard Curle (24 April 1922), regards as 'fatal' to the effects of artistic work: 'Explicitness, my dear fellow, is fatal to the glamour of all artistic work, robbing it of all suggestiveness, destroying all illusion' (Kimbrough 1988: 232).

That Brussels appears to Marlow as a sepulchral city has a proleptic function not only in relation to the brutality and deaths he witnesses in the African jungle, but also in relation to the description of an old woman just a few pages further on in the text. Waiting to be admitted to the company's headquarters, Marlow observes the older of the two women knitting black wool:

> She seemed uncanny and fateful. Often far away there I thought of these two, guarding the door of Darkness, knitting black wool as for a warm pall, one introducing, introducing continuously to the unknown, the other scrutinizing the cheery and foolish faces with unconcerned old eyes. *Ave!* Old knitter of black wool. *Morituri te salutant.* Not many of those she looked at ever saw her again—not half, by a long way. (p. 147)

There is something sinister about the old woman as a guardian of 'the door of Darkness'; later on she appears to Marlow as a premonition of death. It is vital for this effect that Marlow's visual impression of the old woman is linked with two other textual elements in the above quotation: first is the symbol of 'darkness' and then the information in the final sentence. Critics have interpreted 'the door of Darkness' metaphorically as the entrance to the realm of death or hell. The textual basis for such a reading would appear to be strong: compare

Marlow's impression of the up-river journey towards Kurtz as a regressive movement, centrifugally directed towards the centre of the earth.

Although the genre of the epic is actualized in a number of ways in *Heart of Darkness*, the above quotation suggests that two epics are particularly important 'intertexts' for Conrad's novella: Virgil's *Aeneid* (19 BC) and Dante's *Divine Comedy* (1321). From Chapter 4 we recall Julia Kristeva's definition of 'intertextuality' as 'a mosaic of quotations; any text is the absorption and transformation of another' (Kristeva 1980: 66). Her understanding of intertextuality is indebted to Mikhail Bakhtin's notion of 'dialogism' (a term related to 'heteroglossia'). Dialogism means that everything is understood as part of a greater whole: 'there is a constant interaction between meanings, all of which have the potential of conditioning others' (Michael Holquist, in Bakhtin 1982: 426; cf. Holquist 1990). For Kristeva, one essential aspect of dialogism is the attempt to situate 'the text within history and society, which are then seen as texts read by the writer, and into which he inserts himself by rewriting them' (Kristeva 1980: 65). This notion implies that an ancient text such as Virgil's *Aeneid* is potentially as important for the reader's understanding of *Heart of Darkness* as, say, nineteenth-century travel literature. The qualification implied in 'potentially' suggests that (partly since Kristeva's definition of intertextuality may appear impossibly inclusive) it is not equally rewarding to apply the concept of intertextuality to all manner of texts. In a narrative analysis, one determining factor could be that the intertextual relationship is not just thematic but also structural and/or generic.

The significance of the Latin words Marlow uses is enhanced if considered in the light of the *Aeneid*: 'Hail! . . . Those about to die salute you.' Such was the greeting of the gladiators on entering the arena of combat in imperial Rome. The Latin phrase which Marlow incorporates into his first-person narrative, then, originates from a time approximately 1,900 years before his own act of narration. Thus a link is established with Marlow's opening reference to the Romans: 'I was thinking of very old times, when the Romans first came here, nineteen hundred years ago—the other day . . .' (p. 139). As vastly different temporal planes are intertextually forged together, Conrad makes the reader appreciate the affinities between his own novella and Virgil's epic, and also between the historical and cultural formations within which these texts appeared.

As Lillian Feder was one of the first critics to note, Marlow's journey seems fated from the beginning, and though it 'recalls the epic descent in general, it is most specifically related to the visit to Hades in the sixth book of the *Aeneid*' (Feder 1955: 281). In Virgil's epic, Aeneas's descent is part of the learning process he must undergo in order to become the leader of the Roman people. As truth is to be found in the heart of darkness, the sibyl, who, in Virgil's words (*Aeneid* 6. 100), 'obscuris vera involvens' (hides truth in darkness), guides Aeneas. Virgil stresses the importance of Aeneas's descent for his personal development. During his trip to Hades, Aeneas 'learns of the tragedy implicit in the affairs of men . . . [and of] the cost of Rome's imperial power' (Feder 1955: 281). As this cost involves not just the use but also the possible abuse of power, a thematic connection is established between the mechanics of the Roman empire 1,900 years earlier and modern European ones. As Marlow says of the Romans in Britain and suggests of the Belgians in the Congo, they were 'conquerors' engaged in robbery, 'going at it blind—as is very proper for those who tackle a darkness' (p. 140).

Intriguing as the similarities with the *Aeneid* are, the critical interest of such an affinity is strengthened if we compare *Heart of Darkness* not just with Virgil's epic but also with that of Dante written approximately 1,300 years later. An intertextual connection between these two epics is suggested by the novella itself. 'I felt', says Marlow, 'as though, instead of going to the centre of a continent, I were about to set off for the centre of the earth' (p. 150). Now surely the Inferno (or Hell) of Dante's Christian universe is in many ways different from Hades in Virgil's pagan world. In both texts, however, the predominant narrative patterns (associated with Aeneas and Dante respectively) crucially involve forms of descent into darkness as an essential part of the protagonist's learning process. In the *Aeneid* as in *The Divine Comedy*, moreover, the hero's descent complicates and temporarily halts narrative progression while also providing the basis for such progression. That in both texts the dynamics of narrative and the hero's educational process are so intertwined as to become virtually interchangeable is a reminder of the epic's generic affinity with travel literature. Not only does the epic typically involve travel, it also posits the hero's travel adventures as dangerous, challenging, and formative for his development. Just before Dante started composing his epic, the Venetian merchant Marco Polo wrote his account of his journey to Mongolia. An instrumental text in establishing a Western discourse of the Orient, Marco Polo's travel narrative signals the early beginnings of European global hegemony. As Christopher GoGwilt has shown, this hegemony remains remarkably stable until it undergoes a transformation at the turn of the nineteenth century. For GoGwilt, this transformation marks 'the shift from a European to a Western identity' (GoGwilt 1995: 1), just at the time Conrad wrote *Heart of Darkness*.

If the *Aeneid* 'may be regarded as a dramatic allegory of the act of narration and of historical understanding' (Kennedy 1997: 48), Dante's *Divine Comedy* magisterially rewrites the allegory from the Christian vantage-point of medieval Europe. Anticipating *Heart of Darkness*, Dante's epic exploits two interrelated principles of narrative presentation: the association of learning and travel, and the use of Dante as both narrator and main character. Of the epic's three main parts the *Inferno* is more closely related to *Heart of Darkness* than *Purgatorio* and *Paradiso*. To say that Dante's *Inferno* is characterized by stasis is to refer to the fact that those he finds there are condemned to dwell there forever. In the *Inferno*, progression in time and space is limited to Dante and his guide Virgil only. These two are the only travellers here; they are visitors to, not inhabitants of Inferno. For Dante, the intensity of the suffering he meets is further augmented by the thought that it is everlasting. Compare Marlow's impression of the African workers he is suddenly confronted with at a relatively early stage of his Congo journey: 'Black shapes crouched, lay, sat between the trees leaning against the trunks, clinging to the earth, half coming out, half effaced within the dim light, in all the attitudes of pain, abandonment, and despair' (p. 156). 'It seemed to me', says Marlow, 'I had stepped into the gloomy circle of some Inferno' (p. 156).

In *The Divine Comedy*, the *Inferno* is literally the eternal realm of the dead. In the epic's allegorical scheme it 'is the city of man which has become utterly corrupt, where justice and order, fair-dealing and compassion have been totally subverted by loose-living, violence, fraud and treachery' (Higgins in Dante 1998: 16). The 'sins' of the damned in Dante's *Inferno* are largely crimes that would be condemned in any rational society. In Conrad's novella, however, there is no corresponding rationale behind the relationship of crime and punishment. Thus, in one sense the hell encountered by Marlow in the Congo is even more gruesome than that of Dante. The 'crime' of the Africans is to be at this particular spot at this particular point in time. As in *The Divine Comedy*, the sense of 'Inferno' evoked in *Heart of Darkness* involves not just a geographical but also a juridico-political notion. The 'Inferno' Marlow encounters is a *region* which, in addition to mapping a geographical space, also, as Michel Foucault puts it, denotes 'the area controlled by a certain kind of power' (Foucault 1980: 68). If the operative logic in Dante's epic is that of (Christian) justice, in *Heart of Darkness* it is that of war/warfare. This is an intertextual aspect of Conrad's novella which became thematically productive for Francis Ford Coppola as the director of *Apocalypse Now*.

The intertextuality of *Heart of Darkness* is by no means limited to the epic tradition. For example, as Rosalind S. Meyer has shown, the novella 'gains considerably by its distant but perceptible relationship to fairy stories of childhood' (Meyer 1998: 330). *Heart of Darkness* may indeed seem intertextually overdetermined. If, as the above observations suggest, I regard texts such as the *Aeneid* and *The Divine Comedy* as particularly important for our understanding of the novella, this is not only because of the various structural and thematic affinities I have been pointing out, but also because the texts by Virgil and Dante cumulatively contribute to the formation of a literary tradition of which Conrad was acutely aware and to which he was greatly indebted. Part of the originality of *Heart of Darkness* resides in the manner in which the novella engages with—reworks, extends, and problematizes—the European literary tradition.

Arguably, then, our understanding of the symbol of 'darkness' (which is bound to influence our reading of the whole text) is enriched by some basic knowledge of the importance of the darkness metaphor in the *Aeneid* and *The Divine Comedy*. Towards the end of *Heart of Darkness*, 'darkness' is linked to Kurtz's final outburst, 'The horror! The horror!' These are Kurtz's dying words, which Marlow (who claims he hates telling lies) refrains from passing on to the Intended, the lady in mourning in a drawing-room in Brussels: 'I could not tell her. It would have been too dark—too dark altogether . . .' (p. 252). Conrad's use of ellipsis here in itself invites interpretation, as do the numerous repetitions of 'darkness' throughout the novella. It does not follow from this symbol's complexity, however, that we cannot identify several of its most important constituent aspects: brutality, exploitation, racism, false morality, exploitation of natural resources for short-term profit. Through the literary discourse of *Heart of Darkness*, Conrad suggests, most strikingly perhaps through the novella's elaborate pattern of metaphors, that Marlow's understanding of the events he describes is, and indeed cannot possibly be more than, partial. At the same time, Marlow's narrative spiralling downwards towards a centre assuming the form of a blank, emptiness, or vacuity, constitutes a painful learning process ending in resignation and disillusionment. Marlow's discourse, as well as the criteria and attitudes by which it is informed, is destabilized.

This process of destabilization, which Marlow is partly aware of and which culminates with his lie to the Intended, also informs the novella's treatment of race. To make this point is not to claim that *Heart of Darkness* contains no features of racism; it unavoidably does. In an influential essay, the Nigerian novelist Chinua Achebe has asserted that in Conrad's novella the Blacks are dehumanized and degraded—that they are seen as grotesques and denied speech. Conrad, Achebe concludes, 'was a thoroughgoing racist' (Achebe 1998: 117). Now clearly, Achebe's point that the 'natives' Marlow meets with are presented as virtually speechless is, considered as a separate claim, irrefutable. On one textual level, *Heart of Darkness* resembles a large number of contemporary fictional and non-fictional texts about Africa that tended to 'propagate waves of sameness' as Gilles Deleuze and Félix Guattari put it: 'From the viewpoint of racism, there is no exterior, there are no people on the outside. There are only people who should be like us and whose crime it is not to be. The dividing line is not between inside and outside but rather is internal to simultaneous signifying chains and successive subjective choices' (Deleuze and Guattari 1988: 83).

This description of racism can be related to the form of travel (and travel literature) that accompanied imperialist expansion in Africa in the nineteenth century. And yet Conrad's narrative is significantly different from this imperialist discourse if only for the persistent way in which it presents the lack of a measurable exterior, the absence of 'people on the outside' as a problem, thus questioning, or starting to question, the fundamentally racist assumptions of imperialism. It does so, for example, by focusing on its accompanying violence. The ways in which this critique is made, and sustained throughout, are intimately connected with Conrad's innovative and productive use of Marlow as a narrator. Marlow is a first-person narrator who is, frustratingly for the reader, reliable and unreliable at the same time; he is a highly competent narrator who experiences a breakdown of narrativity just as he senses that narration is crucial in order to retain epistemological control and moral integrity. 'It seems to me', Marlow tells his listeners, 'I am trying to tell you a dream'—finding 'it is impossible; it is impossible to convey the life-sensation of any given epoch of one's existence' (p. 172). There is, comments the frame narrator, a 'faint uneasiness inspired by this narrative that seemed to shape itself without human lips in the heavy night-air of the river' (p. 173). And yet, strangely repeating and thus calling renewed attention to the breakdown of Kurtz's report (which ends with the exclamation 'Exterminate all the brutes!', p. 208), the collapse of *Heart of Darkness* as a literary travel narrative represents Conrad's partial, incipient understanding of racism as a parameter of othering in which, as Syed Manzurul Islam puts it, 'the black man's essence is what the white man lacks and abhors within himself' (Islam 1996: 83). Overall, there can be little doubt that the novella's narrative thrust is towards the disillusionment and horror of those who—like Marlow, Kurtz, and *Blackwood's* readers—are the agents of European expansion and 'civilization'.

The Marxist slogan 'Always historicize!' needs consistently to be applied to the concept of racism. We must not forget, but sometimes tend to, that our understanding of 'racism' derives in large part from insights accrued in the twentieth century. The elaborate discussions of race and racism expounded by theorists such as Deleuze and Guattari, Frantz Fanon, and Edward Said, proceed from, and could hardly have been developed without, the historical realities of imperialism, two world wars (the second of which included the Holocaust), and the post-colonial era. Distancing itself from the official ideology of empire by thematizing what in nineteenth-century travel narratives was typically suppressed, *Heart of Darkness* is a literary text which, inspired by and yet problematizing travel narratives from Africa, starts to deliver the premisses on which our present understanding of racism depends. Incorporating a strong critique of European imperialism in Africa, *Heart of Darkness* transcends such a critique in that it dramatizes a series of more or less obscure connections between imperialism as one particular form of human activity and characteristics of the human psyche which may lead human beings of Kurtz's calibre to engage in this kind of activity. Thus *Heart of Darkness* is not essentially, and definitely not only, a story about imperialism, but rather a fictional statement on the human condition and the human psyche provoked by a specific form of exposure to imperialism (and its consequences).

III

Heart of Darkness, then, presents itself as literature, a complex verbal fiction produced by narrators who are part of the fiction and neither of whom unproblematically represents Conrad. Like Kafka's *The Trial*, *Heart of Darkness* is a fascinating, enigmatic, peculiarly parabolic text: insisting on interpretation, it demonstrates that no one reading suffices. Turning to *Apocalypse Now*, a possible first comment on Francis Ford Coppola's film is that its filmic complexity constitutes a sort of parallel to the literary complexity of *Heart of Darkness*. The following comments present no exhaustive analysis of this fascinating, multi-layered, and problematically ambiguous film. My more modest aim is to identify, and briefly discuss, some aspects of *Apocalypse Now* that are interestingly related to Conrad's text, to the challenge of adaptation, and to our discussion of the novella as literary discourse. In so doing I am indebted to the helpful essays on *Apocalypse Now* by Bjørn Sørenssen (1995), Thomas Elsaesser and Michael Wedel (1997), and Seymour Chatman (1997).

Apocalypse Now was presented at the Cannes Film Festival in 1979. It was awarded the Golden Palm for best movie (a prize shared with Volker Schlöndorff's *The Tin Drum*, an adaptation of Günter Grass's novel from 1959). The high expectations aroused by *Apocalypse Now* had been created by the delays and unusually high production costs, by Coppola's status as a 'star director' (following his successes with *The Godfather* (1972) and *The Godfather: Part II* (1974)), and by the participation of actors such as Marlon Brando (as Kurtz). The timing of the film's release was also significant. Four years after the end of the Vietnam War both American and international audiences took a great interest in films about Vietnam—a genre within which *Apocalypse Now* became an instant classic.

Generally speaking, the film was well received by audience and critics alike. Some went as far as to draw comparisons between Coppola and acclaimed directors such as D. W. Griffith and Orson Welles. As Bjørn Sørenssen points out, adverse criticism was mainly confined to those critics who expected, and demanded (as did Sol Yurick in the New York *Screen* magazine), a film about the 'truth' of the Vietnam War. Reasonable or not, such a demand can be related to the fact that *Apocalypse Now*, as is normal with the medium of film but in contrast to Conrad's *Heart of Darkness*, was the aesthetic result of a complicated production process with many players. While Conrad composed *Heart of Darkness* from a unique combination of personal experiences and literary creativity, the completion of *Apocalypse Now* depended on a problematic collaboration between the various, and sometimes changing, members of a large production team. The first draft for *Apocalypse Now* was written by John Milius in 1969. Coppola rewrote the script, and it is unclear to what extent the completed film version is based on Coppola's alterations and how much derives from Milius's original script. Thus Coppola became a co-writer of the script, and since he was also the director of the film and even helped to finance it, we might reasonably regard him as the film's 'author'. Indeed, some critics regarded *Apocalypse Now* as the greatest *auteur*-movie since Griffith's *Intolerance* (1916). Yet there is little doubt that Milius's ideas influenced the completed version, even though both he and Coppola were inspired by *Heart of Darkness* while working on the film. Additionally, Michael Herr, author of *Dispatches* (1977) which at the time was the best-known book about the Vietnam War, provided the film's voice-over narration.

Before proceeding further it may be useful to summarize the plot of *Apocalypse Now*. This summary, which largely follows but condenses that given by Sørenssen (1995: 158–9), can then be compared with that of *Heart of Darkness* presented above.

> Set in Vietnam and Cambodia, *Apocalypse Now* follows the American army captain Willard (Martin Sheen) on a mission which involves finding and liquidating the renegade colonel Walter Kurtz (Marlon Brando). A former Green Beret officer whose 'methods', according to the general who orders Willard to kill him, have become 'unsound', Kurtz has defected and established himself with a private army in the Cambodia border area fighting both the National Liberation Front (NLF) and the Saigon army. Willard boards a patrol boat which is to take him up the Nung river into Kurtz territory, but first the boat has to be taken through the NLF-controlled river delta. There follows a terror air attack by the American airborne cavalry against an NLF village. Led by the cowboy figure Lieutenant-Colonel Kilgore (Robert Duvall), accompanied by deafening blasts of Richard Wagner's 'Ride of the Valkyries', the helicopters spread death and havoc until the US air force finishes the village off with a napalm strike. This gives Kilgore the chance to enjoy the excellent surf of the beach—with the glorious smell of napalm in his nostrils. The first part of the up-river journey incorporates a background sketch of Kurtz's brilliant military career, thus confirming the general's characterization of him as 'one of the most outstanding officers this country has ever produced'. The accompanying presentation of Willard's travelling companions is interspersed with episodes illustrating various aspects of the Vietnam War; in one such episode the highly strung crew of the patrol boat massacre a fisherman's family. After this transitory part of the narrative the boat enters the mystical realm of Kurtz. Here the two black crew members are killed, one by a bullet, the other (the captain) pierced by arrows from Kurtz's tribal mercenaries. Arriving at last at Kurtz's headquarters, a temple ruin in the jungle, they are greeted by a hysterical American press photographer (Dennis Hopper) who has joined Kurtz. Willard is captured by Kurtz's men and is led to the elusive colonel,

who at first appears as nothing but a voice of shadows and only gradually becomes a recognizable character. Kurtz, as it turns out, is aware of Willard's mission and Willard is captured, tortured, and placed in a bamboo cage— but is then released to serve as Kurtz's audience for the latter's musings, monologues, and poetry recitals. When the tribal people are preparing a sacrificial ceremony Willard approaches Kurtz and kills him with an axe at the very moment of the sacrificial slaughter of an ox. The natives bow reverently to Willard as he returns to the patrol boat with the only surviving crew member. The boat departs down the river, accompanied off-screen by Kurtz's final words: 'The horror! The horror!'

If we compare this story version with that of *Heart of Darkness* given above, we can note several points of resemblance. In both narratives, significant parts of the plot revolve round an up-river journey, into the Congo and into Cambodia respectively. In Conrad's novella as in Coppola's film, a complex, tense, and ambiguous relationship beween two male characters is at the centre of the narrative. In both narratives, the 'passive' character (the one who is not travelling but is gradually approached by the other) appears as the driving force of the plot; attitudes to him are mixed (including admiration as well as fear), and he is named Kurtz. The general informs Willard that he regards Kurtz's methods as 'unsound'; the manager tells Marlow that he thinks Kurtz's 'method is unsound' (p. 227). In Coppola's film there is a war going on; in Conrad's novella the Europeans' activities in Africa are repeatedly described as war-like, a 'merry dance of death and trade' (p. 152).

The list could be extended. Yet it could be countered that such a listing of 'parallels' is misleading as it tends to suppress points of dissimilarity that are perhaps equally striking. For example, the film has no frame narrative corresponding to that in *Heart of Darkness*: Willard is no Marlow addressing a group of narratees. Moreover, whereas Marlow is a professional, intelligent, reflective, and eloquent officer who is genuinely shocked by his experiences in the Congo, Willard is a professional killer who, in striking contrast to Marlow, is almost completely inarticulate. Although it is true that Willard *cannot* be as articulate as Marlow—the very different ways in which the two media operate makes this impossible—particularly towards the end of the film our response to, and evaluation of, Willard (and thus of the film as a whole) is complicated by the fact that since he communicates so little of his reactions to the events he encounters we are unsure of his attitudinal distance from these events.

As this list of dissimilarities between the book and the film could also be extended, the essential point to make here is that, rather than looking for points of resemblance and/or difference (which can, as the above examples illustrate, be located at different levels of literary and filmic discourse), it may be more fruitful to consider *Apocalypse Now* as an exceptionally ambitious, impressive yet qualitatively uneven filmic response to a literary text that Coppola clearly admired and was strongly inspired by. The ways in which Coppola activates, combines, and experiments with the large register of means and devices pertaining to the narrative fiction film may be seen as a more indirect, but possibly more productive, response to the complexity of Conrad's text than, say, naming the colonel 'Kurtz'. Paradoxically, then, discussions of *Apocalypse Now as film* may tell us something important about the ways in which the film functions as an adaptation. Ian Watt's concept of 'thematic apposition' (Watt 1980: 285–6) is relevant here. In his discussion of *Lord Jim*, Conrad's next novel, in which Marlow makes a reappearance as the main narrator, Watt uses this term to describe how, for example, different scenes are juxtaposed and added to each other, thus increasing the novel's thematic complexity. Applying the notion of 'thematic apposition' to the involuted relationship between *Heart of Darkness* and *Apocalypse Now*, we might say that the problems probed by Conrad through a literary text are transposed by Coppola to another time and another place in order to be further explored through the medium of film.

I have argued that the film's opening is very different from the beginning of *Heart of Darkness* since there is no corresponding frame narrative. Valid as such a point may seem, it is perhaps indicative of our tendency to equate the two media rather too directly. For there is also a kind of frame narrative in *Apocalypse Now*, and a very effective one at that. One distinct feature of this kind of frame is its 'complex audiovisual texture' (Elsaesser and Wedel 1997: 162) which serves as a prelude to, and an obscure comment on, the horrors of war displayed in the film.

This opening has been well described by Thomas Elsaesser and Michael Wedel:

> *Apocalypse Now* begins with a few seconds of buzzing sound over a dark screen, before a panoramic shot of the jungle fades in and, after another few moments, tentatively locates the source of the sound in the blades of an army helicopter that slowly crosses the screen. After the helicopter has passed, yellow smoke rises from below, and with it the first notes of music are heard. After a second helicopter has crossed the visual field, the jungle bursts into one immense explosion: 'This is the end, beautiful friend . . .' The voice of Jim Morrison accompanies the apocalyptic but silent visual spectacle on the sound track. While The Doors continue to sing, several helicopters pass through the image as the camera pans right. A close-up of Willard's head is superimposed upside down on the left side of the screen, briefly counterpointed first by a ceiling fan and then by the head of a huge Buddha on the right side, before a series of close-ups takes us through Willard's hotel room in Saigon, still superimposed on images of whirring helicopters and burning jungle. (Elsaesser and Wedel 1997: 162)

Note that, as a description of the beginning of the film's *discourse*, this observation is strikingly different from the first couple of sentences in the story version presented above. Interestingly, however, the close attention Elsaesser and Wedel pay to the cinematic devices which serve to constitute the filmic discourse of *Apocalypse Now* does not make *Heart of Darkness* irrelevant as a (possibly rewarding) point of reference—provided, that is, we are prepared to consider not just the novella's themes but also its techniques. For example, the way in which the viewer has to try to locate the sound of the blades of the army helicopter is comparable to the various attempts Marlow makes to understand what is going on in the jungle. We have noted that Ian Watt coined the term 'delayed decoding' to describe Conrad's presentation of such a process of orientation. The concept could also be applied to the beginning of *Apocalypse Now*, as it takes some time before we are able to relate the sound to the moving helicopters. In the film as in the book, moreover, we cannot always be certain that our 'decoding' is correct. That we can only 'tentatively' locate the sound in the helicopter's rotating blades is one of several indications of the way in which Coppola's filmic presentation approximates to an impressionist narrative.

   Film, as we have seen in Part I of this book, is notable for the unique and highly effective manner in which it visualizes events, characters, and action. So obvious as to appear redundant in a discussion of *Apocalypse Now*, this observation can none the less be related to the elaborate combination of visual and auditive effects in the film's opening. This is another way of saying that for all the thematically diverse and technically sophisticated uses Coppola makes of filmic sound here (cf. Fig. 2.4 above), the film's visual qualities are actually strengthened rather than impaired. Yet the relationship between sight and sound is not unproblematic; it is not only informative but also confusing, disorienting. Coppola's experimentation with sound aligns *Apocalypse Now* with those films which, from the 1920s onwards, marked the transition from silent to sound film, 'a period of grave instability as well as great creativity in the history of cinema' (Dibbets 1997: 211). In 1928 Sergei Eisenstein noted that 'the first experimental work with sound must be directed along the lines of its distinct nonsynchronization with the visual images'. Such an approach, Eisenstein argues, 'will later lead to the creation of an orchestral counterpoint of visual and aural images' (Eisenstein 1992: 318). The beginning of *Apocalypse Now* aspires towards such a counterpoint as its complex audiovisual texture 'first offers interpretative strategies and then problematizes and withdraws them from the viewer in order to arrive at an ultimate undecidability between sensual experiences and diegetic motivation' (Elsaesser and Wedel 1997: 163). We first attribute the whirring sound (which, as Elsaesser and Wedel note, we hear *before* the first image) to the helicopters. But then voice (Jim Morrison) and music (The Doors) are added to the first sound (an unidentified noise), and all of these three main variants on film sound are related to, yet also contrasted with, a series of dissolves, superimpositions, and panning movements of the camera. As a result of these complex filmic variations, we are forced to attribute the first sound we hear not just to the helicopters but also to the ceiling fan in the hotel room where Willard is lying on the bed. And yet the first association of unidentified sound and helicopter remains with us. It is rekindled, and in one sense confirmed, in a later filmic segment also notable for its audiovisual texture: the helicopter attack on the coastal village.

I would like to suggest that as filmic discourse, the beginning of *Apocalypse Now* is as complex as that of *Heart of Darkness*. Moving beyond the obvious functions of introducing the viewer to the setting of the Vietnam War and giving a prologue to the film's plot, the opening also serves as a comment on, and postscript to, the film we are about to see. Sound clashes with image: watching the film's first images, the voice we hear is that of Jim Morrison singing 'This is the end'. One interesting feature of this song, which represents the first words in the film, is that in addition to announcing its own title, it offers an attempt at explaining the title of the film. The idea of 'apocalypse' describes our sense of a final ending, such as the doomsday of Christian tradition or the modern-day version of global nuclear war. Long-lived and yet changing, apocalyptic notions are prevalent in many cultures. As Frank Kermode puts it in *The Sense of an Ending*, 'the apocalyptic types—empire, decadence and renovation, progress and catastrophe—are fed by history and underlie our ways of making sense of the world from where we stand, in the midst' (Kermode 1981: 29). Although it does not become clear what role the apocalyptic plays in *Apocalypse Now*, several of the types mentioned by Kermode (including empire, decadence, and catastrophe) are actualized in Coppola's film. Moreover, the insistent way in which both the opening and the film as a whole invite interpretation and yet complicate and defer it suggests a parabolic feature which could be related to the idea of apocalypse as expressed in *Apocalypse Now*.

Coppola's ambitious exploration of the problem of filmic beginning in *Apocalypse Now* calls the opening of Wajda's adaptation of Conrad's *The Shadow-Line* strikingly to mind (see Chapter 4). This is not to say that the filmic techniques of the two directors are similar; in significant ways they are not. But it is to suggest that, inspired as they both are by the literary material of Conrad's novellas, Coppola and Wajda share a common fascination with the problem of how to begin (and, by implication, end) a film. Whereas Coppola explores this problem through a combination of filmic devices of which the uses of sound are particularly important and innovative, Wajda does so not least through the suggestive incorporation of photographs into the film's beginning.

If *Apocalypse Now* is considered as an adaptation of *Heart of Darkness*, critics tend to disagree about how, and to what extent, Willard and Marlow can be compared. As indicated already, to most viewers who have read *Heart of Darkness* Marlow probably seems to be more consistently distanced from, and critical of, the events that confront him than is Willard. Yet it is not always easy to determine the extent to which Willard's dubiously ambivalent attitude to his actions is related to, perhaps in part a result of, the fact that he is so inarticulate. Moreover, Marlow's attitudes are not wholly unambivalent either, and there is after all a great difference between being an officer in the army's secret service during military action and a captain on board an African river steamer belonging to a European power. Considered as a critique of American warfare in Vietnam (and of American imperialism), *Apocalypse Now* is at its most effective in those parts of the film where Willard displays his critical distance from the military action. This comment applies in particular to one sequence in the film. Because one crew member of the patrol boat which is to take Willard up the Nung river happens to be a well-known surfer, the surf-loving officer in charge of the helicopter squadron (Colonel Kilgore) decides that they might just as well combine the task of getting the boat past the delta with a terror air attack on a coastal village. The attack is worthless from a military point of view, but the waves off the coast are excellent for surfing! Elsaesser and Wedel have also written well of this key scene:

> The scene opens with the Air Cavalry going into battle with the bugle call of the traditional John Ford western. There follows a series of extreme long shots of helicopters against the sky, accompanied by atmospheric extradiegetic music, which toward the end gives way to superimposed medium profile shots of Willard, marking a transition to a series of medium close-ups from inside the lead helicopter showing Colonel Kilgore talking to Lance and instructing his pilot. These shots are underlaid by loud engine noise, so that the protagonists have to shout in order to communicate with each other, while the viewer is not meant to understand every detail of the men's exchange. Kilgore, framed in close-up and audible, then gives orders to start the music, followed by a medium close shot of the tape recorder. The shot ends with a slight pan to the right to reveal the set of loudspeakers outside the helicopter, which are thus identified as the diegetic source of the music now swelling in volume. (Elsaesser and Wedel 1997: 167–8)

In this scene, as in the opening one considered above, the film's audiovisual texture is remarkably complex. The rhythm of Wagner's music is used by Coppola as an editing principle; the volume of the music is constant, while the sound of the helicopter's rotor blades (which we think we recognize from the film's beginning) varies. Here as in the opening scene, the effect of sound is visually enhanced as the camera, following the rhythms of the Wagner score, modulates from long shots of the helicopters to various medium and close shots back to two extreme long shots. Then follows an abrupt cut of all sound elements, and a change of image from the helicopters to a Vietnamese village.

If, as several critics have noted, this kind of perspectival change is thematically productive in *Apocalypse Now*, its overall effect largely depends on the visual images and combinations of sound which precede and succeed it. Coppola achieves, to apply a phrase from Eisenstein's introduction to the

Francis Ford Coppola's *Apocalypse Now*—from the helicopter attack on a coastal village in Vietnam.

screenplay for *The Battleship Potemkin,* a transition to 'a sharply opposite quality'. 'The image of the same theme is . . . presented from the *opposite* [perspective] although it *grows out of the theme itself*' (Eisenstein 1988: 10–11, original emphasis). Compared to the approaching helicopters, the everyday life of the village to which the cut relocates the action—with its village square, huts, and schoolchildren—appears to the viewer as a 'sharply opposite quality'. Sound is used first to accentuate the contrast, then to bring the two worlds together in a violent clash resulting in the deaths of many civilians, the loss of a helicopter which provokes Kilgore to ask for a napalm strike, and a closing medium shot of Kilgore preparing for his surfing session ('I love the smell of napalm in the morning'). The first sounds are those of village life: children's voices, adults talking, dogs barking. The sound we then hear is, as Elsaesser and Wedel point out, a faint buzzing sound which reminds us of the very first sound we hear in the film. At first the viewer (like the village inhabitants) has difficulty in identifying the sound; when we manage to do so we relate it not to the helicopters but to the music of Wagner. How are we to understand this constellation of sound, noise, and voices? Are the Valkyries perhaps, as Elsaesser and Wedel suggest, riding to collect dead heroes from the field of battle? The inhabitants of the village are terrified, and the viewer is confronted with the destructiveness of war and its apocalyptic implications. 'If', finds Margot Norris, 'the mass war dead at century's beginning were proletarianized, the mass war dead at century's end are radicalized' (Norris 1996: 159). The context of Norris's discussion is the Persian Gulf War in 1991, a later conflict, different from the one in Vietnam. Yet there are also similarities between these two historical war narratives. Part of the effect of the helicopter attack on the coastal village in *Apocalypse Now* resides in the manner in which Coppola, elegantly and meticulously combining a whole range of filmic devices, displays the attack as an exercise of pure power, thus calling attention to its inherent absurdity and immorality.

On its voyage to the Congo, the boat on which Marlow is a passenger passes a French man-of-war off the coast of West Africa. 'It appears', says Marlow, 'the French had one of their wars going on thereabouts.'

> In the empty immensity of earth, sky, and water, there she was, incomprehensible, firing into a continent. Pop, would go one of the six-inch guns; a small flame would dart and vanish, a little white smoke would disappear, a tiny projectile would give a feeble screech—and nothing happened. Nothing could happen. There was a touch of insanity in the proceeding, a sense of lugubrious drollery in the sight; and it was not dissipated by somebody on board assuring me earnestly that there was a camp of natives—he called them enemies!—hidden out of sight somewhere. (pp. 151–2)

Conrad's discourse here is functionally metonymic, in part oxymoronic. Metonymy consists in the naming of a thing by one of its attributes, as, for example, when we say 'the crown' meaning the king or when we use 'Conrad' to mean all of Conrad's works. Metonymy is created here by the man-of-war being seen as representing, or being equated to, what France/Europe is doing in Africa. Although the metonymy's content is not specified (after all, it is 'incomprehensible'), a possible interpretation of the incident is suggested by Marlow as, resorting to a form of negative dialectic, he uses words such as 'drollery' and 'insanity'. The contrast between the boat firing indiscriminately into the jungle and the immensity of the African continent strikes Marlow as absurd. This kind of contrast highlights the oxymoron in this extract: a juxtaposition of two words or concepts that in ordinary usage are contraries (the man-of-war pitted against an enormous continent).

Calling the African natives 'enemies' is not very different from Kilgore's direct characterization of the Vietnamese villagers as 'fucking savages'. The helicopter attack on the coastal village exhibits also 'a touch of insanity'. Although there is difference in effect, stemming mainly from the use of advanced weapon technology, it is widely acknowledged that the military effect of the extensive bombing in North Vietnam was surprisingly small (though the number of civilians killed was large). The helicopter sequence in *Apocalypse Now* leaves the viewer with the impression of an absurd action with grotesque overtones. In an Academy Award-winning performance, Robert Duvall manages to portray Lieutenant-Colonel Kilgore as credible in spite of all his insanity. Through this spectacular display of systematized insanity within the military system, Kilgore is effectively contrasted with Kurtz, who has defected from the system and perhaps for that very reason is regarded as 'insane' by his superiors.

Martin Sheen gives a more nuanced presentation of Willard in this sequence than later on in the film. Willard's attitude to what he sees is less ambivalent here than towards the end of *Apocalypse Now*; apparently shocked by and distancing himself from Kilgore and his cronies, he even reflects upon the meaninglessness of the attack and the loss of human lives. Even though Willard appears to be more sceptical about the military system here than earlier on, however, he seems to forget, or suppress, his objections to the war in the film's concluding part. To make this point is to draw attention to the problems associated with *Apocalypse Now* being divided into two parts: a magnificently directed, spectacular first half (two sequences of which we have briefly considered), and a more evasive, ambiguous, mystical second half revolving round Kurtz, Kurtz's regime in the Cambodian jungle, and Willard's intrusion into Kurtz's reign of terror. Willard's journey on the patrol boat up the river forms a transition between the two parts, though it is closer to the first than to the second.

Obviously, the up-river journey lasts a shorter time in the film than in the novella. In this mid-section of the film too Coppola activates a number of cinematic devices in order to present the journey in a way reminiscent of Conrad's literary description. Willard's inability to communicate his impressions is still notable; his reflections are extremely restrained compared to Marlow's. Coppola makes use of voice-over in order to transmit some of Willard's thoughts and these are, generally speaking, centred on Kurtz. Although such a restraint is fairly reasonable since Kurtz is the man he has been sent to 'terminate' (not save, as in the case of Marlow), it causes Willard to remain more unfathomable (and in one sense superficial) to the viewer of *Apocalypse Now* than Marlow, through his first-person narration, is to the reader of *Heart of Darkness*. Willard's reluctance, or inability, to communicate his own reactions and thoughts is a problem that increases with his remarkable passivity; he is, as Francis Vanoye has noted, 'above all a viewer' (Vanoye 1991: 160; my translation).

Here as in other parts of the film, our assessment of the filmic techniques Coppola uses (partly to compensate for what is lacking in Willard) will vary depending on the viewer's knowledge, and interpretation, of *Heart of Darkness*. One significant aspect of Coppola's cinematic method here is restriction of camera angle and, by implication, the crew's (and the viewer's) perspective. Mounting a camera on the patrol boat contributes to creating, and gradually intensifying, a picture of the boat as a foreign intruder into an unknown and potentially dangerous territory. A long shot of the river strengthens this impression rather than reducing it: we see a small boat on a river surrounded by a vast jungle. As part of the voice-over narration Willard speaks of a 'main circuit cable leading right into Kurtz'. The viewer is inclined to relate this comment not only to the filmic image of the Nung river but also to Marlow's description of the 'overwhelming realities' (p. 183) of the jungle, with its 'mighty big river . . . resembling an immense snake uncoiled' (p. 142).

Coppola supports perspectival control by presenting the boat's crew as naïve and ignorant. They do not appear to understand anything about the war they themselves are taking part in, nor do they seem to comprehend their situation as dangerous at the beginning (one of them goes water-skiing). As the boat moves up-river, the film shows how the crew, despite their lack of understanding, develop an increasingly forceful impression of the jungle's 'overwhelming realities'. Their sense of impending danger is intensified as a dense fog makes it even more difficult to navigate the river. It all culminates in a stream of arrows pouring on to the boat.

That the narrative of *Heart of Darkness* is stripped of specific geographical reference makes it less problematic for the viewer to compare Coppola's film to Conrad's novella. Cinematographer Vittorio Storaro has claimed that in *Apocalypse Now* he 'wanted to express the main idea of Joseph Conrad, which is the imposition of one culture on top of another culture' (Cowie 1990: 130). Suggesting that Conrad inspired not just Milius and Coppola but other members of his crew as well, this comment draws attention to the challenge of developing filmic equivalents to Conrad's literary impressionism, which is at its most suggestive at this stage of the narrative. ' "Will they attack?" whispered an awed voice. "We will all be butchered in this fog," murmured another' (p. 192). Shortly afterwards Marlow comments: 'Sticks, little sticks, were flying about—thick: . . . We cleared the snag clumsily. Arrows, by Jove! We were being shot at!' (pp. 199–200). Commenting on this passage as an example of delayed decoding, Ian Watt finds that

> *Heart of Darkness* is essentially impressionist in one very special and yet general way: it accepts, and indeed in its very form asserts, the bounded and ambiguous nature of individual understanding; and because the understanding sought is of an inward and experiential kind, we can describe the basis of its narrative method as subjective moral impressionism . . . *Heart of Darkness* embodies more thoroughly than any previous fiction the posture of uncertainty and doubt; one of Marlow's functions is to represent how much a man cannot know. (Watt 1980: 174)

One reason why film has difficulty in conveying this kind of mental impressionism is suggested by its proximity to, if not dependence on, Marlow's sensations and reflections as a narrator. Faced with the challenge of adapting the passage from the novella which describes the attack on the steamer, one possibility could be to exploit the formal conventions of the horror film, to which *Apocalypse Now* is obviously related. Yet as Seymour Chatman points out,

Coppola does not use, for instance, confusing lighting here. Rather, he 'changes the emphasis by assigning the "little sticks" reference to Willard's *dialogue*' (Chatman 1997: 212; original emphasis). When the arrows start hitting the boat Willard shouts: 'They're little sticks; they're just trying to frighten us.' But this reading of the situation is wrong: Chief is pierced by a spear and dies. One effect of Chatman's illustrative example is to draw attention, once again, to the great difference between Willard and Marlow. It is an indication of Willard's limited capacity as a narrator that the impressionist features of this scene of the film are observable elsewhere—particularly, as indicated above, in Coppola's use of extreme camera angles which thus perform essential narrative functions.

The viewer's impression of Willard's position and attitude (to Kurtz and to the war) as problematically ambiguous is strengthened towards the end of the film, especially in the strange final sequence with Kurtz. This is the most controversial part of *Apocalypse Now*. Some critics regard this concluding part as a failure, while most agree that there is a problematic relationship between the film's ending and its earlier parts. Referring again to the statement by Eisenstein which I quoted when discussing the scene of the helicopter attack, we could say that the quality of the film's ending is sharply opposed to the first part. That there is a contrast between the film's two parts is obvious, but it is not made clear what the quality of the last part is, nor does it seem to grow 'out of the theme itself'. Its constituent elements (of form as well as content) are very diverse, and the interpretative signals it provides are conflicting and confusing—especially if, as the film's first part invites us to, we regard *Apocalypse Now* as a forceful critique of the Vietnam War. It needs to be added, however, that although it is unclear in what thematic direction(s) the final part of the film is moving, it becomes clear that Coppola attempts to move beyond, to present something more than, and different from, a relatively specific critique of one particular war. Though the attempt may not be wholly successful, such a generalizing movement is very interesting if the film is considered as an adaptation of *Heart of Darkness*: we have noted a similarly generalizing movement of the thematics in Conrad's narrative. In Conrad's novella, however, the movement beyond imperialist critique (which serves to give the text another, more generalized 'quality') grows 'out of the theme'. Two main reasons for this difference between Conrad's literary narrative and Coppola's filmic one are suggested by the narrative and metaphorical structure of *Heart of Darkness*; the novella is not in two parts and, in contrast to *Apocalypse Now*, it returns to the narrative frame at the end.

Coppola actually produced three different versions of the ending of *Apocalypse Now* and had great difficulty in choosing between them. In the version he eventually chose to use, *Heart of Darkness* continues to be a significant source of inspiration, but aspects of Conrad's novella are blended with allusions to other literary works. Before the actual killing, Coppola presents several scenes where Kurtz reveals some of his thoughts through poems he reads aloud to Willard; he also shares his reflections with Willard in a way that reminds the viewer of the tape-recording of Kurtz's voice at the beginning of the film. If it is hardly credible that Kurtz should recite poetry to his own executioner, this is just one of several events that remove the ending of *Apocalypse Now* from realist film conventions. The poems provide a literary clue, so obvious that it would be more appropriate to call it a reference than an allusion, to three of T. S. Eliot's most famous poems: 'The Love Song of J. Alfred Prufrock' (1917), *The Waste Land* (1922), and 'The Hollow Men' (1925).

The filmic presentation of these three poems varies. 'Prufrock', the most famous of Eliot's earlier poems, is referred to by the American photographer whom Willard encounters at Kurtz's headquarters. An ardent admirer of Kurtz, this strange character is modelled on the Russian Marlow meets who eagerly insists that Kurtz 'has enlarged my mind' (p. 215). The photographer uses the same expression, which is obviously taken from *Heart of Darkness*. The reference to *The Waste Land* is not given as a quotation from the poem, but is nevertheless very clear. During one of Kurtz's soliloquies, the camera pans along the wall of Kurtz's room and then pauses sufficiently long by a table to allow the viewer to read the titles of several books: the Bible, the *Aeneid*, James Frazer's *The Golden Bough*, Jessie Weston's *From Ritual to Romance*. As all of these titles are related to Eliot's poem, we link the presentation of Kurtz and his ideas to a masterpiece of modernist poetry. The most explicit reference to Eliot, however, occurs when Kurtz reads the first twelve lines of 'The Hollow Men' aloud to Willard:

> We are the hollow men
> We are the stuffed men
> Leaning together
> Headpiece filled with straw. Alas!
> Our dried voices, when
> We whisper together
> Are quiet and meaningless
> As wind in dry glass
> Or rats' feet over broken glass
> In our dry cellar

In the filmic situation, Kurtz's reading of this extract has a self-characterizing function. Coppola is inviting the viewer to regard Kurtz as a 'hollow' human being similar to 'The Hollow Men', one of the bleakest poems written by Eliot. Eliot's pessimism is essentially a cultural pessimism that, strengthened by the experience and disillusionment of the First World War, incorporates a critique of modern secularized society—compare the title *The Waste Land*, to which 'The Hollow Men' is thematically related. Ancient rituals and myths (surveyed by Frazer in his pioneer work on magic and religion, published between 1890 and 1915) represent for Eliot a positive contrast to modern society. Moreover, the epigraph to 'The Hollow Men' ('Mistah Kurtz—he dead') is taken from *Heart of Darkness*, and in Conrad's novella Marlow describes Kurtz as 'hollow at the core' (p. 221). If we read the poem's title and epigraph as an invitation to regard Kurtz as a representantive of 'the Hollow Men', then Eliot's poem contributes significantly to the characterization of Kurtz in *Apocalypse Now*. Robert Crawford has observed that '*Heart of Darkness* mattered not for giving Eliot the anthropological reader a better idea of how primitive society worked, but for showing Eliot the poet that the life of the savage and that of the modern urban clerk intersected on the deepest level, the level of "The Horror" which was, essentially for him, the realization of evil within man' (Crawford 1990: 168). This point may be linked to the way in which the symbol of darkness functions in *Heart of Darkness*: it is just as much a part of 'civilized' human beings as of 'primitive' ones. Thus we have returned to the novella's narrative technique, which constitutes a vital link between the two dimensions.

The references to Eliot in the closing sequence of *Apocalypse Now* are an extension of the links with *Heart of Darkness* rather than a replacement. Panning around Kurtz's room, the camera focuses not only on the three books mentioned above but also on a manuscript which is clearly Kurtz's work. On one of the pages of this typed manuscript it says in large handwriting (once again the camera pauses sufficiently long for the viewer to read the sentence): 'Exterminate them all!' That Coppola thus makes the portrayal of Kurtz dependent on the viewer reading a manuscript is an interesting filmic device which, momentarily reducing the difference between literature and film, functions very differently from, say, Willard reading the sentence out loud. The viewer who is familiar with *Heart of Darkness* will connect this manuscript to the report which the 'International Society for the Suppression of Savage Customs' requests Kurtz to compile, 'for its future guidance' (p. 207). Having read this report, Marlow describes it as a rhetorically elegant defence of Europe's colonial involvement in Africa. But, he ironically adds, with a 'valuable postscriptum':

> There were no practical hints to interrupt the magic current of phrases, unless a kind of note at the foot of the last page, scrawled evidently much later, in an unsteady hand, may be regarded as the exposition of a method. It was very simple, and at the end of that moving appeal to every altruistic sentiment it blazed at you, luminous and terrifying, like a flash of lightning in a serene sky: 'Exterminate all the brutes!' (p. 208)

Using the same verb suggests a parallel between film and novella, but the effect of the narrative presentation of the 'postscript' is noticeably greater in the literary text than in the film. In *Heart of Darkness*, the later addition both extends and deconstructs the legitimizing rhetoric of Kurtz's report. It represents a form of insight that is both aggressive and disillusioned, and which may be linked to Kurtz's final exclamation: 'The horror! The horror!' Kurtz's cry of death becomes authoritative for Marlow since it appears to summarize a whole life experience; it is in one sense a final oral remark on the handwritten comment in the report. Marlow claims that his main reason for hating lies is that lying gives him a taste of death. Coppola's Kurtz also informs us that there is nothing he despises more than lies. Coppola uses the closing cry of 'The horror!' twice, first as a direct statement from Kurtz and then as a voice-over comment to emphasize the strong impression the remark makes on Willard. And yet the meaning of 'the horror' in the film is unclear. Although the word's meaning is not unambiguous in *Heart of Darkness* either, in Conrad's novella it is more closely, and more consistently, related to other textual elements (such as the symbol of darkness) and to the novella's overall textual intention. Although it is possible to link the 'horror' of Coppola's Kurtz to, for example, the helicopter attack, the connection is not obvious since the film's ending departs so radically from the first part.

Does this criticism of the adaptation imply too direct a comparison of literature and film? The indirect, distancing, and generalizing manner in which verbal fiction operates makes the reader of *Heart of Darkness* 'visualize' textual events and conflicts. Marlow plays a decisive role in initiating and sup-

Is it 'the horror' Willard sees? Martin Sheen as Captain Willard in Francis Ford Coppola's *Apocalypse Now*.

porting this process of reading. As Marlow draws on the (variously reliable) information provided by others in order to characterize Kurtz, his description is rather indirect; Kurtz is presented as enigmatic and impressive, dangerous and frightening. Sørenssen points out that

> for as long as possible, Coppola attempts to maintain Conrad's indirect description of Kurtz by representing the *figure* of Kurtz as a shapeless shadowed appearance. Initially, Willard is presented with some cryptic static-distorted radio messages from Kurtz; and the images he is presented with are blurred depictions of a towering, human-like form. Following Willard's arrival, Coppola tries to prolong this effect by keeping Kurtz in the shadow. Sooner or later, however, Coppola is forced to portray Kurtz directly, and although Marlon Brando does his Actor's Studio best to maintain the illusion of someone super- or extra-human, from this point on Kurtz loses the mystique that he has in *Heart of Darkness*. (Sørenssen 1995: 161–2)

Despite the series of links with *Heart of Darkness* that I have indicated, the meeting between Willard and Kurtz appears as very different from the meeting between Marlow and Conrad's Kurtz. Many of these differences arise, as Sørenssen indicates, from the different ways in which verbal fiction and film operate. Having said this, it needs to be added that Coppola's presentation of the two main characters' meeting is very suggestive—both in itself (i.e. as filmic presentation) and with a view to *Heart of Darkness*. It is significant, for instance, that for a long while Kurtz is for Willard only a voice; in *Heart of Darkness* the power of Kurtz's voice is repeatedly stressed (pp. 225, 237). Then, as Chatman puts it, 'sections of Brando's totally bald head appear, sliced by totally black shadows, brilliantly visualizing Conrad's description' (Chatman 1997: 212–13): 'And the lofty frontal bone of Mr Kurtz! . . . this—ah—specimen, was impressively bald. The wilderness had patted him on the head, and, behold, it was like a ball—an ivory ball' (p. 205). This scene of the film suggests to Chatman that 'not Marlow, but Colonel Kurtz has become a Buddha—or rather an anti-Buddha, a bloody, unforgiving idol' (Chatman 1997: 213). In the final paragraph of *Heart of Darkness*, the frame narrator compares Marlow to 'a meditating Buddha' (p. 252, cf. pp. 136 and 140), and an image of a large Buddha is also incorporated into the opening sequence of *Apocalypse Now*. At this early stage of the film, however, it is related to Willard, not Kurtz. How are we to understand this complex form of double reference—to Willard and Kurtz, to Buddha and anti-Buddha? The image's import appears to be strengthened through repetition, yet its thematic significance is unclear. Again, part of the problem is associated with the inarticulate Willard. Up to a point, we can perhaps explain Willard's passivity as an unavoidable consequence of the war in which he is engaged (seen thus, the act of killing Kurtz in one sense confirms his passivity, as he has been ordered to do it). His passivity does, however, create a remarkable contrast to Marlow's perceptive reactions to the events he confronts. It is not least the combination of Willard's lack of reflective, attitudinal distance from the events on the one hand, and Coppola's mystification through quasi-ritualistic elements and horror effects on the other, that makes the ending of *Apocalypse Now* so problematically blurred.

Although the concluding part of *Apocalypse Now* makes the film more aesthetically uneven than *Heart of Darkness*, however, it would be both misleading and simplistic to conclude that 'the book is better than the film'. As a literary text *Heart of Darkness* can portray the Congo, the jungle, and Kurtz in the light of Marlow's experiences. In *Apocalypse Now*, Willard's experiences are not relayed to the reader in a similar manner. Although he claims that his story is 'a confession', Willard's account is marginalized by the film's complex blend of images, sound, and a large variety of filmic effects. On the other hand, one could claim that nowhere in Conrad's novella is the absurdity and brutality of war so forcefully exposed as in the scene where the coastal village is being attacked by helicopters in *Apocalypse Now*. One striking effect of all the links between *Heart of Darkness* and *Apocalypse Now* is to illustrate how differently literature and film function.

In 1991, thirteen years after the première of *Apocalypse Now*, several of the questions discussed here were raised again in the documentary *Hearts of Darkness: A Filmmaker's Apocalypse*. Promoting and in part confirming the status of *Apocalypse Now* as a Vietnam classic, this film, directed by Fax Bahr and George Hickenlooper working together with Eleanor Coppola, illustrates how difficult it is for Americans (and partly for Europeans and Asians as well) to put the Vietnam War behind them. Seen in this light, *Hearts of Darkness* is related to films such as *Loin de Vietnam* (A Long Way from Vietnam) from 1967, a French co-production where a number of directors put critical questions about Europe's relationship to the Vietnam War. Indicating the European texture of *Apocalypse Now*, Eleanor Coppola's documentary also confirms the affinity between Coppola and German directors such as Werner Herzog, whose *Aguirre, Wrath of God* (1972) 'visualizes primordial nature as an antagonistic and terrifying force that dwarfs and eventually destroys the colonizer' (Kaez 1997: 620).

The title *Hearts of Darkness*, we notice immediately, expresses a more explicit connection with Conrad's novella than does *Apocalypse Now*. This type of direct connection is confirmed a number of times throughout the film. Eleanor Coppola, who shot the film while her husband Francis was directing *Apocalypse Now*, refers in the introduction to the unsuccessful attempt made by Orson Welles to adapt *Heart of Darkness* in 1939. The purpose of this reference is partly to illustrate how difficult any adaptation of *Heart of Darkness* would be, partly to underline Francis Ford Coppola's level of ambition as a director. The reference to Welles is then linked to a comment made by Coppola himself where he (retrospectively) characterizes *Apocalypse Now* as a 'modern telling of *Heart of Darkness* in a Vietnam setting'. Finally, *Hearts of Darkness* incorporates passages from Welles's 1938 radio broadcast of *Heart of Darkness*. Elsaesser and Wedel find that 'the film Welles did make, *Citizen Kane*, is haunted by the text it had displaced, and the ghost of Welles's *Heart of Darkness* would also haunt Coppola and his collaborators' (Elsaesser and Wedel 1997: 151).

Critics disagree as to whether this documentary tells us anything importantly new about *Apocalypse Now*, or about films as adaptations of literary works. True enough, the links established by this film to *Heart of Darkness* are interesting. Yet as we have seen, such links already exist in *Apocalypse Now*, and it may be more rewarding to discuss them as they are presented in Coppola's film (as elements of adaptation in a narrative filmic discourse) than as statements in a documentary. *Hearts of Darkness* is perhaps most interesting at the level of detail, as when Coppola suddenly compares himself to Kurtz. This comparison can be related to a remark Coppola made speaking to journalists at the Cannes Festival in 1979: 'This film is not about Vietnam.' Read as an indication of what Coppola wanted to achieve, through the medium of film, with *Apocalypse Now*, this statement is given intertextual resonance by a key sentence in Conrad's *Heart of Darkness*: 'All Europe contributed to the making of Kurtz' (p. 207).

8

Virginia Woolf's *To the Lighthouse* and Colin Gregg's *To the Lighthouse*

In his preface to Rachel Bowlby's *Virginia Woolf: Feminist Destinations* (1988), Terry Eagleton points out that whereas male literary critics have tended to celebrate Virginia Woolf's modernism while downplaying her feminism, some feminist critics have gone to the other extreme. It must be added, though, that in feminist scholarship Woolf is referred to and discussed in many different ways (cf. e.g. Moi 1985: 1–18; Dusinberre 1997).

If we roughly divide Woolf criticism into two categories—a 'male discourse' centred on Woolf's modernism and a 'female discourse' focused on problems from the feminist angle—then Bowlby usefully reminds us that neither of these categories is stable, either in Woolf's texts or in interpretations of these texts. For example, while a study of 'Woolf's modernism' may well contain insights and conclusions that are relevant in a feminist perspective, feminist scholarship has clearly helped us to a better understanding of Woolf as a modernist writer.

A narrative analysis will preferably seek to avoid tying itself to *one* of the two main groups just outlined. Although as a 'male author' I cannot of course dissociate myself from the influence of the horizon of cognition (Gadamer) within which I am placed, or from my interests (Habermas) in the text I am working with (see p. 157), I would still argue that a narrative analysis can be relevant and useful in a range of different interpretative contexts—and for readers of both sexes. Psychoanalysis stresses, for instance, that in human development there is no subjectivity without sexual distinction (from the other sex), and there is no natural, 'programmed' development forward towards any final feminine or masculine identity. Since the dominant line of development was the masculine, girls were influenced to define themselves (also sexually) in relation to a norm from which they were in a way excluded. Woolf dramatizes important aspects of this complex of problems in *To the Lighthouse*, particularly in connection with the characterization of Mrs

Virginia Woolf, *To the Lighthouse* [1927], Oxford World's Classics, ed. Margaret Drabble (Oxford: Oxford University Press, 1998). Colin Gregg, *To the Lighthouse* (1983); BBC-TV Colin Gregg Films.

Ramsay and Lily Briscoe. Since this characterization is interwoven with the narrative technique, a discussion of Woolf's narrative can interact with a psychoanalytical criticism of the novel. Similarly, narrative analysis may be linked to other approaches, for example Pierre Bourdieu's anthropological interpretation, to which I shall refer on several occasions.

I

As a starting-point for the analysis I shall quote an excerpt from the presentation of *To the Lighthouse* in Margaret Drabble's *The Oxford Companion to English Literature* (1997):

> The novel is in three sections, of which the first and longest, 'The Window', describes a summer day, with the Ramsays on holiday with their eight children and assorted guests, who include the plump and lethargic elderly poet Augustus Carmichael; the painter Lily Briscoe (who represents in part the struggle and cost of female creativity); and the graceless lower-middle-class academic Charles Tansley. Family tension centres on the desire of the youngest child, James, to visit the lighthouse, and his father's apparent desire to thwart him: the frictions of the day are momentarily resolved around the dinner table, and a triumphant *boeuf en daube*, as Mrs Ramsay reflects that 'something . . . is immune from change, and shines out . . . in the face of the flowing, the fleeting, the spectral, like a ruby' [p. 142]. The second section, 'Time Passes', records with laconic brevity the death of Mrs Ramsay and of her son Andrew, killed in the war, and dwells with a desolate lyricism on the abandoning of the family home, and its gradual post-war re-awakening; it ends with the arrival of Lily Briscoe and Mr Carmichael. The last section, 'The Lighthouse', describes the exhausting but finally successful efforts of Lily, through her painting, to recapture the revelation of shape-in-chaos which she owes to the vanished Mrs Ramsay, and the parallel efforts of Mr Ramsay, Camilla, and James to reach the lighthouse, which they also accomplish, despite the undercurrents of rivalry, loss, and rebellion that torment them. The novel represents a heroic exploration and re-creation of the bereavements and (real or imaginary) tyrannies of the past; it also displays Woolf's technique of narrating . . . at its most assured, rich, and suggestive.

That this plot summary concludes by referring to the novel's narrative technique indicates how important it is in this text. We note the elements of interpretation in the summary, as in the character sketches of Lily Briscoe. We also note that Woolf's narrative method as described here *complicates* a chronologically ordered story version and makes it more misleading than, for example, the one Florence Walzl gives of 'The Dead'. Dominick LaCapra goes so far as to claim that *To the Lighthouse* is not divided into chapters, but rather structured like a piece of music in three movements (LaCapra 1987: 143). The story time in part 1 is concentrated into a September afternoon and evening. Yet this part is five or six times longer than part 2, in which the story time amounts to ten years.

To the Lighthouse turns upside-down and questions 'ordered' or 'structured' time. At the same time the novel presents, or perhaps rather explores, an alternative temporal structure through its own discourse. Consider the novel's opening:

> 'Yes, of course, if it's fine tomorrow,' said Mrs Ramsay. 'But you'll have to be up with the lark,' she added.
>
> To her son these words conveyed an extraordinary joy, as if it were settled the expedition were bound to take place, and the wonder to which he had looked forward, for years and years it seemed, was, after a night's darkness and a day's sail, within touch. (p. 7)

We see that the text starts *in medias res*: it takes us straight into a conversation between two of the characters. 'Yes' indicates that the first sentence in the novel answers a question, but this question lies outside the discourse. The reader is inclined to imagine that it is James who poses the question, and that what he is asking about is whether they are at last going to make the journey to the lighthouse. The interesting thing here is not so much the wording of the question (perhaps it is identical with what Mrs Ramsay hears James asking again towards the end of chapter 10: 'Are we going to the Lighthouse?', p. 84), as the movement beyond the text that the beginning signals. By so clearly indicating that there is something beyond or before the text, the opening of *To the Lighthouse* reflects upon the arbitrariness of its own beginning. Concomitantly, the opening indirectly calls into question more conventional beginnings of novels, in which the author typically makes the third-person narrator begin by introducing the action and the main characters.

It is true that the main characters are presented here too, but more through their utterances, actions, and attitudes than through introductory narrative comments. For when we again read Mrs Ramsay's opening reply with the knowledge of the whole novel, it is striking how charged with meaning it is. The opening utterance has a particularly strong characterizing effect as a contrast to Mr Ramsay's first remark:

> 'But', said his father, stopping in front of the drawing-room window, 'it won't be fine'.
>
> Had there been an axe handy, a poker, or any weapon that would have gashed a hole in his father's breast and killed him, there and then, James would have seized it. Such were the extremes of emotion that Mr Ramsay excited in his children's breasts by his mere presence; standing, as now, lean as a knife, narrow as the blade of one, grinning sarcastically, not only with the pleasure of disillusioning his son and casting ridicule upon his wife, who was ten thousand times better in every way than he was (James thought), but also with some secret conceit at his own accuracy of judgement. What he said was true. It was always true. He was incapable of untruth . . . (p. 8)

Coupled with the opening reply this quotation reveals distinctive features of the novel's narrative, which is third-person and panoramic in the sense that

Woolf does not limit the narrative perspective to a first-person narrator. Since a first-person narrator is active on the text's diegetic level of action, the motivation she or he has for telling the story is existential and linked to her or his own experiences, desires, plans, etc. That in our reading of *To the Lighthouse* we cannot localize the narrator as a participant in the plot is an indication of third-person narrative. We do not know who, or what, the narrator is. Nor does the text tell us where she, he, or it is located. What does gradually become clear, however, and what the quotation above also indicates, is that Woolf's narrator is a flexible and sophisticated instrument. As Hillis Miller puts it:

> Whatever may be said of Woolf herself, the narrator of *To the Lighthouse* has extraordinary powers. The narrator enters at will into the minds of all the characters, or perhaps it might be better to say that the narrator is located already within all those minds and is able to speak for them in that strange, third-person, past-tense form of narration: indirect discourse, *erlebte Rede*, or *style indirect libre* . . . (Miller 1990: 155–6)

Miller here points to significant characteristics of the narrative technique in *To the Lighthouse*. The narration is not first-person, but Woolf develops a form of third-person narration that includes and exploits qualities that we often link to the first-person variant. The most important of these qualities is perhaps the profound effect the presentation gives of being related to the consciousness or perspective of one character. This applies in particular to parts 1 and 2. While the narrative voice remains relatively stable as the text proceeds (with the partial exception of part 2), the narrative perspective varies between different characters, and between these characters and the unidentified third-person narrator.

This rhythmic alternation forms a series of thematically productive narrative variations, and I shall comment on the most important of these. The following analysis focuses on selected extracts from the text and transitions that are important both narratively and thematically. The discussion of Colin Gregg's adaptation of the novel will take up relatively little space, but I shall comment on the film in connection with the discussion of all the three parts of the novel, and also towards the end of the chapter.

Let us return to the text's opening. The narrator quotes two utterances of two of the main characters, Mrs and Mr Ramsay. These utterances clearly have a characterizing function, both in themselves and through the way in which they are linked to the following discourse. In both cases, this discourse is related to James's perceptual perspective. Through its design, the reader gets the impression that James reacts not only to the utterances but also to the positions, not to say the parental attitudes, that they signal. The narrative movement from utterance to personally coloured reaction and association reveals something that turns out to be a central paradox in the novel's narrative technique. The paradox concerns the knowledge and insight of which the third-person narrator is in possession: even if she knows the thoughts and feelings of the characters (and reveals these to the reader), this knowledge is as a rule limited to the character concerned. Thus, the reader gets the impression of a series of subjective and personally coloured perspectives rather than a comprehensive one. It varies from character to character *how* subjective and *how* limited this perspective is. This alternation is a narrative variation constituted by a number of devices including irony, distance, and sympathy. Such narrative devices form an important part of the third-person narration, which is also crucial to establishing the characteristically gliding transitions between different—sometimes complementary, sometimes conflicting—perspectives.

When it comes to the two utterances themselves, Pierre Bourdieu points out that in a strikingly condensed way Mrs Ramsay's opening reply heralds the attitude she has both to James and to her husband. 'Yes' reveals that she does not have the heart to answer 'No' to the question, which she has certainly heard many times before. As early as the first sentence of the novel, however, the two conditions she attaches to this 'yes' allude to her role of mediator, the harmonizing function she has in the Ramsay family. They reflect too what Bourdieu calls her compliance with the husband's 'principle of reality'. We get the first narrative presentation of this principle, which both Mrs Ramsay's opening utterance and James's reaction to her reply in one sense pre-empt, in the sentence ' "But", said his father, stopping in front of the drawing-room window, "it won't be fine" '. Bourdieu comments that 'the father's "no" does not need to be stated or justified, and the initial "but" is there to show that, for a reasonable being, there can be no alternative other than docile submission to the force of circumstance' (Bourdieu 1989: 12). Above all, it is the kill-joy element and the unchallengeable character of the statement that makes James hate his father. In contrast to his reaction to his mother's opening utterance, James's negative response to his father's remark indicates that Mr Ramsay has provoked him in similar ways before. Thus both these utterances, placed right at the opening of the text, point not only forwards but also backwards in time to previous questions and previous answers.

The linking of utterance and reaction to an utterance serves to establish the novel's narrative technique. The narrative communication of James's reactions is third-person, something which shows itself most clearly in informative narrative statements. Still, the narration is clearly character-oriented. Moreover, although the narrator marks the personal perspective through tags such as '(James thought)', she appears not only to understand but even partly to support James's criticism of his father. Woolf achieves this effect through a combination of narrative devices, of which two are particularly important.

The first is linked to the contrast between James's reactions to the two utterances. This contrast is great—it represents the gulf between the 'extraordinary joy' he feels in respect of his mother on the one hand, and the hatred his father provokes in him on the other. The narrator refers to the 'extremes of emotion' Mr Ramsay provokes in his children, but judged as spontaneous (and characterizing) reactions this contrast in response becomes all the more striking on a second reading of the novel. The second narrative device that has an important function here (both in itself and as a supplement to the first) concerns the use of narrative sympathy and distance. As we will remember from Chapter 2, these two concepts may refer to the narrator's attitude to the characters she is presenting. If without further qualification we say that the narrator can have a sympathetic or a critical attitude, we note that Woolf makes the narrator invite the reader to sympathize with James, partly through the contrasting of his responses to the two utterances, partly through the narrative modulating towards James's perspective. This 'invitation', which is a way of influencing the reader, is then confirmed through the use of narrative distance. Here the narrative distancing means that when the third-person narrator switches the perspective from James to Mr Ramsay, the discourse becomes more critically revealing. By way of illustration we can take the quotation above a little further:

> He was incapable of untruth; never tampered with a fact; never altered a disagreeable word to suit the pleasure or convenience of any mortal being, least of all his children, who, sprung from his loins, should be aware from childhood that life is difficult; facts uncompromising; and the passage to that fabled land where our brightest hopes are extinguished, our frail barks founder in darkness (here Mr Ramsay would straighten his back and narrow his little blue eyes upon the horizon), one that needs, above all, courage, truth, and the power to endure. (pp. 8–9)

The character sketch that the narrator gives of Mr Ramsay is authoritative and general; it seems to be based on this character's actions and attitudes throughout the text. If the narration is less character-oriented here, this is because the characterization focuses on Mr Ramsay's principle, and not (as above) on James's feelings. When we read that Mr Ramsay is 'grinning sarcastically', we interpret this as James's reaction to what his father says and the way he grins. But in the latter example we get, to use narrative terms to illustrate one of Bourdieu's points, a distanced third-person presentation of Mr Ramsay's attitude to his children. While earlier the narrator, by modulating her narrative perspective towards James's perceptual perspective, has created an impression of Mr Ramsay's utterance as brutally illusion-shattering, here he is rather presented as a father who forms his attitude to his children on the basis of conscious and considered choices. Mr Ramsay's considered choices, says Bourdieu, include the choice of

> paternal love . . . which refuses to give itself up to the culpable facility of a feminine, blindly maternal indulgence, and is thus duty bound to express everything that is

harshest, most unbending and most pitiless in the necessity of the world (this is, no doubt, what is meant by the metaphor of the knife or of the blade—rendered banal by a naively Freudian interpretation—which locates the masculine role in the domain of cutting, violence, and murder . . .). We start to suspect that the torturer is also a victim. (Bourdieu 1989: 12–13)

By relating what we have said so far to this insightful comment, we can state that Woolf's narrative design of the first two pages of the novel is unusually productive. We have here much more than a technical opening *in medias res*—also *thematically* the novel opens near its own centre. This appears to be the case even though I cannot see any 'thematic core' or an 'overall theme' in the novel. *To the Lighthouse* is too complex both narratively and thematically for me to wish to isolate any single overall theme. Still, there is a lot to be said for a point a number of critics have formulated in slightly different ways: that at the centre of the novel's thematics we find not so much a character as a relationship. The relationship between Mrs and Mr Ramsay—including the complex set of problems it entails and actualizes—is absolutely central to the novel, and it is striking how precisely, and with what characterizing effect, this relationship is sketched right at the text's beginning. The concept of 'relationship' is also thematically interesting (albeit in another way) in part 3, especially in the presentation of Lily's relationship with the late Mrs Ramsay.

We shall have an opportunity to return to the insights in the quotation from Bourdieu, but before taking the analysis any further I specify that even if the discussion of the novel's beginning has been relatively extended, it has by no means been exhaustive. For example, I have not commented on the important intercalation in Mr Ramsay's crushing utterance, ' "But," said his father, stopping in front of the drawing-room window, "it won't be fine" '. At first reading, this insertion may seem like an insignificant narrative variation—an affirmative comment interposed by the third-person narrator in the communication of the utterance. If we look more closely, we will discover that the intercalation is really an integral part of the utterance: the fact that Mr Ramsay stops in front of the window emphasizes and complements what he says. In concrete terms he blocks the view to the lighthouse both for Mrs Ramsay and for James. Within the discourse this is in itself a serious action, for this view opens the text by making James ask the question which Mrs Ramsay answers and which the following comment elaborates. For James, the view of the lighthouse reinforces his intense desire to go there. Thus Mr Ramsay not only blocks the view to the lighthouse in a concrete sense, he also takes from James the joy and hope that the view of the lighthouse awakens in him. We can also note the title of part 1, 'The Window', and the relationship between this part and 'The Lighthouse', which Woolf entitles part 3.

'The Window' signals Mrs Ramsay's perspective in part 1. Through the window, while doing a thousand things at once, she can keep an eye on the children and co-ordinate the family's activities. This she does with tact and with a natural authority that embodies, as Lily reflects towards the end of part 3, 'astonishing power'—'Even her shadow at the window with James was full of authority' (p. 238). In the light of the harmonizing function she has, it is interesting that her reply to her husband's utterance (by which she observantly notices that James is upset) involves a certain amount of criticism: '"But it may be fine—I expect it will be fine," said Mrs Ramsay, making some little twist of the reddish-brown stocking she was knitting, impatiently. If she finished it tonight, if they did go to the Lighthouse after all, it was to be given to the Lighthouse keeper for his little boy . . .' (p. 9). Criticism, but cautious criticism: it is doubly qualified by 'may' and 'I expect'. This utterance is harmonizing both in relation to her husband, with whom she is actually irritated, and James, whom she is anxious to comfort. The clearest indication the narrator gives of her irritation is localized to the adverb 'impatiently', but knitting 'impatiently' is probably much too cautious a signal for Mr Ramsay to perceive it.

Combined with the comments that support them, the three opening utterances in *To the Lighthouse* show a sophisticated and complex variant of third-person narration. While the first two utterances signal two positions which turn out to be central in the novel (and which concern the exercise of power, human attitudes, and ways of functioning socially), through the third utterance Mrs Ramsay starts a dialectic movement forwards in the text. This utterance is thus a good example of Woolf's narrative economy: its harmonizing function is important in relation to characterization. Moreover, this utterance serves to activate the 'dynamic shaping force' (Brooks 1984: 13) of the narrative discourse. What at first may appear to be two deadlocked, static positions is taken further, among other things through the introduction of the minor character Charles Tansley. Thus the beginning of the novel is integrated in the plot that gradually unfolds.

Woolf uses the third-person narrator to structure and embroider this pattern. The insight the narrator has into the characters' thoughts, feelings, and associations is crucial to the flexible and varied perspective with which this insight is correlated. The variation is technically sophisticated, serving several thematic purposes. Over and over again, Woolf makes the narrator convey the subjective impressions of events rather than the events themselves, or more correctly, rather than a 'neutral' version of these events. Through this narrative technique Woolf shows that subjective impressions, even of the same event, are often strikingly different, and that these differences of impression and interpretation actually problematize not only a concept such as 'event' but also questions of identity, direction in life, and stability of human relations. Perhaps, thinks Lily in part 3, Mrs Ramsay is glad in death to be able 'to rest in the extreme obscurity of human relationships. Who knows what we are, what we feel?' (p. 232).

II

How does the adaptation of *To the Lighthouse* begin? If my discussion so far may seem to indicate that significant features of the text's beginning would be difficult to transfer to the screen, Colin Gregg's attempt does go some way to confirming such a hypothesis. The film opens with a shot of James looking towards the lighthouse. Underneath (as superimposed information) we can read 'Cornwall 1912'; thus the plot's setting has been transferred from the Isle of Skye (or possibly the Hebrides) off the coast of Scotland to the south-west of England. Though relatively insignificant, this change of location makes the film more autobiographical than the novel, since Woolf spent childhood summers in Cornwall (see Lee 1997: 21–3). More importantly, however, the adaptation does not develop the image of James looking at the lighthouse. It does not include the possible question James asks his mother ('Can we go to the Lighthouse tomorrow?'). Nor does the film give us Mrs Ramsay's answer (which in Woolf's novel opens the text) or Mr Ramsay's comment. If we link these differences to our discussion

Rosemary Harris as Mrs Ramsay and Christopher Lahr as James (aged six) in Colin Gregg's *To the Lighthouse*. © BBC Picture Library.

of the novel's beginning above, we can see that the film opens in a very different way.

Yet although there are several narrative devices and thematic effects in the literary text that the film version either cannot or does not try to convey, I must again warn against too direct comparison of book and film. Even if, of the four adaptations subjected to discussion in Part II, Gregg's may be the most ordinary, it also has its qualities—as in the attempt to visualize the central part of the novel, 'Time Passes'.

There are two particular characteristics of *To the Lighthouse* that complicate a comparison of the novel and the film. It is true that these factors also apply to the other adaptations, but Gregg's attempt to solve these problems makes them conspicuous in an instructive way. The first characteristic, which concerns the relationship between a first and second reading of the novel, prompts questions about the conditions of comprehension for a literary text in relation to film. *To the Lighthouse* seems to insist on close reading, and rereading. This effect is related to the novel's elaborate pattern of repetition and metaphor; it is also associated with the varied functions the narrative comments have. As we have seen, it is characteristic of the novel that so much lies in and outside the characters' utterances. This aspect of the narration is thematically significant. It shows how much of a personal encounter is felt rather than said (thus providing a basis for associative thought), and how closely aspects of power and feelings of impotence are related to roles and positions. When we see the film, we can no doubt feel some of this, but our impression of what goes on under the visualized surface becomes weaker and more imprecise than that created through Woolf's verbal discourse. That we must necessarily have read the novel to be able to compare what the two media do has a paradoxical effect: it makes it clear what the film does not include, but it also enables us to use our knowledge of the text to supplement the surface visualized in the film.

The second complicating factor when it comes to the adaptation of this novel is related to the narrative presentation of time and perceptions of time. Alongside novels such as Marcel Proust's *In Search of Lost Time* (1913–27) and William Faulkner's *The Sound and the Fury* (1929), *To the Lighthouse* is as persistent as it is innovative in its fictional exploration of time. I shall return to the novel's presentation of time (even if a more thorough analysis of it would require a chapter of its own, at least). The relevant point here is that the novel's presentation of time is greatly simplified in the adaptation. All those who see the film with a knowledge of the book will be able to ascertain this difference, yet it does not follow that the film is 'bad'. What the adaptation's simplified presentation of time primarily actualizes is the relationship between the conveying of time in different media. One aspect of this complex issue concerns the need film has for temporal progression, which is generally greater than the corresponding need in novels. Having said this, it needs to be added that

Gregg's attempt at adaptation is relatively traditional and not very experimental. Had he chosen (and consistently attempted) to be as precise in relation to the literary text as John Huston is with 'The Dead', the film would probably have been more experimental but not necessarily better. The textual starting-points are very different, and a successful adaptation of *To the Lighthouse* much more difficult to achieve than one of Joyce's short stories. Thus Gregg is probably right in not using a stable voice-over in the film. Although such a narrative voice could have communicated more information and reflection, it would rapidly have got out of step with the novel's special variant of third-person narrative.

After Mrs Ramsay's third utterance dialectically opens a deadlocked situation and takes the action further, many of the individual events onward into part 1 have a confirming, yet also refining, function in relation to the novel's opening. Let us consider the narrative presentation of Mr Ramsay's 'war-game' (Bourdieu 1989: 13). Mr Ramsay stamps himself in his first utterance as possessing strong and obstinate paternal authority. On the subsequent pages, Mr Ramsay's academic authority is accentuated through the narrator's presentation of Charles Tansley, a philosopher self-importantly studying 'the influence of something upon somebody' (p. 19). Woolf achieves the slightly ironic tone in the presentation of Tansley by modulating the third-person narrative perspective towards Mrs Ramsay's first-person perspective. Partly she sympathizes with Tansley (because of his difficult background), partly she dislikes him (since he repeats her husband's rejection of James). The narrative perspective is still linked to Mrs Ramsay when this sequence gradually switches to the presentation of Mr Ramsay's war-game:

> Suddenly a loud cry, as of a sleep-walker, half roused, something about
>
> Stormed at with shot and shell
>
> sung out with the utmost intensity in her ear, made her turn apprehensively to see if anyone heard him. Only Lily Briscoe, she was glad to find; and that did not matter. But the sight of the girl standing on the edge of the lawn painting reminded her; she was supposed to be keeping her head as much in the same position as possible for Lily's picture. Lily's picture! Mrs Ramsay smiled. With her little Chinese eyes and her puckered-up face she would never marry; one could not take her painting very seriously; but she was an independent little creature, Mrs Ramsay liked her for it, and so remembering her promise, she bent her head.
>
> 4
>
> Indeed, he almost knocked her easel over, coming down upon her with his hands waving, shouting out 'Boldly we rode and well', but, mercifully, he turned sharp, and rode off, to die gloriously she supposed upon the heights of Balaclava. Never was anybody at once so ridiculous and so alarming. (pp. 25–6)

We note the transition in narrative perspective, from 'her head' to 'her easel'—from Mrs Ramsay's head to Lily's easel. The transition has an elegance characteristic of Woolf and is at first hardly noticeable, although the textual or chapter transition, as marked by the figure '4', in this instance makes it easier for the reader to follow the perspectival shift in the narration. Such typographical marking of shifts of perspective is by no means something the reader can rely on in this novel. Rather in the same way as does Faulkner in *The Sound and the Fury* (in which the temporal shifts in respect of the retarded narrator Benjy are sometimes marked by italics, sometimes not), Woolf uses typographical marking not only to structure the text in a traditional sense, but also to reveal how problematic and arbitrary such structuration can be.

In narrative terms Woolf carries out this variation of perspective by making the third-person narrative voice remain relatively stable, while the narrative *perspective* follows the war-game-playing Mr Ramsay, but without permanently attaching itself to him ('Stormed at with shot and shell' is a line from Tennyson's 'The Charge of the Light Brigade' (1854)—Mr Ramsay seems to identify with the war victims glorified in this poem). Instead the narrative perspective associates itself first with Mrs Ramsay, who observes her husband from the window, and then (when Mr Ramsay almost knocks over the easel in the garden) with Lily. Here as elsewhere, the dominant form of discourse is a past-tense form that seems to indicate that the event—seen from the narrator's unidentified vantage-point—has been completed.

Characteristically, moreover, this mode of discourse mixes reporting of events with reporting the thoughts of those characters with whom the narrator chooses to associate her perspective. There is a significant narrative variation in the exclamatory sentence 'Lily's picture!' This example of free indirect discourse shows how clearly the third-person narrator's perspective is related to Mrs Ramsay's perspective in this paragraph. When the perspective then changes to Lily's, we get a good illustration of Genette's point that narrative perspective refers to the character who is *seeing*, not to the character who is speaking. This type of shift is characteristic of the novel's narrative technique. Such shifts involve a series of perspectival changes in which the third-person narrator associates her presentation with the cognitive perspective of different characters. The degree of personal approach varies: it is clearer in relation to Mrs Ramsay, who is presented sympathetically (but not completely uncritically), than in relation to Mr Ramsay, in respect of whom the narrator is more reserved. Taken together, this combination of narrative devices is structurally formative and thematically productive.

In spite of the general differences between literary language and visualized film language, perspective is one of the narrative terms that it is most natural to link with film. As in the history of art the concept of perspective has been closely associated with painting, its great significance in film illustrates how the functional range of one particular term can be extended as new art forms develop. In *Narration in the Fiction Film*, David Bordwell notes that perspective 'is the central and most fully elaborated concept within the mimetic tradition of narration. Perspective conventions grew up as storytelling devices. [The art historian] E. H. Gombrich has suggested that Greek art took as its purpose the rendition of characters in action at specific moments in a story' (Bordwell 1985: 7; Gombrich 1996: 129–38). Through the medium of verbal fiction, in *To the Lighthouse* Virginia Woolf activates and explores conventions, distinctive features, and artistic possibilities of perspective in a way comparable to that of visual artists. It is not coincidental that Lily is a painter.

When it comes to filmic communication of the event being discussed here, we can imagine that the camera first focuses on Mr Ramsay from the window before cutting to a spot right by Lily in the garden. (Gregg has chosen to delete this scene, and on the whole he does not exploit the possibilities of perspectival change associated with the camera.) It is more difficult to convey filmically the personal associations which are linked to the two perspectives, and which are both narratively and thematically central in the literary text. For it is not a matter of chance that it is Mrs Ramsay and Lily who observe Mr Ramsay playing a private war game with great enthusiasm. They are both distanced observers of this behaviour, not participants in it. What is it that Mr Ramsay, the renowned philosopher and mighty father, is actually doing here? He appears to be engaged in an activity that entails a radical break with the picture we first get of him in his opening utterance, the utterance to which James reacts so violently. Bourdieu offers some perceptive comments:

> So the same Mr Ramsay, who appeared on the very first page of the novel to be a formidable figure, masculine and paternal, the father–king who pronounces judgment, is caught playing like a child.
>
> The whole logic of the character, an archetype of masculinity, is contained in this apparent contradiction. Mr Ramsay, like the archaic king described by Émile Benveniste in his *Vocabulaire des institutions européennes*, is he whose word is law. (Bourdieu 1989: 12)

For Bourdieu, this apparent contradiction in Mr Ramsay's attitude and person relates to what he calls 'the fantasies of the *libido academica*, metaphorically expressed in war-games' (p. 13). Metaphorically we can read Mr Ramsay's war-game as a reconstruction of the intellectual activity he performs as a man. The game then becomes a form of daydream; it gives illusory effect to Mr Ramsay's desire for fame and respect, thus supplementing the later textual passage in which the third-person narrator, with distance and slight irony, presents Mr Ramsay's thought as a precise instrument which—at least in the peace and quiet of his own study—can reach the letter Q, but which then becomes uncertain: 'He reached Q. Very few people in the whole of England ever reach Q. . . . But after Q? What comes next?' (p. 47).

In this sequence the narrative distance from Mr Ramsay is primarily marked through the content and implications of his thoughts, which the third-person narrator omnisciently reveals to the reader. We note that in this instance the use of free indirect discourse has a distancing, ironic effect rather than a sympathizing one (as in the example with Mrs Ramsay above). The supposedly working philosopher is strangely passive here. Suggesting that Mr Ramsay is academically insecure, this passivity is related to the energetic activity he conducts in the war game. A little later in chapter 6, the narrator makes this association clearer through the war metaphors that permeate her characterization of Mr Ramsay. Who can criticize him, thinks Mr Ramsay, if it should happen that he is finally found

> dead at his post, the fine figure of a soldier? Mr Ramsay squared his shoulders and stood very upright by the urn.
>   Who shall blame him, if, so standing for a moment, he dwells upon fame, upon search parties, upon cairns raised by grateful followers over his bones? (p. 50)

Bourdieu sees this extract as an example of Woolf's technique of the 'dissolve'—a form of characterization that entails both contrasting and drawing parallels between Mr Ramsay's private and public spaces (private in his study and in the war game, public in the family and through teaching and publishing). The insight that the third-person narrator has into the private space is revealing. As insights into the private sphere make the outward, public picture of Mr Ramsay start to crack, this kind of narrative knowledge puts Woolf in a position to use characterization as a basis for a more general commentary. This kind of narrative commentary is difficult to summarize since it is closely interwoven with the presentation of both Mr and Mrs Ramsay. However, Bourdieu makes some telling points when he says that through the combined presentation of Mr Ramsay's war game and office 'work' Woolf uncovers

> the heart of the male *illusio*: the one whereby men (as opposed to women) are socially constructed in such a way as to let themselves be ensnared, like children, by all the games that are socially assigned to them, the model of which, *par excellence*, is war . . . Since, among the games that make up our social existence, those considered serious or important are reserved for men, while those reserved for women are children's games, one may forget that a man is also a child playing at being a man. Privilege originates in alienation: it is because they have been brought up to acknowledge the social games in which the stake is domination that men preserve a monopoly in them; it is because they are marked out very early as dominant, and consequently endowed with a *libido dominandi*, that they have the double-edged privilege of participating in games for dominance and of having these games reserved for them alone. (Bourdieu 1989: 13)

Although this generalizing comment may be controversial, it points to significant aspects of the thematics of *To the Lighthouse*. I refer to it partly for that reason, and partly since Bourdieu emphasizes that it is the *narrative presentation* of the novel's thematics that makes it so convincing and engaging. It is also interesting that a number of points in the analysis where Bourdieu refers to Woolf's narrative technique can be commented on more precisely by using narrative terms. As the force of Bourdieu's argument derives in large part from his knowledge of, and contributions to, other disciplines such as sociology and cultural theory, this also exemplifies how interdisciplinary narrative theory is. When, for example, Bourdieu stresses how important it is that the reader should only *gradually* perceive what Mr Ramsay's war game is all about, he is focusing on a variant of the narrative device which the Russian formalists called 'defamiliarization', and which we can also link to Ian Watt's concept of 'delayed decoding'.

'Delayed decoding' refers to a narrative technique that presents the effect of an event or an activity *before* we get to know the cause of the event. When the cause is then presented, it may be obvious (as in the case of the arrows raining on Marlow's boat in Joseph Conrad's *Heart of Darkness*), but it can also be complex and unclear. If we say that the reason why Mr Ramsay plays war games belongs to the latter category, then we imply that what we have here is a complex blend of causes and reasons which needs to be subjected to analysis (as Bourdieu does) in order to be adequately understood. Ironically enough, the philosopher Ramsay does not seem to reflect on why he himself plays. This lack of insight into the reason for the war-game characterizes Mr Ramsay just as much as the game itself, which he expects to be just as private and undisturbed as his work in his study. When in his playful enthusiasm he suddenly comes upon Lily and William Bankes, they both get a feeling of having 'encroached upon a privacy' (p. 27).

The two sequences that present Mr Ramsay in the war game and in his study are among the most important in part 1. In conclusion of the discussion of this part of *To the Lighthouse*, I choose to focus on two textual passages: the first comes in chapter 11, while the latter, in chapter 17 is often called the 'dinner scene'. Even though these passages refine the characterization of Mr Ramsay in the two sequences we have just looked at, it is his wife who is the main character in both of them.

We might ask how much Mrs Ramsay understands of her husband's peculiar war-game. Although the text as a whole indicates that she is the one who understands Mr Ramsay best, for instance when it comes to his insatiable need for sympathy and praise, the text does not provide any clear answer to this question. That she is not particularly surprised at her husband's singing hops and jumps need not mean that she understands the cause, but probably rather comes from the fact that she has seen her husband doing the same thing before. For as the narrative variously indicates, many of Mr Ramsay's activities, both professional and practical, have such a clear character of repetition that Mrs Ramsay can pre-empt what he will do, and not least what he will demand of her. Yet as the discourse presents and elaborates the division of roles between the two, it is not only Mrs Ramsay who can imagine her husband's demands and expectations: he for his part can rely on her positive response. Indeed, perhaps such a positive response, with the acquiescence or submission it implies, is necessary to keep the family together. The novel repeatedly returns to this question, which in narrative terms is usually prompted by the third-person narrator's perspective associating itself with that of Lily. Here, as often elsewhere in the discourse of *To the Lighthouse*, one thematic effect of the narrative variations is to ask difficult questions rather than to give any sure answer. Yet at the same time, particularly through the presentation of Mr Ramsay in relation to Mrs Ramsay and Lily, the narration establishes premises for possible answers. These premises are sometimes stable, sometimes shifting—and they are linked, for example, to those demands and expectations we have of the relationship between two people living as a couple.

It is characteristic that when Mrs Ramsay reads, she reads aloud to James—not like Mr Ramsay, who reads alone in his study or silently to himself in the boat on the way to the lighthouse in part 3. Her actions project into a social context, a social space she establishes through what she does and from which her husband, the children, and the guests benefit. An interesting feature of chapter 11 is a narrative variation that presents Mrs Ramsay not only as acting but also as reflecting. These reflections start while she is still reading to James, and they are taken further in chapter 11 after he has fallen asleep. The narrative transition between the two sequences is designed thus:

> 'And that's the end,' she said, and she saw in his eyes, as the interest of the story died away in them, something else take its place; something wondering, pale, like the reflection of a light, which at once made him gaze and marvel. Turning, she looked across the bay, and there, sure enough, coming regularly across the waves first two quick strokes and then one long steady stroke, was the light of the Lighthouse. It had been lit.
>
> In a moment he would ask her, 'Are we going to the Lighthouse?' And she would have to say, 'No: not tomorrow; your father says not.' (p. 84)

The pivot of this transition—from reading to James, to knitting and thinking to herself for a brief moment—is the light from the lighthouse. Does the transition entail a shift of perspective? No, not as we have hitherto understood it, for the third-person narrator associates her perspective with Mrs Ramsay while she is still reading to James. She thinks how quickly, too quickly, the children are growing up: 'Nothing made up for the loss' (pp. 79–80) is an example of free indirect thought. As I read the paragraph after the transition (signalled by James falling asleep and the lamp of the lighthouse being lit), the third-person narration is nevertheless more strongly linked to Mrs Ramsay's perspective here. Thus, the transition illustrates that in *To the Lighthouse* the third-person narrator associates her perspective not only with different characters, and not only more strongly with some characters (such as Mrs Ramsay and Lily) than others (such as Mr Ramsay and Tansley), but that also the degree of perspectival approach to one and the same character may vary. Chapter 11 in part 1 is perhaps the point in the novel where the third-person narrative associates itself most closely with the reflections and feelings of one character. The reader is given signals of such an approach through the metaphorical quality of the lighthouse and the light coming from it, through the seriousness and realism of Mrs Ramsay's reflections, and through the peculiar descriptive pause that arises when she

> stopped knitting; she held the long reddish-brown stocking dangling in her hands a moment. She saw the light again. With some irony in her interrogation, for when one woke at all, one's relations changed, she looked at the steady light, the pitiless, the remorseless, which was so much her, yet so little her, which had her at its beck and call (she woke in the night and saw it bent across their bed, stroking the floor), but for all that she thought, watching it with fascination, hypnotized, as if it were stroking with its silver fingers some sealed vessel in her brain . . .
> (pp. 88–9)

The way in which Woolf here combines narrative devices and effects complicates analysis. I want to comment on some narrative variations that all interconnect with one another and that are thematically formative. We have already observed that the light is associated with the lighthouse, and thus also with the novel's title. As narrative repetition contributes to making the light into a symbol, the symbol of the light is complicated as its range of possible meanings is extended. It is still related to the lighthouse, but also appears more independent and is more closely connected to Mrs Ramsay: 'She praised herself in praising the light, without vanity, for she was stern, she was searching, she was beautiful like that light' (p. 87). By associating Mrs Ramsay with the light, both with the light from the lighthouse and with the light as a symbol, the third-person narrator emphasizes her key position in the novel's plot as well as in its thematics. Values that our cultural environment has long connected with the symbol of light are thus linked with Mrs Ramsay. From the Christian tradition we know light as an expression of God's leadership (as in Exodus 13) or of Jesus's salvation (as in John 1: 4–5), or in literary form as in Dante's *The Divine Comedy* and in the hymn

> Lead, Kindly Light, amid the encircling gloom
>   Lead Thou me on!
> The night is dark, and I am far from home—
>   Lead Thou me on! . . .

Even if chapter 1 of *To the Lighthouse* were to contain an allusion to this classic hymn written by John Henry Newman, however, this does not mean that

Mrs Ramsay feels as secure as he did in his Christian belief. What Woolf does here is rather to use the third-person narrator's insight into Mrs Ramsay's reflections to dramatize a form of doubt and disillusionment that characterizes much of European modernism:

> How could any Lord have made this world? she asked. With her mind she had always seized the fact that there is no reason, order, justice: but suffering, death, the poor. There was no treachery too base for the world to commit; she knew that. No happiness lasted; she knew that. (p. 87)

It is characteristic of the narrative presentation of this sequence that the third-person narrator, to the extent that she indicates her own position, seems to share Mrs Ramsay's reflections. The narrator in *To the Lighthouse* has insight into and conveys Mrs Ramsay's questions, yet by not answering (or not being able to answer) them she reinforces their seriousness and forceful relevance. This comment also applies to the function the questions have in relation to the reader: rather than providing firm interpretative guidelines associated with a given tradition of faith or understanding, they invite diverse responses and interpretations.

The difficulty of giving a confirming answer is correlated with a complicating extension of the meaning of the light symbol. In chapter 11 as in the novel as a whole, 'the light . . . the steady light' refers primarily to a set of qualities that the text itself, as narrative discourse, presents as important. These qualities are related to Mrs Ramsay's character and to her relations with other people. This does not mean that the third-person narrative necessarily presents Mrs Ramsay uncritically. The narrative linking with Lily's perspective can express criticism, for instance by indicating that Mrs Ramsay's conciliatory attitude on several occasions leads to her (as Lily sees it) compromising herself in relation to her husband. Yet although there is a good deal of truth in such an assessment, Mrs Ramsay's activities also include an element of managing control. Some critics find that the positive influence she has on others is surprisingly small, and is perhaps greatest after she is dead.

Broadly speaking, however, the association of the light symbol in chapter 11 (and in the whole novel) with Mrs Ramsay's reflections is a strong indication of her importance as a character situated at the centre of the narrative. Two narrative devices in the examples above support such a reading. They are related to one another, partly because they are both proleptic. The first is linked to the final sentence I have quoted from chapter 11: 'No happiness lasted; she knew that.' This sentence is important because of the way in which the assertion it formulates is supported by two later plot sequences: the dinner scene and part 2. The dinner scene is Mrs Ramsay's triumph, when for a brief moment she feels really happy. But this scene is placed towards the end of part 1; in part 2 not only is Mrs Ramsay dead, but two of her children are too.

The quotation depicting the light as 'stroking with its silver fingers some sealed vessel in her brain . . .' embeds a second prolepsis. While the first prolepsis points forward to the contrast between the ending of part 1 and part 2, the proleptic effect here is suggested by the way in which the light is personified. That in part 2 it is the dark that is personified rather than the light is meaningful in relation to the fact that Mrs Ramsay, who in one sense is the novel's bearer of light, is now dead. The essential point to make here, however, is that the use of personification has a distinctly proleptic effect as it points forward to one of the most important constituent aspects of the narrative technique in part 2. If, as Hillis Miller tends to do, we see a connection between the extensive use of personification in part 2 and its striking absence of characters, can we then consider this personification as a premonition of death for Mrs Ramsay? At any rate, it seems reasonably clear that the way in which the light symbol is related to Mrs Ramsay's reflections indicates an insight on her part which is associated with, and significantly contributes to, the novel's thematics. That she afterwards dislikes being reminded 'that she had been seen sitting thinking' (p. 93) does little to change this impression, and the marginalized position Mr Ramsay has in chapter 11 ('He could do nothing to help her', p. 89) strengthens it.

While Colin Gregg's adaptation brings out relatively few of the textual qualities of chapters 10 and 11, it concentrates on the dinner scene towards the end of part 1. Gregg's design of this film sequence draws on, and is inspired by, the following passage:

> Now all the candles were lit, and the faces on both sides of the table were brought nearer by the candle light, and composed, as they had not been in the twilight, into a party round a table, for the night was now shut off by panes of glass, which, far from giving any accurate view of the outside world, rippled it so strangely that here, inside the room, seemed to be order and dry land; there, outside, a reflection in which things wavered and vanished, waterily. (pp. 131–2)

The dinner scene, which this passage introduces, extends over many pages. The narrator communicates selectively excerpts from the conversation and details of the '*Boeuf en Daube*', the dish that is being served. The narrator's associations around, and provoked by, the family dinner are related to the perspectives of Lily and Mrs Ramsay—the first as attending guest and keen observer, the latter as organizer and leading mid-point in the conversation.

Here, as in Joyce's 'The Dead' (and also Blixen's 'Babette's Feast'), the presentation of the dinner scene creates an impression of relative harmony, and in both cases this impression is reinforced by the contrast with what comes afterwards: the scene with Gretta and Gabriel in the hotel room in 'The Dead', part 2 in *To the Lighthouse*. Moreover, in both cases the narration is third-person, but since Woolf puts more personally coloured reflection into the presentation than Joyce does, Joyce's presentation is more obviously 'scenic' in relation to the definition given in Chapter 3 above. It is also interesting that since in both texts latent conflicts 'underwrite' the conversation, it has to be managed and adjusted by (some of) those contributing to it. Finally, we may note that in both 'The Dead' and *To the Lighthouse* the dinner scene serves to establish a contrast between the light and warmth inside and the darkness and cold outside. In both texts the window marks the boundary between these two areas, but if we then ask what qualities they stand for or are associated with, the differences between the two texts become apparent—thus complicating (though in one sense inviting) further comparison.

A candle is also a light, but very different from the white, penetrating light from the lighthouse. As Gregg's adaptation shows, candlelight can illuminate the dinner table, create atmosphere, and shut out the night in such a way that in the room there 'seemed to be order and dry land'. The verb 'seemed' has a key function in this paragraph. On the one hand, it indicates distance between the characters and the third-person narrator, especially if we assume that she knows what is to come in part 2. On the other hand, the 'seemingly' safe and stable can also be linked to the more subjective impression the characters have of the positive atmosphere and harmony during the dinner as something that becomes more valuable *because* it is so unexpected and rare. In the next paragraph the narrator invites such a linking when she states that 'they were all conscious of making a party together in a hollow, on an island . . .'.

From this introductory paragraph there goes a narrative line through the whole textual segment up to the point towards the end of the dinner when Mrs Ramsay thinks that

> there is a coherence in things, a stability; something, she meant, is immune from change, and shines out (she glanced at the window with its ripple of reflected lights) in the face of the flowing, the fleeting, the spectral, like a ruby; so that again tonight she had the feeling she had had once today already, of peace, of rest. Of such moments, she thought, the thing is made that remains for ever after. This would remain. (p. 142)

These thoughts of Mrs Ramsay's have been interpreted very differently, yet everybody agrees that this is one of the central paragraphs in part 1. Many critics believe that these reflections, as the third-person narrator presents them, establish a positive contrast to the gloomy part 2. We should not forget, however, that earlier in the evening Mrs Ramsay has thought other thoughts, and as I have tried to show, chapter 11 in part 1 also contains important paragraphs about Mrs Ramsay. What Mrs Ramsay thinks appears to be influenced by the situation she is in and those she is together with; thus the ways in which Mrs Ramsay relates to others contribute to Woolf's overall characterization of her. As Martha C. Nussbaum has observed, 'Mrs Ramsay's identity for the reader is fundamentally constituted by her care for others, her public doings and actings' (Nussbaum 1995: 740). The free indirect discourse Woolf uses to convey

Mrs Ramsay's impression that 'This would remain' indicates on the one hand narrative distance, a sort of narrative reservation (cf. 'seemed' in the introductory paragraph), especially in relation to part 2. Yet the free indirect discourse also suggests a form of support for Mrs Ramsay's thoughts. The dinner has a value of its own that remains by virtue of the fact that it has been realized, and if we associate 'This' with Mrs Ramsay herself, part 3 of the novel shows her influence to be considerable and memories of her enduring.

III

While in part 1 of *To the Lighthouse* Woolf takes 160 pages to present the events, thoughts, and feelings within a family on *one* September afternoon and evening, in the narration of part 2 she goes to the opposite extreme. This part, which takes only twenty-four pages of text, covers a period of approximately ten years. Although there is still reference to the Ramsay family, part 2 is just as much a meditation—about time, absence, and loss of people—as it is a continuation of the plot presented in part 1. 'Absence', notes Gillian Beer in an essay on *To the Lighthouse*, 'gives predominance to memory and to imagination. Absence may blur the distinction between those who are dead and those who are away' (Beer 1996: 29). The ways in which time, absence, and loss are interrelated and explored in part 2 call the term 'elegy' to mind, a word used by Virginia Woolf in 1925 when she wrote in her diary that 'I will invent a new name for my books to supplant "novel". A new —— by Virginia Woolf. But what? Elegy?'

In Beer's phrase, 'in elegy there is a repetition of mourning and an allaying of mourning. Elegy lets go of the past, formally transferring it into language . . .' (Beer 1996: 31). As her essay demonstrates, elegy is a critically productive term to use when analysing *To the Lighthouse*, and part 2 in particular. And yet its relevance to a work of fiction partly explains why 'Time Passes' is unusually difficult to analyse. Not only does this part of the text establish a number of interwoven relations (linguistically, narratively, and thematically) with parts 2 and 3, it is also experimental and thematically productive in applying devices, techniques, and generic characteristics more commonly associated with poetry than with narrative fiction. Such devices and characteristics (of which elegy is one) challenge narrative theory in an area where it is relatively weak; yet they are so central to part 2 that I cannot avoid discussing them. If narrative theory has problems getting to grips with the complex discourse Woolf constructs here, the fault is with the theory and not with Woolf. Key terms for the selective and incomplete discussion that follows are narrative positioning and perspective, personification, repetition, and use of round and square brackets.

In part 2 Woolf also uses a third-person narrator. This narrator is a central narrative instrument for her in the whole novel. Combined with other literary means the narrator performs a series of functions which to a high degree are thematically creative, but, as the concept 'third person' indicates, it is unclear who or what the narrator is. As Hillis Miller puts it, the narrator in *To the Lighthouse* has

> none of the characteristics of a person except voice and tone. The reader learns nothing of the narrator's history, dress, opinions, or family relations. She, he, it is anonymous, impersonal, ubiquitous, subtle, penetrative, insidious, sympathetic, and indifferent at once, able to plunge into the depths of any character's thoughts and feelings but liable to move without warning out of one mind and into another in the middle of a sentence . . . The narrator, it seems, is a ubiquitous mind, present everywhere at all times of the past, but condemned to know and feel only what the characters know and feel . . . (Miller 1990: 156)

The critical value of the way in which Miller considers the third-person narrator lies just as much in the difficulties he mentions in localizing the narrator and understanding her functions, as in what he in fact says about her. The difficulties associated with the narrator present a challenge to both the reader and the critic of *To the Lighthouse*; they also illustrate how important the question of narrative technique is in this text. From Chapter 2 we will recall that Miller, in the same essay, warns against relating the narrator too closely to Woolf (see p. 18 above). The narrator in *To the Lighthouse* is not just a 'different person', she is an advanced narrative instrument combining many qualities. It is illustrative of this form of narrative flexibility that parts of the quotation above characterize the narrator in parts 1 and 3 better than they do the narrator in part 2. For in 'Time Passes' the narrator does not associate her perspective with the characters in the same way as before. As Miller stresses, this change is important thematically, both in itself and through the way in which it is combined with devices such as repetition and personification. If in part 1 we get the impression that the narrator articulates thoughts via a character, this does not apply to part 2. In a way this is a logical narrative variation, since the characters to whom the narrator has usually linked her perspective are now dead or absent. 'Time Passes' demonstrates that the novel's third-person narrative can function just as well without character-related points of reference, but the lack of such an attachment to the characters makes the narrator stand out as more impersonal—as a neutrally recording witness:

> Night after night, summer and winter, the torment of storms, the arrow-like stillness of fine weather, held their court without interference. Listening (had there been anyone to listen) from the upper rooms of the empty house only gigantic chaos streaked with lightning could have been heard tumbling and tossing, as the winds and waves disported themselves like the amorphous bulks of leviathans whose brows are pierced by no light of reason, and mounted one on top of another, and lunged and plunged in the darkness or the daylight (for night and day, month

and year ran shapelessly together) in idiot games, until it seemed as if the universe were battling and tumbling, in brute confusion and wanton lust aimlessly by itself. (p. 183)

The house was left; the house was deserted. It was left like a shell on a sand-hill to fill with dry salt grains now that life had left it. The long night seemed to have set in; the trifling airs, nibbling, the clammy breaths, fumbling, seemed to have triumphed. The saucepan had rusted and the mat decayed. Toads had nosed their way in. Idly, aimlessly, the swaying shawl swung to and fro. (p. 187)

These two examples are characteristic of what we can call the main narrative level in part 2. We see how Woolf creates linguistic and narrative rhythm through words that are identical or opposite ('night after night', 'night and day'), words characterized by alliteration ('winds and waves', 'life had left it'), and words which semantically mark rhythm ('waves', 'daylight'). The effect thus achieved is reinforced through the use of comma and semicolon. Rhythm is often looked upon as a stylistic means more than a narrative one, but the close connection between rhythm and repetition in these examples shows that the transition between these two constituent elements of a literary text can be hard to pinpoint. Repetition operates here at the word level, through the way in which the sentences are divided up, and in the references to the rhythmically repeating natural forces.

What kind of narrator expresses herself in this way? On the one hand, she appears completely impersonal and distanced; on the other, she can hardly function as a neutral, observant witness without leaving personal or human traces, as in 'seemed' in the second example. Hillis Miller argues that Woolf 'attempts a hyperbolic fulfillment of the project of Mr Ramsay's books' (Miller 1990: 161). As Andrew tells Lily, his father's books investigate 'subject and object and the nature of reality' (p. 33). When Lily says she does not understand what that means, the intelligent Andrew provides this example: 'Think of a kitchen table . . . when you're not there.' That it is difficult, not to say impossible to do so is something everyone who has tried knows. The context here is the British philosophers of the eighteenth century (Locke, Berkeley, Hume) in whom Virginia Woolf's father, Leslie Stephen specialized, for example in *History of English Thought in the Eighteenth Century* (1876). If a tree falls without anybody being there to hear it, asks the philosopher Berkeley, does it make any noise? While Berkeley answers that God guarantees that He hears all noise, Woolf tries in *To the Lighthouse* to confront the problem without any such metaphysical explanation. That the narrator in part 2 is central to this attempt may in part explain why her reflections continually circle around in their own language, their own narrative rhythm, rather than linking up with a character. How impersonal is the narrator's voice or language? Miller believes that 'the narrator of *To the Lighthouse* is not a ubiquitous mind but language itself; that language therefore takes precedence over consciousness here' (Miller 1990:

163). Although in one sense this explanation is persuasive, I see the third-person narrator as a narrative instrument that is linguistic but also 'narrative', since through prose fiction it can be variously presented and structured in relation to a (however distorted and incomplete) plot sequence. When in part 2 Woolf makes the narrator less personal, she not only stands out more clearly *as* language, she also makes visible more of the human traces *in* language (and, interestingly and perhaps unavoidably, Miller also ascribes personal qualities to the narrator).

Miller puts emphasis on Woolf's use of personification in part 2. Personification is a form of prosopopoeia: a figure of speech that entails our talking about what is absent, dead, or about an object as if it were alive—as if it had a human face, voice, and consciousness. The discussion of part 1 has given one example of personification; in part 2 this trope is central to the narration.

> Only through the rusty hinges and swollen sea-moistened woodwork certain airs, detached from the body of the wind (the house was ramshackle after all) *crept* round corners and *ventured* indoors. Almost one might imagine them, as they *entered* the drawing room, *questioning and wondering, toying* with the flap of hanging wallpaper, *asking,* would it hang much longer, when would it fall? Then *smoothly brushing* the walls, they passed on *musingly* as if *asking* the red and yellow roses on the wallpaper whether they would fade, and *questioning* (gently, for there was time at their disposal) the torn letters in the wastepaper basket, the flowers, the books, all of which were now open to them and *asking, Were they allies? Were they enemies? How long would they endure?* (p. 172, my emphasis)

The italicized verbs in this quotation all express *human* actions. Ascribing such actions to the wind entails personifying it. One sees it as a person or an individual who can wonder, play, ask. This personification is reinforced through repetition, and the narrator even gives examples of questions that the wind asks. What thematic purpose does the personification serve here, and what does it tell us about the narrator? We note that the expression 'almost one might imagine' has a function comparable to that we have already ascribed to 'seemed': both verbs give the third-person narrator a personal quality. Appearing impersonal, she records in a personal manner. The personifications stress the personal element, since the narrator associates her perspective with that of the wind. The reason why she can do so is that the wind is personified—thus the narrator makes it capable of posing questions that resemble those she lets the characters ask in part 1. The use of personification is in other words closely related to narrative functions. By personifying the wind, the narrator reflects Woolf's reflections on the limited ability we have, or the limited ability language has, to represent the house when it is empty, the kitchen table when we are not there, the world when we are dead. Through her depiction of the relationship between James and Mr Ramsay (who uses language to hurt his son), Woolf shows that human worth is not dependent on knowledge of language. Yet language is a prerequisite for reflective thought and experience, and it always seems to imply a perspective from which it is uttered or written. Combined with the variation in perspective and the use of personification, the person-related words in the quotation illustrate how embedded in each other are the narrative and thematic aspects of *To the Lighthouse*.

To the extent that the absence of a human perspective is an aim of the narrative technique of part 2, we might think of the film camera (as a mechanical instrument) as capable of presenting the empty house more 'directly' than can Woolf's prose. Gregg attempts to do so as the camera pans along the walls and furniture of the empty summer house, conveying its dilapidation—raw and cold, leaking and with furniture protected by makeshift coverings. The use of extradiegetic music strengthens the viewer's impression of slow, descriptively rhythmic camera movements in this sequence. This kind of filmic rhythm is related to the adaptation's temporal presentation of part 2. It illustrates that while the camera records and passes on to the viewer each individual image, it is guided—by the cinematographer, the director, and others involved in the production of a film. Although the camera objectively records and visualizes each image, the choice of images entails human selection, and so do the combination of images, the tempo of the presentation, the combination of light and sound, and so forth. Thus the film medium too illustrates, in its own way, the difficulty of representing the external, physical world with no human observer there.

To the Lighthouse strongly resists the kind of selective, chronologically ordered summary presented at the beginning of this chapter. Woolf's use of square brackets in part 2 is one of the most visible signs the novel gives of such resistance. For in these embedded textual fragments we find information, or what we might call fictional facts, which allow themselves to be much more easily arranged in a story version than the third-person narrator's reflections which here constitute the main text. This does not imply that what is contained in square brackets in part 2 is unimportant; on the contrary, they provide necessary information about events on the novel's diegetic level. Consider the last two pieces of text in square brackets in chapter 6:

[A shell exploded. Twenty or thirty young men were blown up in France, among them Andrew Ramsay, whose death, mercifully, was instantaneous.] (p. 181)

[Mr Carmichael brought out a volume of poems that spring, which had an unexpected success. The war, people said, had revived their interest in poetry.] (p. 183)

One effect such information has on the reader is to relate part 2 more closely to part 1, and an effect of this again is that the third-person narrator's observations and reflections in part 1 are more closely linked to the plot and the main characters. Although they are short (partly *because* they are short), the fragments of information in square brackets suggest what has prompted the narrator's reflections, thus situating them more clearly in a historical and cultural context. Presented as the most intelligent of the Ramsay children, Andrew has exceptional gifts in mathematics in particular. Since the unusually beautiful Prue Ramsay also dies young (something we are told in square brackets a little earlier in chapter 6), the two children who most clearly resemble their parents will be absent in part 3.

Dominick LaCapra notes that, as explicit marks of punctuation, square brackets can 'represent the way in which major and often negative forces of ordinary time and history are self-consciously contained, in a sense suppressed' (LaCapra 1987: 139). Yet as he also says, it is characteristic of Woolf's narrative technique that the negative events are not suppressed, silenced, or eliminated. Rather, the use of brackets constitutes a way of keeping events at a distance in order thus to be able to reflect on them and perhaps become reconciled with them. The narrative reflections gathered round the empty house are not essentially, and definitely not only, focused on general philosophical issues such as questions about time and the relationship between subject and object. These general questions are specified, dramatized, and intensified through the way in which they are related to a group of people, and by the story which provokes them: as part 2 places the Ramsay family in the context of the Great War, it reflects not only on time but on war as a form of man-made disaster, a 'gigantic chaos' (p. 183).

IV

Some of the loss on which part 2 dwells resurfaces when those members of the Ramsay family who are still alive meet again in the summer house in part 3. The definitive absence of Mrs Ramsay is central to this final part of *To the Lighthouse*, and the characters give expression to this loss in different ways. When Mr Ramsay in the opening of part 3 asks 'What's the use of going now?' (p. 197), it shows his irritation at their not getting to the boat (which is to take them out to the lighthouse) as early as agreed. Yet the 'now' in the question also has other implications. First, it is remarkable that Mr Ramsay is now so keen to get to the lighthouse, since he was the major obstacle to any possibility of the trip being undertaken in part 1. Second, 'now' not only refers to the delay on this particular morning, it also implies a 'then' that refers back to part 1. If we read the sentence in this way, we can supplement the question with the reflections the narrator conveys from Lily's perspective in the paragraph above: 'what did she feel, come back after all these years and Mrs Ramsay dead?'

As the third-person narrative in part 3 contains relatively few variations beyond those in the novel's first two parts on which we have already commented, the discussion of this final part can be relatively brief. The chapter will conclude with some more general comments on the novel's presentation of time and on Gregg's adaptation of it.

For Dominick LaCapra, the composition of *To the Lighthouse* is reminiscent of a piece of music in three movements. Employing another concept from musicology, we might say that part 3 serves as a counterpoint in relation to part 1. By this I mean that various 'points' in this final part take up and return to corresponding questions in the novel's first part, but in a manner that involves contrast and difference rather than—and in addition to—direct continuation. The main reason for this contrast lies in part 2, which occupies a key position in the novel both structurally and thematically. For example, the lighthouse is important in both parts 1 and 3, but given the ten years that have passed and the loss of Mrs Ramsay, it no longer has quite the same meaning for the characters (certainly not for James) or for the reader. Mrs Ramsay is dead, but the influence that part 3 shows she has had on the others (in particular Lily) paradoxically strengthens her position as the novel's main character. Mr Ramsay seems not to have changed very much, but he has aged, and his family authority is not quite what it used to be. Although the family has again gathered in the same summer house, both the house and the place appear different after the description in part 2.

Since Lily is the character in part 3 to whom the third-person narration is most often linked, she takes over some of the narrative functions Mrs Ramsay has in the first part. This we can illustrate with a couple of examples, but first it must be mentioned that the striking spatial quality of part 3 largely stems from the alternation in the third-person narration between two points: a fixed point on land where Lily is standing painting, and a point that is in motion at sea—the boat on its way out to the lighthouse. This alternation too constitutes a form of counterpoint, which, as it is performed here, has third-person narration as a precondition.

Before this narrative alternation is established, Lily and Mr Ramsay have a silent confrontation in the garden in front of the house:

> Mr Ramsay sighed to the full. He waited. Was she not going to say anything? Did she not see what he wanted from her? Then he said he had a particular reason for wanting to go to the Lighthouse. His wife used to send the men things. There was a poor boy with a tuberculous hip, the lightkeeper's son. He sighed profoundly. He sighed significantly. (p. 205)

> They stood there, isolated from the rest of the world. His immense self-pity, his demand for sympathy poured and spread itself in pools at her feet, and all she did, miserable sinner that she was, was to draw her skirts a little closer round her ankles, lest she should get wet. In complete silence she stood there, grasping her paint brush.
>
> Heaven could never be sufficiently praised! She heard sounds in the house. (p. 207)

In the way it is presented, the situation in this example resembles situations with Mr and Mrs Ramsay in part 1, in which the philosopher Ramsay constantly expects support and sympathy from his wife. His need for such sympathy does not appear to be less now; the difference lies in the fact that Lily is much less inclined to satisfy it than was Mrs Ramsay. Lily's reasons for rejecting Mr Ramsay's desire for sympathy are complex; they are in part presented in the third-person narrative which in part 3 is associated with her thoughts, feelings, and opinions. One reason for her rejection of Mr Ramsay is that she is not inclined to play up to him to the same extent as Mrs Ramsay, or more generally to satisfy the wishes and demands that men make in respect of women. Yet if Lily is consciously less conciliatory than Mrs Ramsay, she is also intelligent enough to realize that she can more easily stand up to a confrontation with Mr Ramsay than his wife could. Mrs Ramsay lived in the previous generation, and was the uniting and organizing central point on which a large family was dependent.

The effective use of free indirect discourse is linked both to Mr Ramsay's and to Lily's perspective. 'Was she not going to say anything?' signals the expectations Mr Ramsay has of Lily. One effect of the free indirect discourse here is that since the narrator formulates Mr Ramsay's question, his expectations are made clearer to the reader. At the same time it is uncertain to what extent Mr Ramsay is himself aware that he is transferring to Lily expectations and demands he had in respect of his late wife. The exclamation 'Heaven could never be sufficiently praised!' is also free indirect discourse, but we note that the narrator has now shifted the perspective from Mr Ramsay to Lily. Mr Ramsay's desire for sympathy is not satisfied: by using free indirect discourse the narrator inserts into the presentation of the meeting an explanation of why it develops into a silent confrontation.

Lily does not reject Mr Ramsay completely, however; as a kind of compromise she allows herself to comment on what fine boots he has. The main reason for the ambivalent attitude she has to Mr Ramsay lies in her great respect for his wife. Through a series of narrative reflections—which are related to Lily's perspective and thoughts, and which in part are clearly analeptic—this respect is presented and qualified. One constituent aspect of Woolf's presentation of the relationship between the two main female characters is to relate Lily's attempts at painting to the varied activities Mrs Ramsay performed. As early as part 1 Lily tries to paint (her motif is Mrs Ramsay framed by the window), but in part 3 her attempts are more concentrated and enduring, and in the end also more successful. She finds painting tiring, however, and in the breaks she has to take the narrator reports the thoughts Lily has about herself and about Mrs Ramsay. Thus, the analeptic jumps back to part 1 (in particular to a scene with Mrs Ramsay on the beach) provide the basis for Lily's reflections about her own situation in life and her future. On several occasions it is as if the memory of Mrs Ramsay helps Lily to greater self-insight:

> What is the meaning of life? That was all—a simple question; one that tended to close in on one with years. The great revelation had never come. The great revelation perhaps never did come. Instead there were little daily miracles, illuminations, matches struck unexpectedly in the dark; here was one. . . Mrs Ramsay saying 'Life stand still here'; Mrs Ramsay making of the moment something permanent (as in another sphere Lily herself tried to make of the moment something permanent)—this was of the nature of a revelation. In the midst of chaos there was shape; this external passing and flowing (she looked at the clouds going and the leaves shaking) was stuck into stability. Life stand still here, Mrs Ramsay said. 'Mrs Ramsay! Mrs Ramsay!' she repeated. She owed this revelation to her. (p. 218)

The use of quotation marks here signals that Lily not only thinks of Mrs Ramsay but even pronounces her name. This actualizes the rhetorical term *apostrophe*: the addressing of a person who is absent. As the narration in part 3 approximates to presenting the late Mrs Ramsay as present and alive, the sense of loss, and of people missing her, are reinforced. As I read part 3, it is Mrs Ramsay's influence that makes it possible to complete the projects that the narration alternates in presenting in counterpoint form: the painting Lily is working on and the trip to the lighthouse. The function the parentheses have in this example is characteristic: they relate the reflections in which Lily indulges to the present situation in which she finds herself.

This sudden, epiphany-like experience Lily has of something that is stable and enduring points both backwards and forwards in the discourse. In relation to part 1, it links up with the feeling Mrs Ramsay has during the dinner party that something 'is immune from change' (p. 142). It also points forward to the end, when Lily finishes her painting just as (she believes) the boat reaches the lighthouse. The analeptic narrative variations are related to Lily's perspective, to her memory, and to the strenuous effort she makes with the painting.

James has a double narrative function here towards the end. First, the narrator reports omnisciently how well James remembers his father's scepticism about the trip: ' "It will rain," he remembered his father saying. "You won't be able to go to the Lighthouse" ' (p. 251). As Mrs Ramsay comments in part 1, there are things children cannot forget. This sentence refers directly back to the opening of the novel, it marks a limit on how complete reconciliation between father and son can be. Second, James asks whether the lighthouse he now at last sees coming closer is the same one he wanted to go to as a little boy:

> So that was the Lighthouse, was it?
>   No, the other was also the Lighthouse. For nothing was simply one thing. The other was the Lighthouse too. (p. 251)

The lighthouse both is and is not the same one, it is identical with the one James remembers and yet different. In this paradox Woolf concentrates important aspects of both the symbolism and the presentation of time in *To the Lighthouse*.

One such aspect concerns the relationship between the lighthouse as a symbol and Mrs Ramsay as the novel's main character. I have related the narrative and thematic functions Mrs Ramsay has, and the values for which she stands, to the symbol of light as it is presented in the narrative discourse. In a certain sense the trip to the lighthouse is a journey to, or at any rate towards, those qualities Mrs Ramsay represented, and which the loss of her has made clearer to those who are left. Although the positive aspect of the fact that they actually reach the lighthouse is doubly qualified by the long time that has elapsed and by the absence of several family members, the ending of *To the Lighthouse* suggests a resigned reconciliation of the remaining members of the Ramsay family. The way in which the narrator associates her perspective with Lily's confirms this impression. Although it is important that—inspired by the fact that the others reach the lighthouse—she manages to finish her painting, the use of the perfect form in the final sentence seems to place a question mark against her future as a painter: 'Yes, she thought, laying down her brush in extreme fatigue, I have had my vision' (p. 281). The end is not definitive, however, as it opens up the possibility of different interpretations. Some critics see the picture Lily completes as a metaphorical expression for the novel Woolf finishes, pointing out that all artistic activity is tiring and demanding. Supplementing the many other elements in part 3 that refer back to part 1, the perfect form in the final sentence contributes to concluding the text, including its presentation of time and exploration of human perceptions of time.

In common with other novels, *To the Lighthouse* presents time through a combination of narrative devices and techniques of which this analysis gives an outline. LaCapra (1987: 138) illustrates by means of a diagram (see Fig. 8.1) part of the reason for the novel's resistance to chronologically ordered story time. The horizontal level refers to the 'diachronic' movement 'external' events have in 'real' story time, as it is conventionally understood. On this horizontal level we have, for instance, Mrs Ramsay's project of bringing clothes to the people in the lighthouse; we can also place the First World War here. As LaCapra puts it, 'time in this dimension is a matter of change that can be chronicled in terms of a succession of now-points' (LaCapra 1987: 138). The vertical level, however, refers to the more 'synchronic' and structural dimension: 'an aesthetic immobilization and perception in depth of the random

Figure 8.1

event or moment *seems* to provide a fleeing passage outside time and a recon-ciliation between "inner" experience and the impersonal symbolic form' (LaCapra 1987: 138, original emphasis). Again and again, the narration in *To the Lighthouse* dwells on *one* event or *one* point of time, so that the diachronic temporal progression seems to come to a stop. One example that I have dis-cussed is the presentation of Mrs Ramsay's thoughts after James has fallen asleep in part 1.

To the Lighthouse combines these two forms of temporal presentation in strikingly original fashion. The insights that are presented on the synchronic level are problematized by elements or 'intrusions' from the diachronic, but without their thereby losing all value. 'Thus time is not simply spatialized, and the moment is not simply eternalized' (LaCapra 1987: 139). It is characteristic of the narrative technique of *To the Lighthouse* that the two temporal levels are both separated from each other and joined together again. The novel's nar-rative is a well-suited instrument for achieving this alternation in the presen-tation of time, with the unidentified third-person narrator placed at an unspecified point in time after the events have been played out.

V

The fact that Colin Gregg's adaptation has no narrative instance corres-ponding to the novel's third-person narrator may in part explain why the alternation between the synchronic and diachronic temporal levels becomes less clear (and does not appear so important either) in the film. Yet it is difficult to determine how much of this difference arises from conscious choices that Gregg has made, and how much stems from differences of media between ver-bal fiction and film. The pressure of action in film may be one reason why the diachronic temporal level appears more important in the adaptation than in the novel.

It is more productive to ask how the adaptation presents time and human perception of time, which is indisputably an important part of the thematics of Woolf's *To the Lighthouse*. Since the novel's presentation of time is difficult to show filmically, the viewer appreciates the attempt Gregg makes: rather than shrinking from the problem, he reshapes parts of it for the film medium with which he himself works. Although all the attempts may not be equally successful, we should not forget that our judgement is all the time coloured by the literary text which constitutes the starting-point for the comparison (and which has in one sense already been visualized by us in the process of reading).

When it comes to part 1, the most striking variation is that Gregg's adapta-tion stretches over a markedly longer period of time—at least several days, compared with an afternoon/evening in the novel. Such a variation is unusual since an adaptation's selective use of literary materials often gives the viewer the impression of temporal compression. One reason why the first part of the film covers a relatively long period of time is suggested by the shortness of the story time in the novel's part 1. One major effect of the variation is to reduce the text's synchronic dimension, thus also reducing the narrative alternation, and contrast, between this dimension and the diachronic.

This commentary primarily concerns part 1. If part 2 of the adaptation is the most interesting in relation to the literary original, part of the reason is suggested by the way in which the novel's synchronic dimension comes out here. Gregg achieves this partly through the descriptive camera use on which I have already commented, and partly by linking these descriptive sequences with images of events which in the literary part 2 are presented in square brackets. Since these events (such as an image of Andrew who is killed at the front in the First World War) can be related to the diachronic level of action, Gregg manages to present on film one of the most important narrative devices in part 2 of the novel. An additional effect of the way in which the film here combines diachronic information with synchronic description is to convey how far part 2 extends in time. In a way that conforms well with Woolf's text, a diachronic film segment shows the wedding of Prue Ramsay. After a descriptive sequence another shot then communicates that she dies giving birth the following year.

Both the first and second parts of the film bring out how helpless and alone Mr Ramsay is after his wife's death. An interesting feature of part 3 of the film is Gregg's use of analeptic shots in the presentation of Lily. In the adaptation, as in the novel, Lily is the most important character in this final part. In addition to focusing analeptically on Mrs Ramsay together with James, the adaptation of part 3 includes a repeating cut from the dinner scene in part 1. This narrative variation is thematically productive as it visualizes how strongly felt is the loss of Mrs Ramsay, both in relation to Lily's painting activity and for those who now at last are on their way out to the lighthouse.

The film's presentation of the confrontation between Mr Ramsay and Cam should also be mentioned. Even if it does not represent a direct filmic representation of any passage in Woolf's text, this confrontation illustrates the tense relationship Cam has with her father. It is an unresolved relationship that places her in an intermediate position between Lily and the late Mrs Ramsay. The parcel she is preparing for the boy in the lighthouse continues Mrs Ramsay's action early in the novel's part 1: 'the reddish-brown stocking she was knitting, impatiently. If she finished it tonight, if they did go to the Lighthouse after all, it was to be given to the Lighthouse keeper for his little boy. . .' (p. 9). When Mr Ramsay (in the adaptation) refuses to take the parcel with them, Cam is upset. Mr Ramsay thinks she overreacts, but the viewer relates Cam's violent reaction to her father's rejection of a project she knows her mother would have supported.

Suzanne Bertish as Lily Briscoe in Colin Gregg's *To the Lighthouse*. © BBC Picture Library.

When it comes to the overall presentation of Mr and Mrs Ramsay, Gregg's adaptation is uneven. Gregg succeeds best with the presentation of Mr Ramsay, while Mrs Ramsay loses much of the complexity she has as a character in the literary text. To make this point is not to say that the quality of the acting is very different: the performances of Rosemary Harris (as Mrs Ramsay) and Michael Gough (as Mr Ramsay) are both competent and well executed. The problem is rather that Mr Ramsay is simpler to present filmically, both because he behaves in a manner that is partly typically repetitive (for example his insatiable need for sympathy, which the film brings out well), and also because the presentation of him is not so integrated in the novel's narrative comments and reflections as is the case with Mrs Ramsay. This factor may in part explain why the presentation of Mrs Ramsay is simplified in the adaptation. However, this is not to deny that the film does have some excellent passages and sequences—

Michael Gough as Mr Ramsay in Colin Gregg's *To the Lighthouse*. © BBC Picture Library.

also when it comes to the presentation of Mrs Ramsay in relation to the problematic complexity of time. Two variants are particularly interesting. While the first is in my judgement not very productive, the second is unusually exciting.

The first variant concerns the presentation of Mrs Ramsay's death. The information that she is dead comes as a shock to the reader of the novel. The narrative use of square brackets to convey this information strengthens this effect, while also providing a context for the narrator's reflections in much of part 2. One reason why we are so violently surprised is that in part 1 Mrs Ramsay is presented as being strong and healthy: this reinforces the reader's feeling of contrast between the presentation of her in part 1 and the information that she is dead early in part 2. The adaptation reduces this contrast by showing (as an addition to the literary text) a scene in which Mrs Ramsay is suddenly taken ill. This brief sequence, a filmic prolepsis of her death in part 2, is thematically unproductive as it reduces the effect of shock-like surprise associated with Mrs Ramsay's death.

Productive, however, is the other variant, which also constitutes a change in relation to the literary original. Gregg chooses to end the presentation of the dinner—Mrs Ramsay's achievement, centrally placed towards the end of part 1—with Mr and Mrs Ramsay reading aloud to the others at the table. Mrs Ramsay does not say what she is reading, but we can identify the poem as a sonnet (no. 60) by Shakespeare:

> Like as the waves make towards the pebbled shore,
> So do our minutes hasten to their end,
> Each changing place with that which goes before,
> In sequent toil all forwards do contend.
> Nativity, once in the main of light,
> Crawls to maturity; wherewith being crowned
> Crooked eclipses 'gainst his glory fight,
> And time, that gave, doth now his gift confound.
> Time doth transfix the flourish set on youth,
> And delves the parallels in beauty's brow;
> Feeds on the rarities of nature's truth,
> And nothing stands but for his scythe to mow.
>> And yet to times in hope my verse shall stand,
>> Praising thy worth, despite his cruel hand.

We cannot here analyse this masterly sonnet, but it is striking how clearly the questions the poem raises are related to the problematic complexity of time that Virginia Woolf—several hundred years later and in another literary genre—presents in *To the Lighthouse*. In this sonnet, 'the speaker considers the inevitable process of maturity and decay in the natural world, only to be counteracted by his own verse in praise of the young man' (Katherine Duncan-Jones in Shakespeare 1998: 230). If we look for example at the concluding couplet, which in the Shakespearian sonnet usually tends towards a form of summary or aphoristic conclusion, we see the contours of questions which are also central in the novel, and which Woolf explores through the presentation of Mrs Ramsay and Lily in particular. What is the relationship between the stable, the enduring, on the one hand and that which changes, that which is lost, on the other? Can art resist, or help us to resist, the continual changes and the many losses that the process of time brings with it? If the conclusion of this sonnet seems to express a hope that the poet's verse will defy time, this hope is strongly qualified in Woolf. Yet, as I read *To the Lighthouse*, it is not *totally* absent.

The thematic affinity between Shakespeare's sonnet and Woolf's novel becomes even more interesting as some of the literary devices Shakespeare uses can be related to Woolf's narrative technique. Although the difference in literary genre means that we must be cautious about direct comparison here, it is striking how strongly the use of metaphor and personification in the sonnet reminds us of part 2 of *To the Lighthouse*. This applies not least to the wave metaphor which opens the sonnet, and which through simile is then linked with personifications of time. Because, as Duncan-Jones shows, the sonnet's opening echoes Ovid's *Metamorphoses* (15. 181–4), there is a sense in which this sonnet is intertextually related to reflections on time in, on the one hand, a much earlier literary work by Ovid (43 BC–AD 18), and, on the other hand, a modernist novel and a film. In Woolf the waves are a central metaphor. The title of one of her later novels is *The Waves* (1931). In part 2 of *To the Lighthouse* 'the winds and waves' (p. 183) are powerful images of time, and they are personified in a way that reminds us of the personification of time in the sonnet. For the viewer, it is as if Mrs Ramsay, by reading this sonnet to the other characters in the adaptation of *To the Lighthouse*, communicates Shakespeare's poetic reflections on time by relating them to her own understanding of time (and to that explored in the novel as aesthetic structure). For the *reader* of the sonnet, as I have presented it in written form, this effect is reinforced. The poem encourages a form of reflective response that the film's pressure of action complicates; furthermore, the poem's character of commentary becomes clearer if one knows the whole film—and even clearer if one has read the novel. Yet although this difference in interpretative response says something about how differently film and literature operate, the sonnet works as an integral part of the film. In its concise form the sonnet expresses, as it is presented in the adaptation of this novel, how productive and thought-provoking the relationship between the two media can be.

References

Abrams, M. H. (1999). *A Glossary of Literary Terms*. 7th edn. Fort Worth: Harcourt Brace College Publishers.

Achebe, Chinua (1998). 'An Image of Africa: Racism in Conrad's *Heart of Darkness*' [1st pub. *The Massachusetts Review*, 18 (1977)]; repr. in Andrew Michael Roberts (ed.), *Joseph Conrad*. London: Longman, 109–23.

Adorno, Theodor W. (1970). *Ästhetische Theorie*. Frankfurt am Main: Suhrkamp.

——(1982). 'Notes on Kafka', in *Prisms*. Cambridge, Mass.: MIT Press.

Allende, Isabel (1991a). *Eva Luna* [1987]. Harmondsworth: Penguin.

——(1991b). *The Stories of Eva Luna*. Harmondsworth: Penguin.

Altman, Robert, and Barhydt, Frank (1993). *Short Cuts: The Screenplay*. Santa Barbara: Capra Press.

Andrew, Dudley (1992). 'Adaptation', in Gerald Mast, Marshal Cohen, and Leo Braudy (eds.), *Film Theory and Criticism*. Oxford: Oxford University Press, 420–8.

Annals of Saint Gall (1963). In *Monumenta Germaniae Historica*, series *Scriptores*, ed. George Heinrich Pertz. Stuttgart.

Arabian Nights' Entertainments (1998). Oxford World's Classics, ed. Robert Mack. Oxford: Oxford University Press.

Aristotle (1995). *Poetics*, ed. and trans. Stephen Halliwell. Loeb Classical Library. Cambridge, Mass.: Harvard University Press.

Armstrong, Paul (1990). *Conflicting Readings: Variety and Validity in Interpretation*. Chapel Hill: University of North Carolina Press.

Arnheim, Rudolf (1957). *Film as Art*. Berkeley: University of California Press.

Auerbach, Erich (1959). 'Figura', in *Scenes from the Drama of European Literature*. New York: Meridian, 11–76.

Austen, Jane (1998). *Pride and Prejudice* [1813], Oxford World's Classics, ed. James Kinsley. Oxford: Oxford University Press.

Bakhtin, M. M. (1982). *The Dialogic Imagination: Four Essays*, ed. Michael Holquist. Austin: University of Texas Press.

Bal, Mieke (1997). *Narratology: Introduction to the Theory of Narrative*. 2nd edn. Toronto: University of Toronto Press.

Balzac, Honoré de (1974). 'Sarrasine' [1830], in Barthes (1974). New York: Hill & Wang, 221–54.

Baroja, Pía (1943). *La casa de aigorri*. Madrid: Colección Austral.

Barthes, Roland (1974). *S/Z* [1970]. New York: Hill & Wang.

——(1982a). *Camera Lucida: Reflections on Photography*. London: Jonathan Cape.

——(1982b). 'Introduction to the Structural Analysis of Narratives', in *A Barthes Reader*, ed. Susan Sontag. London: Jonathan Cape, 251–95. [Original title: 'Introduction à l'analyse structurale des récits'. *Communications* (1966).]

——(1988). 'The Death of the Author' [1968], in *Modern Criticism and Theory: A Reader*, ed. David Lodge. London: Longman, 167–71.

Beckett, Samuel (1972). *Malone Dies* [1958]. Harmondsworth: Penguin.

Beer, Gillian (1996). *Virginia Woolf: The Common Ground*. Edinburgh: Edinburgh University Press.

Benjamin, Walter (1979a). *Illuminations*, ed. Hannah Arendt. London: Fontana.

—— (1979b). *Über Literatur*. Frankfurt am Main: Suhrkamp.

Bjørnson, Bjørnstjerne (1969). 'Faderen' [The Father]. In *Perler i prosa* [Pearls in Prose], ed. Edvard Beyer. Oslo: Den Norske Bokklubben, 45–7.

Blanchot, Maurice (1995). *The Work of Fire*. Stanford: Stanford University Press.

Blixen, Karen (Isak Dinesen) (1986). *Anecdotes of Destiny* [1958]. Harmondsworth: Penguin.

Booth, Wayne C. (1974). *A Rhetoric of Irony*. Chicago: University of Chicago Press.

—— (1983). *The Rhetoric of Fiction*. 2nd edn. Chicago: University of Chicago Press.

Bordwell, David (1985). *Narration in the Fiction Film*. Madison: University of Wisconsin Press.

—— and Thompson, Kristin (1997). *Film Art: An Introduction*. 5th edn. New York: McGraw-Hill.

Borges, Jorge Luis (1979). *Labyrinths: Selected Stories and Other Writings*. Harmondsworth: Penguin.

Bourdieu, Pierre (1989). 'He Whose Word is Law', *Times Literary Supplement* (6–12 Oct.), 12–13.

Bowlby, Rachel (1988). *Virginia Woolf: Feminist Destinations*. Oxford: Blackwell.

Braaten, Lars Thomas (1984). *Filmfortelling og subjektivitet* [Film Narrative and Subjectivity]. Oslo: Universitetsforlaget.

Branigan, Edward (1992). *Narrative Comprehension and Film*. London: Routledge.

Brill, Lesley (1997). *John Huston's Filmmaking*. Cambridge: Cambridge University Press.

Brontë, Charlotte (1998). *Jane Eyre* [1847], Oxford World's Classics, ed. Margaret Smith. Oxford: Oxford University Press.

Brontë, Emily (1998). *Wuthering Heights* [1847], Oxford World's Classics, ed. Ian Jack. Oxford: Oxford University Press.

Brooks, Peter (1984). *Reading for the Plot: Design and Intention in Narrative*. Oxford: Clarendon Press.

Bullough, Edward (1957). 'Psychical Distance' [1912], in *Aesthetics: Lectures and Essays*, ed. E. Wilkinson. Stanford: Stanford University Press.

Bunyan, John (1998). *The Pilgrim's Progress* [1684], Oxford World's Classics, ed. N. H. Keeble. Oxford: Oxford University Press.

Burke, Kenneth (1975). ' "Stages" in "The Dead" ', in Robert Scholes and A. Walton Litz (eds.), *Dubliners: Text, Criticism, and Notes*. New York: Viking, 410–16.

Camus, Albert (1983). *The Outsider* [1942]. Harmondsworth: Penguin.

Carver, Raymond (1995). *Short Cuts*. London: Harvill Press.

Cavell, Stanley (1979). *The World Viewed: Reflections on the Ontology of Film*. Cambridge, Mass.: Harvard University Press.

Cervantes, Miguel de (1998). *Don Quixote* [1605, 1615], Oxford World's Classics, ed. E. C. Riley. Oxford: Oxford University Press.

Chatman, Seymour (1978). *Story and Discourse: Narrative Structure in Fiction and Film*. Ithaca: Cornell University Press.

—— (1985). *Antonioni: Or, the Surface of the World*. Berkeley: University of California Press.

—— (1990). *Coming to Terms: The Rhetoric of Narrative in Fiction and Film*. Ithaca: Cornell University Press.

——(1997). '2½ Film Versions of *Heart of Darkness*', in Gene M. Moore (ed.), *Conrad on Film*. Cambridge: Cambridge University Press, 207–23.

Cixous, Hélène (1984). 'Joyce: The (r)use of Writing', in Derek Attridge and Daniel Ferrer (eds.), *Post-structuralist Joyce*. Cambridge: Cambridge University Press, 15–30.

Close, A. J. (1990). *Cervantes' Don Quixote*. Cambridge: Cambridge University Press.

Cohen, Keith (1979). *Film and Fiction: The Dynamics of Exchange*. New Haven: Yale University Press.

Cohn, Dorrit (1983). *Transparent Minds: Narrative Modes for Presenting Consciousness in Fiction*. Princeton: Princeton University Press.

Connors, Martin, and Craddock, James (eds.) (1998). *Videohound's Golden Movie Retriever*. New York: Visible Ink.

Conrad, Joseph (1978). *Congo Diary and Other Uncollected Pieces by Joseph Conrad*, ed. Zdzisław Najder. New York: Doubleday.

——(1989). *Under Western Eyes* [1911], Oxford World's Classics, ed. Jeremy Hawthorn. Oxford: Oxford University Press.

——(1992). *The Shadow-Line* [1916], Oxford World's Classics, ed. Jeremy Hawthorn. Oxford: Oxford University Press.

——(1995). *Nostromo* [1904], Oxford World's Classics, ed. Keith Karabine. Oxford: Oxford University Press.

——(1998a). *Heart of Darkness* [1899, 1902], Oxford World's Classics, ed. Cedric Watts. Oxford: Oxford University Press.

——(1998b). *The Secret Agent* [1907], Oxford World's Classics, ed. Roger Tennant. Oxford: Oxford University Press.

Corngold, Stanley (1988). *Kafka: The Necessity of Form*. Ithaca: Cornell University Press.

Cowie, Peter (1990). *Coppola*. London: Faber & Faber.

Crawford, Robert (1990). *The Savage and the City in the Work of T. S. Eliot*. Oxford: Clarendon Press.

Dante Alighieri (1998). *The Divine Comedy* [1321], Oxford World's Classics, ed. David Higgins. Oxford: Oxford University Press.

Davies, Norman (1984). *God's Playground: A History of Poland*, 2 vols. Oxford: Clarendon Press.

Deleuze, Gilles (1969). *Logique du sens*. Paris: Minuit. English trans. *The Logic of Sense*. New York: Columbia University Press, 1990.

——(1989). *Cinema 2: The Time-Image*. London: Athlone Press.

——and Guattari, Félix (1988). *A Thousand Plateaus*. London: Athlone Press.

de Man, Paul (1979). 'Semiology and Rhetoric', in *Textual Strategies*, ed. Josué V. Harari. London: Methuen, 121–40.

Derrida, Jacques (1984). 'Two Words for Joyce', in Derek Attridge and Daniel Ferrer (eds.), *Post-structuralist Joyce*. Cambridge: Cambridge University Press, 145–59.

——(1985). 'Préjugés, devant la loi', in *La Faculté de juger*. Paris: Minuit, 87–139.

Dibbets, Karel (1997). 'The Introduction of Sound', in Geoffrey Nowell-Smith (ed.), *The Oxford Dictionary of World Cinema*. Oxford: Oxford University Press, 211–19.

Dickens, Charles (1998). *Hard Times* [1854], Oxford World's Classics, ed. Paul Schlicke. Oxford: Oxford University Press.

——(1998). *Great Expectations* [1861], Oxford World's Classics, ed. Margaret Cardwell and Kate Flint. Oxford: Oxford University Press.

Diderot, Denis (1967). *Le Neveu de rameau* [1805]. Paris: Flammarion.

Diderot, Denis (1970). *Jacques le fataliste et son maître* [1795]. Paris: Flammarion.

Dos Passos, John (1938). *U.S.A.* New York: Modern Library.

Dostoevsky, Fyodor (1998a). *Crime and Punishment* [1866]. Oxford World's Classics. Oxford: Oxford University Press.

——(1998b). *The Karamazov Brothers* [1879–80]. Oxford World's Classics. Oxford: Oxford University Press.

Drabble, Margaret (ed.) (1997). *The Oxford Companion to English Literature.* Oxford: Oxford University Press.

Dusinberre, Juliet (1997). *Virginia Woolf's Renaissance: Woman Reader or Common Reader?* London: Macmillan.

Eco, Umberto (1984). *Semiotics and the Philosophy of Language.* London: Macmillan.

——(1989). *The Aesthetics of Chaosmos: The Middle Ages of James Joyce.* Cambridge, Mass.: Harvard University Press.

——(1990). *The Limits of Interpretation.* Bloomington: Indiana University Press.

——(1992). *Interpretation and Overinterpretation,* ed. Stefan Collini. Cambridge: Cambridge University Press.

Eikhenbaum, Boris (1973). 'Literature and Cinema' [1926], in *Russian Formalism: A Collection of Articles and Texts in Translation,* ed. Stephen Bann and John Bowlt. Edinburgh: Edinburgh University Press, 122–7.

Eisenstein, Sergei (1986). *The Film Sense* [1943]. London: Faber & Faber.

——(1988). *The Battleship Potemkin.* London: Faber & Faber.

——(1992). 'Dickens, Griffith, and the Film Today', in Gerald Mast, Marshall Cohen, and Leo Braudy (eds.), *Film Theory and Criticism.* Oxford: Oxford University Press, 395–402.

——Pudovkin, V. I., and Alexandrov, G. V. (1992). 'A Statement [on Sound]', in Gerald Mast, Marshall Cohen, and Leo Braudy (eds.), *Film Theory and Criticism.* Oxford: Oxford University Press, 317–19.

Eliot, Thomas Stearns (1974). *Collected Poems.* London: Faber & Faber.

Ellis, John (1989). *Visible Fictions: Cinema, Television, Video.* London: Routledge.

Ellmann, Richard (1982). *James Joyce.* Oxford: Oxford University Press.

Elsaesser, Thomas (ed.), with Adam Barker (1994). *Early Cinema: Space, Frame, Narrative.* London: BFI Publishing.

——and Wedel, Michael (1997). 'The Hollow Heart of Hollywood: *Apocalypse Now* and the New Sound Space', in Gene M. Moore (ed.), *Conrad on Film.* Cambridge: Cambridge University Press, 151–75.

Emrich, Wilhelm (1981). *Franz Kafka.* Königstein: Athenäum.

Erlich, Victor (1981). *Russian Formalism: History—Doctrine.* 3rd edn. New Haven: Yale University Press.

Faulkner, William (1950). *Collected Stories of William Faulkner.* New York: Random House.

——(1994). *The Sound and the Fury* [1929]. 2nd edn., ed. David Minter. New York: Norton.

——(1995). *Absalom, Absalom!* [1936]. London: Vintage.

Feder, Lillian (1955). 'Marlow's Descent into Hell', *Nineteenth-Century Fiction,* 9: 280–92.

Flaubert, Gustave (1998). *Madame Bovary* [1857]. Oxford World's Classics. Oxford: Oxford University Press.

Fleishman, Avrom (1992). *Narrated Films: Storytelling Situations in Cinema History.* Baltimore: Johns Hopkins University Press.

Fludernik, Monika (1996). *Towards a 'Natural' Narratology.* London: Routledge.

Forster, E. M. (1971). *Aspects of the Novel* [1927]. Harmondsworth: Penguin.

Fothergill, Anthony (1989). *Heart of Darkness.* London: Open University Press.

Foucault, Michel (1980). *Power/Knowledge.* Brighton: Harvester.

Gadamer, Hans-Georg (1975). *Wahrheit und Methode: Grundzüge einer philosophischen Hermeneutik* [1960]. Tübingen: J. C. B. Mohr. English trans. *Truth and Method.* London: Sheed & Ward, 1975.

Genette, Gérard (1980). *Narrative Discourse.* Oxford: Blackwell. [Original title: 'Discours du récit: essai de méthode', in *Figures III.* Paris: Seuil, 1972, 67–273.]

—— (1988). *Narrative Discourse Revisited.* Ithaca: Cornell University Press.

GoGwilt, Christopher (1995). *The Invention of the West: Joseph Conrad and the Double-Mapping Europe and Empire.* Stanford: Stanford University Press.

Gombrich, E. H. (1996). *Art and Illusion: A Study in the Psychology of Pictorial Representation* [1960]. London: Phaidon.

Gordimer, Nadine (1983). *Selected Stories.* Harmondsworth: Penguin.

Greimas, A. J. (1966). *Sémantique structurale.* Paris: Larousse.

Habermas, Jürgen (1973). 'Zu Gadamers *Wahrheit und Methode*', in *Hermeneutik und Ideologiekritik,* ed. Karl-Otto Apel *et al.* Frankfurt am Main: Suhrkamp, 45–56.

Hamburger, Käte (1968). *Die Logik der Dichtung.* 2nd edn. Stuttgart: Ernst Klett.

Hamsun, Knut (1996). *Hunger* [1890]. Edinburgh: Rebel.

—— (1998). *Mysteries* [1892]. London: Condor.

Hansen, Erik Fosnes (1998). *Psalm at Journey's End* [1990]. London: Vintage.

Hayman, David (1987). *Re-forming the Narrative: Towards a Mechanics of Modernist Fiction.* Ithaca: Cornell University Press.

Hawthorn, Jeremy (ed.) (1985). *Narrative: From Malory to Motion Pictures.* London: Edward Arnold.

—— (1997). *Studying the Novel: An Introduction.* 3rd edn. London: Arnold.

—— (1998). *A Glossary of Contemporary Literary Theory.* 3rd edn. London: Arnold.

Hemingway, Ernest (1965). *Men Without Women* [1928]. Harmondsworth: Penguin.

Herr, Michael (1977). *Dispatches.* New York: Alfred Knopf.

Holquist, Michael (1990). *Dialogism: Bakhtin and his World.* London: Routledge.

Iser, Wolfgang (1980). *The Act of Reading: A Theory of Aesthetic Response.* Baltimore: Johns Hopkins University Press.

Islam, Syed Manzurul (1996). *The Ethics of Travel: From Marco Polo to Kafka.* Manchester: Manchester University Press.

Jakobson, Roman (1987). *Language in Literature,* ed. Krystyna Pomorska and Stephen Rudy. Cambridge, Mass.: Harvard University Press.

Jameson, Fredric (1992). *Signatures of the Visible.* London: Routledge.

Joyce, James (1992a). *Dubliners* [1914]. Harmondsworth: Penguin.

—— (1992b). *A Portrait of the Artist as a Young Man* [1914–15]. Harmondsworth: Penguin.

—— (1992c). *Ulysses* [1922]. Harmondsworth: Penguin.

Kaez, Anton (1997). 'The New German Cinema', in Geoffrey Nowell-Smith (ed.), *The Oxford History of World Cinema.* Oxford: Oxford University Press, 514–27.

Kafka, Franz (1981). *Sämtliche Erzählungen,* ed. Paul Raabe. Frankfurt am Main: Fischer.

—— (1988). *The Trial,* trans. Douglas Scott and Chris Walker. London: Picador.

—— (1997). *Das Schloss* [1922]. Frankfurt am Main: Fischer.

Kafka, Franz (1998). *Der Process* [1914–15]. Frankfurt am Main: Fischer.

Kayser, Wolfgang (1971). *Das sprachliche Kunstwerk*. Berne: Francke.

Kennedy, Duncan (1997). 'Virgilian Epic', in Charles Martindale (ed.), *The Cambridge Companion to Virgil*. Cambridge: Cambridge University Press, 145–54.

Kermode, Frank (1979). *The Genesis of Secrecy: On the Interpretation of Narrative*. Cambridge, Mass.: Harvard University Press.

——(1981). *The Sense of an Ending: Studies in the Theory of Fiction*. Oxford: Oxford University Press.

Kimbrough, Robert (ed.) (1988). *Joseph Conrad's Heart of Darkness*, Norton Critical Edition, 3rd edn. New York: Norton.

Kittang, Atle (1884). *Luft, vind, ingenting: Hamsuns desillusjonsromanar frå Sult til Ringen sluttet* [Air, Wind, Nothingness: Hamsun's Novels of Disillusionment]. Oslo: Gyldendal.

Kobs, Jörgen (1970). *Kafka: Untersuchungen zur Bewusstsein und Sprache seiner Gestalten* [Kafka: Investigation of his Characters' Consciousness and Language]. Bad Homburg: Athenäum.

Koelb, Klayton (1989). *Kafka's Rhetoric: The Passion of Reading*. Ithaca: Cornell University Press.

Kozloff, Sarah (1988). *Invisible Storytellers: Voice-over Narration in the American Fiction Film*. Berkeley: University of California Press.

Kristeva, Julia (1980). *Desire in Language*. London: Blackwell.

Kundera, Milan (1995). *The Unbearable Lightness of Being* [1984]. London: Faber & Faber.

LaCapra, Dominick (1987). *History, Politics, and the Novel*. Ithaca: Cornell University Press.

Larsen, Peter (1989). 'TV: historie og/eller diskurs?' [TV: Story and/or Discourse?]. *Edda*, 75: 9–25.

Laxdæla Saga (1968). Oslo: Det Norske Samlaget.

Lee, Hermione (1997). *Virginia Woolf*. London: Vintage.

Lefebvre, Henri (1991). *The Production of Space*. Oxford: Blackwell.

Lessing, G. E. (1998). *Laokoon: Oder über die Grenzen der Malerei und der Poesie* [1766]. Stuttgart: Reclam.

Lie, Sissel (1986). *Tigersmil* [Smile of the Tiger]. Oslo: Gyldendal.

Livingstone, David, and Livingstone, Charles (1866). *Narrative of an Expedition to the Zambesi*. New York: Harper.

Lodge, David (1966). *Language of Fiction*. London: Routledge.

Lothe, Jakob (1985). 'Repetition and Narrative Method: Hardy, Conrad, Faulkner', in Jeremy Hawthorn (ed.), *Narrative: From Malory to Motion Pictures*. London: Edward Arnold, 116–31.

——(1989). *Conrad's Narrative Method*. Oxford: Clarendon Press.

——(1996a). 'Andrzej Wajda's Adaptation of Conrad's *The Shadow-Line*', in Alex S. Kurczaba (ed.), *Conrad and Poland*. New York: Columbia University Press, 217–32.

——(1996b). 'Conradian Narrative', in J. H. Stape (ed.), *The Cambridge Companion to Joseph Conrad*. Cambridge: Cambridge University Press, 160–78.

——(1997). 'Narrative, Character, and Plot: Theoretical Observations Related to Two Short Stories by Faulkner', in Hans H. Skei (ed.), *William Faulkner's Short Fiction*. Oslo: Solum, 74–81.

—— (1999). 'Variants on Genre: *The Return of the Native, The Mayor of Casterbridge, The Hand of Ethelberta*', in Dale Kramer (ed.), *The Cambridge Companion to Thomas Hardy*. Cambridge: Cambridge University Press, 112–29.

Lubbock, Percy (1973). *The Craft of Fiction* [1921]. New York: Viking.

McDougal, Stuart Y. (1985). *Made into Movies: From Literature to Film*. New York: Holt, Rinehart, and Winston.

McEwan, Ian (1998). *Enduring Love*. London: Vintage.

McFarlane, Brian (1996). *Novel to Film: An Introduction to the Theory of Adaptation*. Oxford: Clarendon Press.

McHale, Brian (1978). 'Free Indirect Discourse: A Survey of Recent Accounts', *Poetics and Theory of Literature*, 3: 249–87.

Maclean, Ian (1992). 'Reading and Interpretation', in Ann Jefferson and David Robey (eds.), *Modern Literary Theory*. London: Batsford, 122–44.

Madsen, Peter (1995). 'Modernity and Melancholy: Narration, Discourse, and Identity in *Heart of Darkness*', in Jakob Lothe (ed.), *Conrad in Scandinavia*. New York: Columbia University Press, 127–54.

Maltby, Richard (1998). 'Casablanca', in John Hill and Pamela Church Gibson (eds.), *The Oxford Guide to Film Studies*. Oxford: Oxford University Press, 283–6.

Martin, Wallace (1986). *Recent Theories of Narrative*. Ithaca: Cornell University Press.

Mast, Gerald (1983). *Film/Cinema/Movie: A Theory of Experience*. Chicago: University of Chicago Press.

—— Cohen, Marshall, and Braudy, Leo (eds.) (1992). *Film Theory and Criticism: Introductory Readings*. 4th edn. Oxford: Oxford University Press.

Mayer, David (1972). *Sergei M. Eisenstein's Potemkin*. New York: Da Capo Press.

Metz, Christian (1974). *Film Language: A Semiotics of the Cinema*. New York: Oxford University Press.

Meyer, Rosalind S. (1998). 'Literary Sources of *Heart of Darkness*', *Modern Language Review*, 93: 330–44.

Miller, J. Hillis (1981). 'The Two Allegories', in Morton W. Bloomfield (ed.), *Allegory, Myth, and Symbol*. Cambridge, Mass.: Harvard University Press, 355–70.

—— (1982). *Fiction and Repetition: Seven English Novels*. Oxford: Blackwell.

—— (1985). '*Heart of Darkness* Revisited', in Ross C. Murfin (ed.), *Conrad Revisited: Essays for the Eighties*. Alabama: University of Alabama Press, 31–50.

—— (1990). 'Mr. Carmichael and Lily Briscoe: The Rhythm of Creativity in *To the Lighthouse*', in *Tropes, Parables, Performatives*. London: Harvester Wheatsheaf, 151–70.

—— (1992). *Ariadne's Thread: Story Lines*. New Haven: Yale University Press.

Moi, Toril (1985). *Sexual/Textual Politics: Feminist Literary Theory*. London: Methuen.

Muecke, D. C. (1969). *The Compass of Irony*. London: Methuen.

Najder, Zdzisław (1983). *Joseph Conrad: A Chronicle*. Cambridge: Cambridge University Press.

—— (1997). *Conrad in Perspective: Essays on Art and Fidelity*. Cambridge: Cambridge University Press.

Nietzsche, Friedrich (1974). *The Gay Science*. New York: Vintage.

Nøjgaard, Morten (1976). *Litteraturens univers: Indføring i tekstanalyse* [The Universe of Literature: Introduction to Textual Analysis]. Odense: Odense University Press.

Norris, Margot (1996). 'The (Lethal) Turn of the Twentieth Century: War and Popula-tion Control', in Robert Newman (ed.), *Centuries' Ends, Narrative Means*. Stanford: Stanford University Press, 151–9.

Nussbaum, Martha C. (1995). 'The Window: Knowledge of Other Minds in Virginia Woolf's *To the Lighthouse*', *New Literary History*, 26: 731–53.

Onega, Susana, and Landa, José Ángel García (eds.) (1996). *Narratology: An Introduc-tion*. London: Longman.

Orr, John, and Nicholson, Colin (eds.) (1992). *Cinema and Fiction: New Modes of Adapting, 1950–1990*. Edinburgh: Edinburgh University Press.

Ovid (1998). *Metamorphoses*, Oxford World's Classics, ed. E. J. Kenney. Oxford: Oxford University Press.

Pascal, Roy (1982). *Kafka's Narrators: A Study of his Stories and Sketches*. Cambridge: Cambridge University Press.

Pecora, Vincent (1989). *Self and Form in Modern Narrative*. Baltimore: Johns Hopkins University Press.

Phelan, James (1989). *Reading People, Reading Plots: Character, Progression, and the Interpretation of Narrative*. Chicago: University of Chicago Press.

——and Rabinowitz, Peter J. (eds.) (1994). *Understanding Narrative*. Columbus: Ohio State University Press.

Politzer, Heinz (1966). *Franz Kafka: Parable and Paradox*. Ithaca: Cornell University Press.

Pratt, Mary Louise (1994). 'Travel Narrative and Imperialist Vision', in James Phelan and Peter J. Rabinowitz (eds.), *Understanding Narrative*. Columbus: Ohio State University Press, 199–221.

Prince, Gerald (1991). *A Dictionary of Narratology*. Aldershot: Scholar Press.

Propp, Vladimir (1968). *Morphology of the Folktale* [1928]. Austin: University of Austin Press.

Proust, Marcel (1992). *In Search of Lost Time*, 6 vols. [1913–27]. London: Chatto & Windus.

Ricoeur, Paul (1981). 'Narrative Time', in *On Narrative*, ed. J. W. T. Mitchell. Chicago: University of Chicago Press, 165–86.

Rimmon-Kenan, Shlomith (1983). *Narrative Fiction: Contemporary Poetics*. London: Methuen.

Robbe-Grillet, Alain (1957). *La Jalousie*. Paris: Minuit.

——(1966). 'The Beach', in *French Short Stories*, ed. Pamela Lyon. Harmondsworth: Penguin, 12–23.

Robertson, Ritchie (1985). *Kafka: Judaism, Politics, and Literature*. Oxford: Clarendon Press.

Rothman, William (1988). *The 'I' of the Camera: Essays in Film Criticism, History, and Aesthetics*. Cambridge: Cambridge University Press.

Rushdie, Salman (1992). *Imaginary Homelands: Essays and Criticism 1981–91*. London: Granta.

——(1995). *Midnight's Children* [1981]. London: Vintage.

——(1998). *The Satanic Verses* [1988]. London: Vintage.

Russell, D. A., and Winterbottom, Michael (eds.) (1998). *Classical Literary Criticism*, Oxford World's Classics. Oxford: Oxford University Press.

Sandberg, Beatrice, and Speirs, Ronald (1997). *Franz Kafka*. London: Macmillan.

Scholes, Robert (1985). 'Narration and Narrativity in Film', in Gerald Mast and

Marshall Cohen (eds.), *Film Theory and Criticism*. 3rd edn. Oxford: Oxford University Press, 390–403.

—— and Litz, A. Walton (eds.) (1975). *Dubliners: Text, Criticism, and Notes*. New York: Viking.

Shakespeare, William (1997). *Hamlet*, The Arden Shakespeare, ed. Harold Jenkins. London: Methuen.

—— (1998). *Shakespeare's Sonnets*, The Arden Shakespeare, ed. Katherine Duncan-Jones. London: Nelson & Sons.

Shklovsky, Viktor (1973). *Theorie der Prosa*, ed. G. Drohla. Munich.

Showalter, Elaine (1977). 'Virginia Woolf and the Flight into Androgyny', in *A Literature of their Own: British Women Novelists from Brontë to Lessing*. Princeton, NJ: Princeton University Press.

Sophocles (1998). *Oedipus the King*, Oxford World's Classics. Oxford: Oxford University Press.

Sørenssen, Bjørn (1995). 'An Uneasy Relationship: *Heart of Darkness* and *Apocalypse Now*', in Jakob Lothe (ed.), *Conrad in Scandinavia*. New York: Columbia University Press, 155–69.

Stanzel, Franz K. (1986). *A Theory of Narrative*. Cambridge: Cambridge University Press.

—— (1992). 'Consonant and Dissonant Closure in *Death in Venice* and *The Dead*', in Ann Fehn *et al.* (eds.), *Neverending Stories*. Princeton: Princeton University Press, 112–23.

Sturrock, John (1993). *The Language of Autobiography: Studies in the First Person Singular*. Cambridge: Cambridge University Press.

Tate, Allen (1975). 'The Dead', in Robert Scholes and A. Walton Litz (eds.), *Dubliners: Text, Criticism, and Notes*. New York: Viking, 404–9.

Todorov, Tzvetan (1978). 'Connaissance du vide: *Cœur des ténèbres*'. In *Les Genres du discours*. Paris: Seuil, 161–73.

—— (1981). *Introduction to Poetics*. Brighton: Harvester.

—— (1984). *Mikhail Bakhtin: The Dialogical Principle*. Manchester: Manchester University Press.

Togeby, Knud (1957). *La Composition du roman 'Don Quijote'*. København: Munksgaard.

Uspensky, Boris (1973). *A Poetics of Composition*. Berkeley: University of California Press.

Vanoye, Francis (1991). *Scénarios modèles, modèles scénarios*. Paris: Nathan.

Walker, John (ed.) (1998). *Halliwell's Film and Video Guide*. 1999 edn. London: HarperCollins.

Walzl, Florence L. (1975). 'Gabriel and Michael: The Conclusion of "The Dead"', in Robert Scholes and A. Walton Litz (eds.), *Dubliners: Text, Criticism, and Notes*. New York: Viking, 423–44.

Watt, Ian (1980). *Conrad in the Nineteenth Century*. London: Chatto & Windus.

Watts, Cedric (1977). *Conrad's Heart of Darkness: A Critical and Contextual Discussion*. Milan: Mursia.

—— (1984). *The Deceptive Text: An Introduction to Covert Plots*. Brighton: Harvester.

—— (1998). Introduction to Conrad, *Heart of Darkness*, Oxford World's Classics, ed. Cedric Watts. Oxford: Oxford University Press, pp. vii–xxiii.

Welles, Orson, and Bogdanovich, Peter (1998). *This is Orson Welles*. New York: Da Capo Press.

White, Hayden (1990). *The Content of the Form: Narrative Discourse and Historical Representation.* Baltimore: Johns Hopkins University Press.

Wilder, Thornton (1976). *The Bridge of San Luis Rey* [1927]. New York: Avon.

Woolf, Virginia (1998). *To the Lighthouse* [1927], Oxford World's Classics, ed. Margaret Drabble. Oxford: Oxford University Press.

Filmography

Apocalypse Now (1979)

Director, Francis Ford Coppola; script, John Milius and Francis Ford Coppola; narration, Michael Herr; photography, Vittorio Storaro; music, Carmine and Francis Coppola. With Marlon Brando (Col. Walter E. Kurtz), Martin Sheen (Capt. Benjamin Willard), Robert Duvall (Lt.-Col. Kilgore), Frederic Forest (Chef), Albert Hall (Chief), Dennis Hopper (Photo Journalist), G. D. Spradlin (General). Production, Francis Ford Coppola (Omni-Zoetrope). Video, Zoetrope Studios; Paramount Video.

Babette's Feast (1987)

Director and script, Gabriel Axel; photography, Henning Kristiansen; music, Per Nørgaard. With Stéphane Audran (Babette), Bodil Kjer (Philippa), Birgitte Federspiel (Martine), Jean-Philippe Lafont (Papin), Jarl Kulle (General Loewenhielm). Production, Panorama Film International/Nordic Film/Danish Film Institute. Video, Braveworld.

The Battleship Potemkin (1925)

Director and script, Sergei Eisenstein; photography, Edouard Tissé. With A. Antonov, V. Barski, G. Alexandrov, M. Gomorov. Production, Goskino. Video, Hendring Ltd.

Citizen Kane (1941)

Director, Orson Welles; script, Herman J. Mankiewicz and Orson Welles; photography, Gregg Toland; music, Bernard Herrmann. With Orson Welles (Charles Forster Kane), Joseph Cotten (Jedediah Leland), Dorothy Comingore (Susan Alexander Kane), Everett Sloane (Bernstein). Production, Orson Welles (RKO). Video, Heron Films.

Crime and Punishment (1970)

Director and script, Lev Kulidzhanov; photography, Vyacheslav Shumsky. With Georgi Taratorkin (Raskolnikov), Innokenti Smoktunovsky (Porfiry), Viktoria Fyodorova, Tatjana Bedova. Production, Gorky Studio.

The Dead (1987)

Director, John Huston; script, Tony Huston; photography, Fred Murphy; music, Alex North. With Anjelica Huston (Gretta), Donal McCann (Gabriel). Production, Zenith Production/Liffey Films. Video, First Rate.

Hearts of Darkness (1991)

Director and script, Fax Bahr with George Hickenlooper and Eleanor Coppola. Documentary footage with Eleanor Coppola, Francis Ford Coppola, John Milius, *et al.* Production, George Zaloom and Les Mayfield/ZM Productions. Video, Paramount Video; Tartan.

To the Lighthouse (1983)

Director, Colin Gregg; script, Hugh Stoddart; photography, Ken Westbury; music, Julian Dawson-Lyell. With Rosemary Harris (Mrs Ramsay), Michael Glough (Mr Ramsay), Suzanne Bertish (Lily Briscoe), Kenneth Branagh (Charles Tansley). Production, Alan Shallcross/BBC-TV/Colin Gregg Films.

The Shadow-Line (1976)

Director, Andrzej Wajda; script, Bolesław Sulik and Andrzej Wajda; photography, Witold Sobociński; music, Wojciech Kilar. With Marek Kondrat (Korzeniowski), Graham Lines (Burns), Tomas Wilkinson (Ransome), Martin Wyldeck (Capt. Giles). Production, Film Polski and Thames Television.

Short Cuts (1993)

Director, Robert Altman; script, Robert Altman and Frank Barhyydt; photography, Walt Lloyd; music, Mark Isham. With Andie MacDowell, Bruce Davidson, Julianne Moore, Matthew Modine, Anne Archer, Fred Ward, Jack Lemmon, *et al.* Production, Cary Brokaw. Video, Spelling Films International.

Sult (Hunger) (1966)

Director, Henning Carlsen; script, Peter Seeberg and Henning Carlsen; photographer, Henning Kristiansen; music, Krzystof Komeda. With Per Oscarson (main character), Gunnel Lindblom (Ylajali). Production, ABC-Film/Henning Carlsen/Sandrew/Swedish Film Institute.

The Trial (1962)

Director and script, Orson Welles; photography, Edmond Richard; music, Jean Ledrut. With Anthony Perkins (Joseph K.), Jeanne Moreau (Ms Brüstner), Orson Welles (the lawyer). Production, Paris Europe Productions/FI-C-IT/Hisa-Films. Video, Art House Productions.

Index

Numbers in **bold** refer to definitions or extended discussions